Whitmarsh

Senior French Composition

From O to A Level

Senior French Composition

From O to A Level

W. F. H. WHITMARSH M.A.

Licencié ès Lettres

LONGMAN

LONGMAN GROUP LIMITED
London

*Associated companies, branches and
representatives throughout the world*

© Whitmarsh Publications Ltd 1969

First published 1969
Sixth impression 1977

ISBN 0 582 36072 2

*Printed in Singapore by
Huntsmen Offset Printing Pte Ltd.*

Contents

Foreword

With the growth of Sixth Forms, an increasing number of young people take French at the Advanced Level. Most of these pupils have done reasonably well at the Ordinary Level: for the most part they were in the 60+ range. This means that they probably made a fair fist at translating into French a short passage of English containing only common words and carefully contrived to avoid any serious difficulties of rendering.

This then is their attainment in this field when they embark upon Sixth Form studies. If, for lack of suitable material, they are at once switched to much more difficult composition, the effect is in most cases bad. They encounter a host of troubles they have had no training to face and simply flounder; they get discouraged and lose even what they had, sprinkling their work with the most elementary blunders. From this unhappy state many never recover.

There is then a case for a book which does effect more smoothly the transition from elementary to more advanced composition. In the present work we offer quite a wide range of material, beginning with easy passages and working up to really difficult pieces. The proses are divided into two groups. Those in the First Group (numbers 1 to 60) have been specially composed to drill essential constructions with the maximum frequency. Since the subjunctive is usually considered beyond the powers of O Level candidates, it is avoided in the first sixteen passages, but it occurs frequently from number 17 onwards.

The pieces of the Second Group (61–95) have been drawn from various sources. Some have actually been set for the 'A' Level test, some have been selected from contemporary literature, including extracts from books translated from French, retranslation being always a good exercise.

The Grammar (Part Three) deals with a fair range of essential constructions, but we have avoided cluttering it up with unnecessary things. Even when we were considering the rendering of the most difficult passages, the Grammar was found adequate for all occasions.

To provide separate drill in the various constructions, we give twenty-two groups of Practice Sentences (Part Two). These examples do not follow *pari passu* the whole of the Grammar, but pick out special points which often arise in composition and need stressing. The fewer the examples, the more frequently they can be worked through.

A Key of suggested translations of all the prose passages is available to teachers.

W.F.H.W.

Acknowledgements

We are grateful to the following for permission to reproduce copyright material:

W. H. Allen & Co. for extracts from *Mr. Pepys of Seething Lane* by C. Abernathy; author, author's agents and Houghton Mifflin Co. for an extract from *Life at the Top* by John Braine; Constable Publishers for extracts from *Winston Churchill: The Struggle for Survival* by Lord Moran; Faber & Faber Ltd for extracts from *The Catalyst* by G. O. Jones; author's agents for an extract from *White Sand and Grey Sand* by Stella Gibbons; author's agents and Hutchinson Publishing Group Ltd for extracts from *The Ram in the Thicket* by Anthony Glyn; William Heinemann Ltd, Harold Ober Associates and Little Brown & Co. for an extract from *A Question of Upbringing* by Anthony Powell, published in U.S.A. as *A Dance to the Music of Time*, Copyright © 1957, 1960, 1962 by Anthony Powell; Macmillan & Co. Ltd and Charles Scribner's Sons for extracts from *Time of Hope* by C. P. Snow; Perpetua Ltd for extract from *La vie de Manet* by Henri Perruchot (trans. by Humphrey Hare); Martin Secker & Warburg Ltd and Simon & Schuster Inc for extracts from *Clochemerle-les-Bains* by Gabriel Chevallier; Georges Simenon and Hamish Hamilton Ltd for extracts from *The Patient* (Les Anneaux de Bicetre) copyright © 1963 by Georges Simenon; translation by Jean Stewart copyright © 1963, Hamish Hamilton; Mrs. Helen Thurber and Hamish Hamilton Ltd for 'The Tiger Who Would be King' from *Further Fables for our Time* by James Thurber, Copyright © 1956 James Thurber, published by Simon & Schuster; New York, originally printed in *The New Yorker*; *The Sunday Times* for an extract from 'The Manor Gates are Open' by Vincent Cronin, from *The Sunday Times*; and the Joint Matriculation Board, Scottish Certificate of Education Examination Board, University of Cambridge, University of London, Welsh Joint Education Committee for questions from past examination papers.

Part One

English
Prose Passages
for Translation
into French

First Group (1–60)

The Subjunctive is not required until number 17

1 On the way to Nice

Denis left London at ten in the morning and reached Paris at about six o'clock in the evening. At the Gare du Nord there was a wait of three quarters of an hour, so he got out of the train and walked up and down the platform[1].

Suddenly he heard a voice: "You are Denis, aren't you?" He turned round and, to his great surprise, he saw before him an old friend of his father's, Monsieur Roche, who lived in Paris. The latter explained that he had received a letter telling[2] him that Denis would be at Paris at that time, and[3] so he had come to see him and wish him luck.

Denis was[4] very pleased to see a friend of his family. It was the first time he had travelled[5] abroad and he felt lonely and rather depressed. To[6] him it was a new experience to[7] travel in a French train and to hear all round him people speaking[8] very rapidly in French. He had listened and had tried to understand what was being said[9], but he caught[10] only a sentence here and there.

Monsieur Roche told him that at Nice he would meet a lot of English people, and that if he wanted to speak French really well, he ought not to[11] spend his time[12] speaking English with his countrymen. He advised[13] Denis to look for friends among the French.

1 'on the platform'. 2 Better to say: 'which told him'; use *informer* or *apprendre*. 3 Unnecessary to translate 'and'. 4 Past historic or imperfect? § 12. 5 French tends to use the imperfect in such cases. 6 *pour*. 7 *de*. 8 'who were speaking'. 9 'one was saying'. 10 Use *saisir* (like *finir*). 11 Conditional of *devoir*. 12 'to spend one's time (doing)' = *passer son temps à (faire)*. 13 Construction with *conseiller*? § 31.

2 Monk

After dinner we went into the hotel lounge, we sat down and slowly drank a glass of port. Next to me Dr. Paul was sitting[1] chatting[2] to a lady. As usual his dog was lying at his feet. Monk, as he was called[3], was a big black labrador. He was[4] a fine dog, intelligent, marvellously trained. When you stroked him his eyes thanked you, but at the same time he looked ashamed as though he feared he was being[5] unfaithful to his master.

After a few minutes the door opened and a man came in, holding on a leash a young dog about six months old[6], which immediately took interest in Monk lying two or three yards away[7]. I recognized the newcomer. He was[4] a well known man; I had often seen him on[8] television. He sat down and began to read a magazine.

The two dogs were watching each other[9] intently. Soon Monk decided that he did not like the other dog and he gave a low growl. Hearing this growl the doctor turned round and said sharply, "Monk, shut up!"

But Monk growled a second time. This time the doctor was[10] furious. He raised his hand and gave Monk a cuff, saying, "I told[11] you to shut up, didn't I?" The blow only[12] skimmed the dog's head, but the doctor's hand, continuing its sweep, struck my nose[13].

The doctor jumped up, his face crimson[14]. "Oh," he exclaimed, "I beg your pardon! I am so[15] sorry to have hit you like that. Of course it was an accident. Please[16] forgive me."

---

1 Invert: 'was sitting Dr. Paul'. 2 'who was conversing'. 3 'as one called him'. 4 *il était* or *c'était*? § 67(a). 5 Express by an infinitive: 'he feared to be'; § 22(c). 6 'of about six months'; or one could use *âgé de*. 7 'at two or three metres from him'; § 87(b). 8 *à*. 9 Expressed by reflexive; § 3(a). 10 *était* or *fut*? § 12. 11 Construction with *dire*? § 31. 12 For 'only' used with a verb, see § 79. 13 Cp. *La balle le frappa au visage*. 14 'the face crimson'. 15 *tellement*. 16 Expressed by *je vous en prie*, e.g. *Entrez, je vous en prie*.

3 About to move[1] house

We have been living[2] in this house for seven years. In[3] a few days we are going to leave it, having bought another house a hundred miles away[4].

I have always liked this house. We had it built[5]. It is comfortable, light, with plenty of windows; it is well heated in the winter. Being of modern construction, it is very well appointed, especially the kitchen.

I have just come up into my study. I sit before my desk and look out of the window overlooking[6] the garden. I can[7] see the rose-bushes and the trees I planted[8] five or six years ago, the lawns I have mown dozens of times.

In[3] seven years a lot of things happen[9]. Of course, our family has greatly changed. When we came[8] here our daughter still lived with us; now she is married and has two children. Our son was a school-boy of thirteen; now he is[10] a tall young man who is at the University most of the time. Formerly he liked to spend his holidays with us, now he goes abroad with other students.

We shall be sorry, too, to leave so many good friends. All our neighbours are congenial, and we have had many merry gatherings to celebrate Christmas and the New Year. Yesterday evening our neighbours opposite called on us. They were about to[1] go on holiday and had come to say goodbye. I was very moved, and when I shook hands with them[11] I could hardly get out a word.

1 § 15, note 2.   2 Tense? § 17(a).   3 *en* or *dans*? § 88.   4 'situated at 100 miles from here'.   5 Construction? § 24(c).   6 'which overlooks'.   7 Unnecessary to use *pouvoir*; § 26, note 1.   8 Perfect tense.   9 Use the impersonal form *il arrive*; § 9.   10 *il est* or *c'est*? § 67(a).   11 Cp. *je lui serre la main.*

4 A hotel in Brittany

At Pornec I knew a little hotel kept by a couple named Monsieur and Madame Guertin. I had known[1] the Guertins for years. When I wanted to spend a few days on the Breton coast, I had only to[2] telephone, and they did everything possible[3] to give me a room. Occasionally, when the hotel was full, they found me a room elsewhere for a day or two.

The Hôtel Ker-Fur was a rather modest establishment, but the bedrooms were excellent and the food was good[4]. What I liked was[5] the family atmosphere and the cordiality of the proprietors.

The Guertins were not Bretons[6], they were Parisians[6]. One had only to[2] listen to Léon talking[7] for a minute to guess where he came from[8]: he had a very marked Paris accent. These people lived half the year at Pornec, the other half in Paris. In April they left their Montmartre flat[9] and went off to Pornec to get the hotel ready for the season. In the early days of October they would[10] close everything up again and return to the capital. I do not know what they lived on[11] there, whether either of them[12] had a job. Perhaps[13] the money they earned at Pornec sufficed for the whole year.

Léon had a red face and a purple nose. Doubtless[14] he owed this florid complexion to the many aperitives which customers got[15] him to drink in the little bar. Madame Guertin did most of the serious work. She was[16] a very nice woman. She spoke slowly and distinctly, so that it was[17] easy for foreigners to understand what she said.

1 Tense? § 17(b). 2 *à*. 3 'I do everything possible to', *je fais tout mon possible pour*. 4 'the food is good', *on mange bien*. 5 'it was'; § 65. 6 No article; § 46(b). 7 Infinitive. 8 'from where he came'. 9. 'flat of Montmartre'. 10 Tense? § 10. 11 'what do they live on?', *de quoi vivent-ils?* 12 'the one or the other'; § 75. 13 Inversion after *peut-être*; § 82(c). 14 Inversion after *sans doute*; § 82(c). 15 'made him drink'; § 24(b). 16 *elle était* or *c'était*? § 67(a). 17 *il était* or *c'était*? § 67(b).

5 The young organist

On leaving[1] the car park we passed under an archway and entered the old town which was surrounded on all sides by high walls several metres thick[2]. These[3] dated, I believe, from the eleventh century. In the Middle Ages this town must have been[4] a stronghold. Most of the streets were narrow and flanked by ancient houses.

It was market day. On the square hundreds of peasant women dressed in black were moving round between the stalls, on which goods of all kinds were exhibited. There was a constant hubbub: women talked loudly in[5] groups, traders shouted to attract customers.

After walking about[6] for some time we went into the church. Inside it was rather dark. At the far end, above the altar, the light was filtered by fine stained-glass windows; a few tapers were burning. We sat down to rest. Some one was playing the organ softly. Here and there women were kneeling, looking towards the altar and murmuring prayers. One by one they got up[7] and went out; others came in.

When my eyes got used to the half-light I noticed that the person who[8] was playing[9] the organ was a lad of about sixteen. After a while he stopped playing, got up and walked through the nave. He was[10] a handsome young fellow, with[11] a frank and earnest expression. Before going out, he turned towards the altar, knelt and prayed.

I said to myself, "It is[12] almost certain that one day that boy will be a priest."

1 § 8(c). 2 For dimensions, see § 87(c). 3 Pronoun? § 69(c). 4 Pluperfect of *devoir*; § 27. 5 *par*. 6 Perfect infinitive; § 23. 7 Tense for continuing process? 8 You could use *celui qui*. 9 'to play the piano', *jouer du piano*. 10 *il était* or *c'était*? § 67(a). 11 *à* in such descriptive expressions; § 47(a). 12 *il est* or *c'est*? § 67(b).

6 The unhappy accomplice

When Odile went in, Léon was sitting before his desk looking[1] dejected and miserable.

"What is the matter with you?" Odile asked him. "You don't look well[2]. You must have[3] eaten something which has upset your stomach[4]."

"No," answered Léon, "it isn't that. I eat almost nothing, I don't sleep[5], I am worried all the time."

"Well, my friend," went on Odile, "you must take a holiday. Why don't you go out more[6]? Why don't you enjoy yourself a bit? You stay in your flat day after day, you never see anybody[7]! I've told you not to[8] worry about your work. I've asked you several times to take me to the theatre, but you never want to do anything[7]."

"No," said Léon sadly, "I don't feel like going out, I don't want to meet people; I'm afraid."

"What are you afraid of?":

"You know very well what[9] I'm afraid of. I realize that all the business we do[10] here is dishonest. One day we shall have to deal with the police. The boss is a scoundrel. Every day I see the most shameless dishonesty, the worst[11] corruption ... And you ask me why I'm worried! If I could[12] get away I should do so[13], but I can't, I'm caught in the trap. If I'd known[12] at the outset what I know now, I should never have accepted this job."

"You're talking nonsense!" exclaimed Odile impatiently. "What[14] are you complaining about? You ought[15] to take advantage of your position. You've been lucky."

1 Cp. *il entra, l'air content.* 2 'to look well', *avoir bonne mine.* 3 What form of *devoir*? § 27. 4 Construction? § 47(b). 5 When the idea of 'no longer' is present, use *ne . . . plus.* 6 *davantage*; § 57. 7 Two negatives together; § 80(a). 8 Negative with infinitive; § 80(b). 9 Pronoun? § 65. 10 The expression is *traiter des affaires.* 11 *pire* or *plus mauvaise*? § 58(b). 12 Tense? § 16. 13 *le*; § 60(a). 14 'Of what are you complaining?' 15 Form of *devoir*? § 27.

7 Do you know Maigret?

As he was passing[1] the café, Louis spotted his friend Chauliat sitting on the terrace, chatting with another man of about his own[2] age. Naturally he went up to shake hands with Chauliat. The latter said to him:

"Louis, allow me to[3] introduce to you my brother-in-law, Maurice Leplat. He is a[4] chief inspector of police in Paris."

"Delighted, sir," said Louis, smiling. "I must say you don't look[5] at all like a policeman. If you are a[4] chief inspector in Paris, you must know Maigret?"

All three burst out laughing. Maurice said:

"It isn't the first time I've been asked[6] if I know Maigret. For many people he has become almost a living person. But, you know, we[7] chief inspectors don't act like Maigret. We don't stay out all hours of the night to watch a house or to seek information in shady bars. We don't often visit the scenes where crimes have taken place. Most of the time we stay in our offices. We question suspects brought[8] to us by our men, and we have to do a lot of administrative work."

"I have been told[6]," went on Louis, "that the setting and the atmosphere of Simenon's stories are quite authentic."

"Oh yes, it's true. That is explained[9] by the fact that formerly Simenon was a[4] newspaper reporter at the Law Courts. He observed[10] very exactly the premises and those[11] who worked in them . . . and obviously he knew his Paris marvellously well."

1 'passing before the café'. 2 Unnecessary to translate 'own'. 3 Construction with *permettre*? § 31. 4 No article required; § 46(b). 5 Use *avoir l'air de*. 6 Construction? § 7(a). 7 Cp. *nous autres Français*. 8 Turn: 'whom our men bring to us'. 9 Use the reflexive; § 7(b). 10 Perfect tense. 11 Pronoun? § 69(b).

8 An accident in the dark

It had been raining[1] for hours. There were puddles on the road, and each vehicle which passed us spattered our windscreen with mud. I hate journeys in those conditions. I should like to have[2] stayed at home, but our visit to the Martins had been agreed[1] for a long time and we were obliged to go[3].

The grey[4] November afternoon drew to its close; dusk fell; lights showed in the houses, cars put on their sidelights. Soon it was quite dark.

Then something unexpected happened[5]. We were going down a hill. Suddenly Bernard, who was driving, said, "What are all those lights on the road?" About[6] three hundred yards ahead of us we could[7] see a group of lights which seemed to indicate the presence of half-a-dozen cars, several of which[8] must be[9] barring the road.

As soon as he had[10] noticed these lights, Bernard slowed down, and when we got near the spot he stopped the car and got out. Without any[11] doubt there had been an accident. We could[7] dimly see people coming[12] and going in the darkness. It was horrible.

My wife was trembling. "I don't want to wait here," she said, "I shall be ill." I didn't like staying near the scene of an accident either[13].

Bernard came back. "Yes," he said, "two cars have collided. There is a man who is seriously injured. The police and the ambulance are about to[14] arrive; a doctor has been sent for[15]. We can do nothing. I am going to turn; we shall have to find another road."

1 Tense? § 17(b). 2 Form of *vouloir*? § 25. 3 Add 'there'. 4 For place of adjective, see § 53. 5 Use the impersonal form *il arriva*. 6 'At about . . .' 7 Unnecessary to use *pouvoir*: § 26, Note 1. 8 Position of *dont*? § 64(b). 9 Imperfect of *devoir*. 10 *avait* or *eut*? § 14. 11 *aucun*; § 78. 12 'who were coming and going'. 13 *non plus*; § 81(a). 14 § 15, Note 2. 15 'one has sent for . . .'

9 A cruel joke

"I've bad news for you," said Panard, looking[1] very grave. "Our poor Falla has just been drowned."

For a moment Matou stood[2] dumbfounded, then he said in[3] a faint voice, "Oh no! it isn't possible ... But tell me, how[4] did that poor chap get drowned?"

"You know[5] as well as I do," replied Panard grimly. "You sold him a boat, didn't you? You sold him Dr. Verrier's old boat, the one[6] that capsized every time it went out of the harbour."

"Well," said Matou, seeking to justify himself, "he insisted on[7] buying it. I warned[8] him that the boat had capsized several times, but that was because it needed ballast."

"You didn't tell him that it capsized at the slightest puff of wind?"

"But it isn't true!" protested Matou. "I myself went fishing with Dr. Verrier and I came back safe and sound!"

"Yes, because there was no wind. You had to use the engine, which took the boat along[9] at one kilometre an[10] hour."

Matou covered his face[11] with his hands.

"Oh!" he moaned, "it's true, I oughtn't to have[12] sold Falla that boat. He was such[13] a good fellow ... But are you sure he's dead? Have they tried to revive him?"

"I tell you he is lying over there on the quay. There is something still ticking[14], but we don't know whether it's his heart or his watch."

"Then perhaps[15] he isn't dead!" exclaimed Matou.

Just then the door opened and in walked Falla, drenched to the skin.

---

1 Cp. *Il entra, l'air mécontent.* 2 Use *rester* or *demeurer*. 3 *de.* 4 Form of question? § 82(b). 5 'You know it'; § 60(b). 6 Pronoun? § 69(b). 7 'to insist on (doing)', *insister pour (faire).* 8 Tense? § 13. 9 'to take along', *faire marcher.* 10 § 87(b). 11 Construction? § 47(b). 12 Form of *devoir?* § 27. 13 Not *tel*; § 74. 14 Use *battre.* 15 Inversion after *peut-être*; § 82(c)

10 Ideas of a Swiss guide

One day an English climber asked Francis, "Have you ever made the ascent of the north face of the Eiger?"

"No, sir," the guide replied, "I have never done that and it is[1] probable that I never shall[2]. As you already know[3], we are obliged by the Government to go to the help of people lost or injured on the mountains. Well, the Eiger is an exception, the only one, I believe. The ascent is so dangerous that the Government will not[4] take the responsibility of forcing guides to attempt it."

"You know, sir," Francis went on, "if people want to risk their lives[5], it's their affair. When they take it into their heads to[6] attempt that north face, they think: 'We are strong enough to[7] do it, we are well trained, we are prepared for[8] everything.' But they don't know the terrible conditions and the awful difficulties they will encounter up there. If they are resolved to go[9], you can't prevent them[10]. It isn't forbidden. Switzerland is a free country. In my opinion it shouldn't be forbidden.[11]"

"It is[1] possible to make a name for oneself[12] by doing that climb. Your portrait and articles describing your exploit appear in the newspapers, and that helps you in your job. Doubtless[13] there are plenty of guides who could[14] do it—I know a few[15]—but why risk[16] one's life? When you[17] think that nearly half of those who have attempted it have perished, it isn't encouraging."

1 *il est* or *c'est?* § 67(b). 2 'I shall never do it'. 3 *le* necessary; § 60(b).
4 Means 'is unwilling to'. 5 Use the singular; § 47 (b). 6 'to take it into one's head to (do)', *s'aviser de (faire)* or *se mettre en tête de (faire)*.
7 Preposition? § 22(d). 8 *à.* 9 Add 'there'. 10 *en* required; § 62.
11 'one ought not to forbid it'. 12 *se faire une réputation.* 13 Inversion after *sans doute*; § 82(c). 14 Tense of *pouvoir?* § 26. 15 'a few of them'.
16 Infinitive; § 22(a). 17 *on.*

11 When we are[1] married

SHE: When we are[1] married, I'm wondering how we are going to live, I mean when we have[1] a family. It is[2] true that for the moment we both have a job and we could[3] live on what we earn together. But what will happen when we have[1] children? I shouldn't[4] have a job and we should need much more money.

HE: Don't worry[5], we shall manage. Perhaps[6] you are forgetting that I have a father. I'm sure he will help us; he is[7] a generous man. A few weeks ago he told me that when I got married[8] he would sell his house and buy a smaller one[9]. Don't you see, he probably intends giving us a nice little house as a wedding present!

SHE: It[10] displeases me to hear you talk like that. We mustn't rely on other people; I[11] prefer independence. Besides, you never know what those[12] who have money will do with it[13]. It's like my mother's rich uncle. That old fool used to say that when he had retired[14] from business he would share out a good part of his money among his relations. But he never did it and when he died the State took nearly half his capital. So don't count too much on your father.

HE: Come now, don't get annoyed[15], darling!

SHE: I'm not getting annoyed, I'm just[16] telling you what I think.

---

1 Tense? § 15. 2 *il est* or *c'est*? § 67(b). 3 Tense of *pouvoir*? § 26. 4 When the idea of 'no longer' is present, use *ne . . . plus*. 5 Use 2nd person singular (*tutoyer*). 6 Inversion after *peut-être*; § 82(c). 7 *il est* or *c'est*? § 67(a). 8 'when I should get married'; § 15. 9 *en* necessary; cp. *j'en prends un plus grand*. 10 Pronoun? § 68. 11 Emphasise; § 63(b). 12 Pronoun? § 69(b). 13 Cp. *Que fait-il de son argent? Qu'en fait-il?* 14 Means 'would have retired'; § 15. 15 Imperative of reflexive; § 3(b). 16 Use *seulement* or *simplement*.

12 A man hard to[1] catch

Someone had seen the glimmer of an electric torch coming and going in the offices. As soon as the alarm was[2] given, the police hastened up and surrounded the building.

As usual, a crowd had gathered, but most of the people did not know what was happening.

Several policemen managed to get into the premises and went up into the offices, where they chased the intruder from room to room, without however being able to catch him. Seeing himself in danger of being cornered, the latter got out through an open window and began to climb up[3] a vertical pipe.

Meanwhile, inside the building, policemen were running about, going up from floor to floor, opening windows, looking out.

The burglar went on up[4], whilst down below in the street women shrieked with fright. Finally the man reached the roof, where he paused and made gestures of defiance. It was a sloping roof, on which the constables hesitated to follow him.

The firemen had just[5] arrived with their long ladders. A search-light was[2] trained on the man, but he leapt nimbly on to the next roof and disappeared.

When he was[2] arrested half-an-hour later, he was not even[6] out of breath. Then, just as the policemen were getting him into[7] the van, he somehow or other[8] slipped from their[9] hands and disappeared into the crowd.

1 *à.*   2 *était* or *fut*? § 6.   3 *le long de.*   4 'continued to go up'.   5 § 18. 6 Place of adverb? § 81(a).   7 Use *faire monter*.   8 Phrase? § 77.   9 Not the possessive adjective; § 47(b).

13 A picture

Yes, I like that little picture very much. It is an original. I bought[1] it in Montmartre. Last year we went[1] to Paris just[2] after Easter and spent a pleasant week exploring[3] the capital and making[3] excursions in the neighbourhood.

One morning we decided to go to Montmartre. On coming out of the Metro we walked up several narrow streets and reached the foot of those stone steps leading to the Sacré-Cœur on[4] the top of the hill. We didn't feel inclined to climb all those steps, so we took the funicular.

After visiting the Sacré-Cœur we went to the Place du Tertre, which my wife had never seen before[5]. It is a fairly large square, round which there are numerous cafés and restaurants brightened with coloured parasols. As you already know[6], it is a place where artists gather and work. Everywhere you[7] see young men standing before their easels[8], brush in hand[9], or talking in[10] noisy groups on the café terraces[11].

We bought that picture in a little shop at the corner of the square, and I don't regret having bought[12] it. I often look at it, wondering[13] how the artist managed to communicate that sensation of warmth and sunshine without using any bright colours. All the tints are neutral: indefinite greys and browns, with here and there a little green on the trees. Yet, looking[13] at this picture, I feel again the charm of a hundred mornings when I have walked across squares bathed in sunshine and shadow like that one[14].

---

1 Perfect tense suitable here. 2 *un peu.* 3 *à* + infinitive. 4 French would prefer: 'which stands on the top' ... 5 Unnecessary to translate 'before'. 6 *le* required; § 60(b). 7 *on.* 8 Singular; § 47(b). 9 For expressions descriptive of attitude, see § 47(a). 10 *par.* 11 'on the terrace of the cafés'. 12 Perfect infinitive; § 23. 13 *en* + present participle. 14 Pronoun? § 69(c).

14 The city councillor

When he was[1] elected a[2] city councillor, Marin was[3] very proud of himself[4]. At last he was somebody important, a man whose name appeared in the newspapers. At the Town Hall he soon got to know[3] the heads of the different departments; he called on them in their offices, he talked to them familiarly, always ready to exert his influence.

One day when[5] Marin was walking along the main street, it began to rain in torrents, so, having no umbrella, Marin sheltered under the awning of a shop. The next moment[6] he was[1] joined by a middle-aged man, with whom he began to chat.

"When the rain stops[7]," said this individual, "I am going to the Town Hall."

"Really!" said Marin, "and whom are you going to see at the Town Hall?"

"I hope I shall[8] see M. Bonnet. I haven't an appointment. I have written to that gentleman several times but he hasn't replied."

"Don't worry," went on Marin, "I'll see to it[9]. M. Bonnet is a good friend of mine[10]."

When the rain had[11] stopped they went together to the Town Hall. In the corridor they happened to pass[12] M. Bonnet, and Marin had[3] the impression that, on seeing his companion, Bonnet frowned.

Marin told the man to wait[13] while he talked[14] with the chief.

When he entered Bonnet's office, the latter, looking[15] furious, said to him, "Why do you bring that individual to me? He wants to see me about his dustbin. If his dustbin isn't emptied on Monday, he wants to see me on Tuesday, or else he writes me a rude letter. I've had enough of it! Tell him to go away[13]!"

1 *était* or *fut*? § 6. 2 No article required. 3 Tense? § 12. 4 Just *lui*. 5 Not *quand*; § 88. 6 § 56(b). 7 Tense? § 15. 8 Use an infinitive; § 22(c). 9 'to see to', *veiller à*. 10 'one of my good friends'. 11 Tense? § 14. 12 'You could use *par hasard*: 'they passed by chance'. 13 Construction with *dire*? § 31. 14 Tense? § 15. 15 Cp. *Il resta là, l'air honteux.*

15 On the water (I)

That day Bernet had gone fishing. Late in the afternoon he had gone up[1] the river a few hundred yards, he had found his favourite spot and had thrown out the anchor. Sitting alone in his boat, he had fished for several hours with great patience[2] and had caught a few nice perch. Finally, when he saw that evening was falling, he raised anchor and let the boat go down gently with the current.

It was a delightful evening. The air was calm and soft; the sunset sky was still red, but the moon was already shining.

When he was[3] near the place where he usually moored his boat, Bernet, charmed by the beauty of the evening, was[4] tempted to stay on the water a little longer, so he cast anchor again, lay down in the bottom of the boat and lit his pipe. The air was still warm. Bernet felt comfortable; he was perfectly happy. As he smoked[5], he felt his eyelids gradually close and finally[6] he dozed off.

When he awoke several hours later he was[4] surprised to see that the river was covered with thick mist[7], so that he could[8] no longer see the banks. The moon had disappeared, the air was chilly.

Bernet stood up in the boat, grasped the anchor chain and pulled, but he felt a resistance. He pulled hard, but the anchor did not come; it must have[9] caught in something on the river-bed. It was[10] impossible to break the chain, and Bernet had no[11] tool to unfasten it from the boat. He had to resign himself to wait for daybreak, when other fishermen would come to his help.

1 Use *remonter*. 2 Article required; § 46(a). 3 Tense? § 12. 4 *était* or *fut*? § 6. 5 'While smoking'; § 8(c). 6 You could use *finir par*: 'he finished by dozing off'. 7 'a thick mist'. 8 Unnecessary to use *pouvoir*; § 26, Note 1. 9 What tense of *devoir*? § 27. 10 *il était* or *c'était*? § 67(b). 11 Use *ne . . . aucun*.

16 On the water (II)

So Bernet relit his pipe, lay down in the boat and soon[1] dozed off again. He slept several hours. When at last he opened his eyes, he saw something extraordinary. The mist had retreated from the river and had massed along the banks, so that on[2] either side there[3] rose a sort of long, white cliff about thirty feet high[4].

This sight was so strange that Bernet was[5] frightened by it[6]. He had never seen anything[7] like it[8]. It[9] looked like something supernatural, out of this world. Bernet noticed, too, that the night, which had been absolutely quiet, was now filled with mysterious little sounds. Something gently tapped the side of the boat. It was probably only a piece of drifting wood, but that shook Bernet's nerves.

Then, suddenly, he thought[10] he saw[11] a shadow gliding[12] over the water a few yards away[13]. He shouted and a voice replied. It was a fisherman who had set out before dawn. Bernet told him of his misadventure and asked him to help him. Together they grasped the chain, but pull as they might[14] the anchor did not shift.

Now daylight was coming[15], grey and cold. Another fisherman passed. They hailed him and he came up in his boat to see what was the matter. Then all three pulled hard on the chain and gradually the anchor yielded. It came up slowly, as though weighted with some heavy object. Finally there[16] came to the surface a dark mass: it was a body with a big stone tied to the neck.

1 You could use *ne pas tarder à (faire)*; § 21. 2 Preposition? 3 Use the impersonal form with *il*; § 9. 4 Dimensions, § 87(c). 5 Tense? § 6. 6 Since we say *avoir peur de, être effrayé de*, what will the pronoun be? 7 Combined negatives; § 80(a). 8 Use *pareil*. 9 *Cela*. 10 Tense? § 12. 11 Use an infinitive; § 22(c). 12 'which was gliding'. 13 'at a few mètres from him'. 14 Use the idiom *avoir beau (faire)*, e.g. *il avait beau crier*. 15 Use *se lever*. 16 The impersonal *il*; § 9.

17 What had become of[1] the father?

"Will you sit down?" Riolle said to the girl.

"Do you intend keeping me long?" she asked. "I am in a hurry."

"That will depend on you," said Riolle quietly. "Although you are[2] in a hurry, I am nevertheless obliged to ask you a certain number of questions, and that will take time. I want you to realize[3] that I shall attach great importance[4] to what you tell[5] me."

"Is it necessary that I should answer[6] your questions? I've done nothing wrong and there's no[7] reason for me to[8] tell you things that concern only myself."

"Let me tell you, mademoiselle, that it is not a question of trying to incriminate you. I shall ask you only for information which might[9] help us. But I want you to[3] tell me the truth and nothing but the truth, you understand. . . . Now tell me, how long had you known[10] that your father hadn't a job?"

She did not appear surprised by this question, she must have[11] anticipated it. She hesitated a moment, as though she were trying to remember exactly.

"About six months," she finally said. "We're now in May. I am sure it was in November, because it was cold and it was dark at five o'clock. I chanced[12] to be in the district, so I went to the factory where we believed he worked. There were no lights, everything was locked up and I was told[13] that the firm no longer existed."

"Is it possible that your mother knows[14] all this?"

"I don't think so[15]. If she had known[16] she would have told me; at least she wouldn't have been able to conceal it from me[17]."

---

1 § 70.   2 Subjunctive; § 38.   3 Expressed by subjunctive; § 40.   4. Article required; § 46(a).   5 Tense? § 15.   6 Subjunctive; § 39.   7 Use *ne . . . aucun*.   8 Express by *pour que* + subjunctive.   9 Tense of *pouvoir*? § 26.   10 Tense? § 17(b).   11 Tense of *devoir*? § 27.   12 Make use of *par hasard*, 'by chance'.   13 Construction? § 7(a).   14 Subjunctive; § 41. 15 § 81(a).   16 'it' must be supplied; § 60(b).   17 Construction with *cacher*? § 30.

18 Free lessons

The headmaster walked slowly round the room with[1] his hands in his pockets, pausing a moment to look out of the window. Finally he turned to Frilin and said in[2] a stern voice:

"Mr. Frilin, I am surprised."

Frilin opened his eyes wide and stammered:

"You are suprised, sir? At[3] what?"

"Listen, my friend," went on Mr. Croutte, laying his hand on Frilin's shoulder, "tell me, how long have you been[4] a master in this school?"

"Four years," replied Frilin, wondering if he was going to be sacked. "I hope, headmaster, that my work here has given you satisfaction?"

"Oh yes, oh yes, it is not a question of your work. I am happy that our pupils are able[5] to profit by[6] your excellent instruction. But I want you to tell[7] me something. You give private lessons in your classroom don't you?"

"Yes, sir, it is[8] true that I give a few lessons, but ..."

"One moment, please. Allow me to finish what I was going to say. Before you give[9] private lessons, you should[10] tell me, so that I know[11] what is going on in the school. May I remind you, too, that masters who give private lessons have to pay me twenty per cent of their fees? I regret that you do not observe[12] this rule. ... By the way, how much do you charge an[13] hour?"

"I don't charge anything, headmaster! The lessons I give are free."

"What, free lessons!" yelled Mr. Croutte. "If you give free lessons, my good sir, what will become of your colleagues, including myself? We shall all[14] starve!"

1 § 47(a). 2 *de*. 3 Remember that 'surprised by' is *surpris de*. 4 Tense? § 17(a). 5 Subjunctive; § 40. 6 *de*. 7 Expressed by subjunctive; § 40. 8 *il est* or *c'est*? § 67(b). 9 Use an infinitive; § 38, Special Note 1. 10 Means 'you ought to'. 11 Subjunctive after *pour que*. 12 Subjunctive; § 40. 13 *par*. 14 § 73.

19 Political murder at Vichy

I was about[1] two hundred yards from the boulevard when I thought I heard[2] several bangs. The next moment I saw men running[3] along[4] the boulevard, shouting and waving their[5] arms. Obviously something serious had happened.

When I reached the broad avenue, there were groups of people standing at the street corners, talking excitedly and all[6] looking in the direction of the bridge.

As I learned[7] later, this is what took place:

At about five o'clock, in the main street, which was crowded at that time, two young terrorists shot down an Algerian senator and a French politician who were strolling and chatting together. As soon as they had[8] carried out their crime, the terrorists fled.

As often happens[9] in these moments of unexpected violence, nobody knew what to do. Passers-by stood[10] bewildered, hardly realizing what had just taken place. Then a few men started in pursuit, shouting[11] "Murder! Murder!" The terrorists turned on them and fired several shots, but luckily nobody was[12] hit.

Meanwhile, the policeman on duty at the crossroads by the bridge heard the shots and the shouting, and soon saw the terrorists running[3] towards him. He made as though to[13] stop them, but one of them fired at him and he fell wounded in the thigh.

But then a police car came along at full speed, drove past the men and stopped. Armed policemen got out[14]. The terrorists were[12] pinned down against a wall and were[12] arrested.

---

1 'at about'. 2 Use an infinitive; § 22(c). 3 'who were running'. 4 *sur*. 5 Not *leurs*; § 47(b). 6 *tous* after verb. 7 Supply 'it'; §60(b). 8 Tense? § 14. 9 Use the impersonal form with *il*; § 9. 10 Use *rester* or *demeurer*. 11 *en* + present participle. 12 Tense? § 6. 13 'to make as though to', *faire mine de*. 14 'got out of it'.

20 The eavesdropper

Brigitte was about to[1] open the door, when she heard a sound of voices in the room. Two people were talking. She listened. One of the voices was her father's[2], the other Anne's[2]. Hearing her own name pronounced[3], she pressed her ear to the crack of the door and listened to what was being said[4].

"You know, Maurice," Anne was saying, "Brigitte doesn't look well. It's a pity she's[5] so pale and thin. When she's in a bathing costume you can see her ribs. I'm not surprised she's always got[5] a pale face, seeing that she seldom goes to bed before midnight. And then she smokes too much. You ought[6] to tell her not to[7] smoke more than two or three cigarettes a[8] day. Besides, those[9] who smoke a lot don't eat."

There was a moment's silence, then Brigitte heard her father's voice:

"I know, I know. Brigitte is seventeen, and at that age plenty of girls are thin. But what do you expect me to[10] do? If she wants to smoke, I can't stop her[11]; I can't watch her all the time. If I forbid her to smoke she will do it without my knowing[12]."

Anne's voice went on:

"So you are going to wait until[13] she's really ill? There is nothing to stop you from sending her to bed earlier. Then there's her exam. After failing in June she hopes to succeed in November. She ought[6] to work more[14] before it is[15] too late. She pretends to work in the afternoon, but I know she does nothing."

Brigitte had heard enough[16]. She stole away.

---

1 § 15, note 2. 2 Pronoun? § 69(a). 3 Cp. *J'entendais vider les poubelles*, I heard the dustbins being emptied. 4 This could be expressed by the reflexive; § 7(b). 5 Subjunctive; § 40. 6 Form of *devoir*? § 27. 7 Negative with infinitive, § 80(b). 8 *par*. 9 Pronoun? § 69(b). 10 Use *vouloir que* + subjunctive. 11 *en* required; § 62. 12 *sans que* + subjunctive. 13 *attendre que* + subjunctive. 14 *davantage*. 15 Subjunctive; § 38. 16 Add 'of it'.

21 The unexpected visitor

Suddenly Françoise thought[1] she heard[2] a knock on the shutter. She sat[3] still and listened. There was another knock[4], this time louder. She was[5] frightened. Without getting up she called out in a voice which trembled a little:

"What is it? Who's knocking?"

"It's a friend, open the shutters," said a man's voice. "It's Jean."

Françoise sat up with a start. The shock was[1] such that she nearly[6] fainted. It was three years since[7] she had seen Jean. They had been engaged, but one day Jean had told her bluntly that he was too young to get married and that, before settling down, he wanted to see the world. He had gone away on a ship and she had had no more news of him[8]. Then, a year later, although deep down she still loved[9] Jean, she had married Philippe, and they had a child. And now Jean had come back.

Françoise made up her mind. She could not refuse to see him, so she called out:

"Wait for me to[10] come and open [11] the door, it's locked."

"Don't bother about[12] the door," was the reply, "just[13] open the shutters."

She opened the window and the shutters, and Jean jumped into the room. He held out his arms, smiling[14], he wanted[1] to kiss her, but she pushed him off, saying[14] sharply:

"None of[15] that, Jean! Don't forget I'm married. You must be stupid to think that, after leaving me like that you can come back and court me as though nothing had happened!"

---

1 Tense? § 12.   2 Use an infinitive; § 22(c).   3 Use *rester* or *demeurer*. 4 'one knocked again'.   5 Tense? § 6.   6 Express by *faillir*; § 22(e). 7 Construction? § 81(b).   8 § 56(a).   9 Imperfect subjunctive.   10 Use *attendre que* + subjunctive.   11 Infinitive; § 22(b).   12 'to bother about', *s'occuper de* or *se soucier de*.   13 *seulement*.   14 *en* + present participle. 15 *Pas de*.

22 Visit to a doctor

Usually a doctor's waiting room is a dreary place, but this one[1] was different. The people didn't look sad or bored; some of them[2] were smiling and soon I realized why. The consulting-room door was half-open and you could[3] hear the doctor talking[4] to a woman patient. He talked loudly so that[5] everybody should hear him.

"Come now, madame," he was saying, "you say it is[6] impossible for you to rest? You think that if you don't work it will be the end of the world; the government will resign, the factories will close, the hens won't lay any more eggs!" And so on. He was[7] a witty man and he joked all the time. Evidently he considered laughter and cheerfulness as an essential part of his treatment, and I think he was right.

When it was[8] my turn, I went into the consulting-room. The doctor shook hands with me and asked me to sit down. I looked at him. Although his nose was[9] a little askew, he was[7] a handsome man; he had lively and intelligent eyes[10].

I told[11] him about my catarrh. He didn't take it seriously.

"You know, monsieur," he said, "it isn't a cold, it's hay fever. I will write you a prescription."

"So you are touring?" said the doctor, as I got up to go. "It's very pleasant. If I had time I should do the same. . . . Is that your car behind mine[12]? It's a nice car. It's an English make, isn't it?"

I thanked him, paid and went out. As I was closing the door I heard the doctor's voice: "Whose turn[13], please?"

1 Pronoun? § 69(c). 2 § 63(a). 3 Unnecessary to use *pouvoir*; § 26, Note 1. 4 'who was talking'. 5 *pour que* + subjunctive; § 38. 6 *il est* or *c'est*? § 67(b). 7 *il était* or *c'était*? § 67(a). 8 Tense? § 12. 9 Subjunctive after *bien que* or *quoique*. 10 § 47(a). 11 Use *parler*. 12 Pronoun? § 71. 13 Expressed as: 'To whom the turn?'

23 A moment of frankness

"But what do you want me to[1] tell you?" asked Mousse, getting up from his chair.

"Sit down!" Berthe said to him in a sharp tone. "Now listen to me. We've got to[2] understand each other. Tell me first of all, have you given us away?"

"Of course not!" answered Mousse. "How could[3] I do that? If I denounced Pache, it would be denouncing[4] you too[5], and I wouldn't[6] do that for anything in the[7] world."

"Good!" went on Berthe. "But you simply must[8] keep quiet about[9] what you have seen and heard here. Is that understood?"

"Oh! it's so difficult," groaned Mousse. "But why go on[10] like this? Why don't you leave this crook?"

"Because I don't want to[11]," retorted Berthe without hesitating. "The life I lead suits me. I have money, I know people, I am invited everywhere, I can dress with taste. Let me tell you that I hate poverty. I have been poor, I know what it is, and I had to work hard to get out of it[12]. Don't you see how ungrateful[13] you are? Money has come to you without your making[14] any[15] effort to earn it."

"Oh!" sighed Mousse, "I'm sorry I spoke[16] to you like that."

"Don't worry," said Berthe, lighting a cigarette. "I'm afraid you are[17] a bit simple, but you are a likeable fellow all the same. I just[18] ask you for your friendship, as I gladly offer you mine."

---

1 *vouloir que* + subjunctive; § 40. 2 Use *il faut que* + subjunctive. 3 Tense? § 26. 4 Infinitive. 5 § 63(b). 6 Means 'would not be willing to'. 7 *au*. 8 *il faut absolument que.* . . . 9 *sur*. 10 Infinitive; § 22(a). 11 'to' not translated. 12 Pronoun? § 62. 13 Order: 'how you are ungrateful'. 14 *sans que* + subjunctive. 15 Use *ne . . . aucun*. 16 Infinitive may be used: 'I am sorry to have spoken . . .' 17 Subjunctive; § 40. 18 Use *seulement*.

24 A time of mourning

When the doctor and the priest had[1] gone, Dupeu felt the need to get out of the house of mourning and to be alone for a while, so he put on his hat and coat and walked down towards the Seine. The familiar street, with its rows of old houses, the shutters of which[2] were all closed, was quiet and deserted.

When he reached the bridge he turned to the right. There was the river flowing[3] quietly between the screens of tall poplars. The sky was clear and the stars seemed to be swimming on the water. Wisps of whitish mist drifting[4] over the banks brought to Dupeu's lungs a damp smell which stirred in his heart very old memories.

He suddenly saw[5] his mother kneeling by[6] the brook which flowed past their little house away there in Normandy. She was doing the washing. In the quiet of the country-side he could[7] hear the sound of her platter and her voice calling out[8], "Alfred, bring me some soap!" And he remembered that there[9] came from the brook and the sodden fields that same river smell that was now rising from the Seine.

He was[10] seized with deep despair. It was as though a flash of light had just lit up the full[11] extent of his sorrow and his irrevocable loss. Life appeared to him suddenly in all its briefness and wretchedness, full of sufferings and misunderstandings. Although he was[12] a little ashamed of it, he wept. But afterwards he felt relieved and he slowly walked back home.

1 Tense? § 14. 2 Position of *dont*? § 64(b). 3 'which was flowing'.
4 'which were drifting'. 5 Use *revoir*. 6 Means 'on the bank of'.
7 Unneccessary to use *pouvoir*; § 26, Note 1. 8 'which was calling out'.
9 Expressed by the impersonal *il*; § 9. 10 Tense? § 6. 11 'the whole extent'. 12 Subjunctive after *bien que* or *quoique*.

25 Handshakes

Yes, Hamel is a curious man. At bottom he is shy, but he tries to overcome his shyness by[1] doing his best to please everybody. You must have[2] noticed that he talks incessantly, but he never says what he really thinks; he hides behind a cloud of words, so to speak. After listening to him for a few minutes, you[3] ask yourself what he has said, and you remember nothing. But, above all, he loves shaking hands with people. Wherever[4] he is, if he sees an outstretched hand, he shakes it. I remember the day[5] his nephew got married. The church was by[6] the market place, and it was market day. Seeing that a wedding was taking place, a crowd of onlookers had gathered before the gates. Hamel arrived in his car, he got out[7] and at once began shaking hands with all these people. A few[8] of the men laughed at him a bit, but most of the women seemed to think he was[9] a charming gentleman.

A friend of mine told me a funny story about Hamel. This young man was going to Paris by train. At the station he met Hamel, who was going there too[10]. They got into a compartment together. As usual, Hamel talked throughout the journey. When they got out of the train Hamel was still talking. They reached the exit. There was the ticket-collector holding out his hand. Hamel couldn't help grasping this hand, saying[11] "How are you today?" The man said laughingly[11], "Very well, sir . . . your ticket, please."

1 *en* + present participle. 2 What form of *devoir*? § 27. 3 *on*. 4 *Où que* + subjunctive; § 44. 5 'the day when'; § 88. 6 Means 'near to'. 7 'he got out of it'. 8 Pronoun? § 72. 9 *il était* or *c'était*? § 67(a). 10 'he too'; § 63(b). 11 § 8(c).

26 Too late

"But," protested Pertuis, "when I asked you for your daughter's hand, you refused me and gave me the sack!"

"Ah!" said Louche with a sigh[1], "it's a pity we had[2] that little misunderstanding. Let us forget what I said then. It appears that you have been successful[3] in business; I am told[4] you are now a rich man. But I must[5] tell you how much my daughter misses you. The poor child has gone[6] all[7] pale and thin. In a word she still loves you."

"But really . . ." exclaimed Pertuis, but Louche would not let him get in a word.

"No, my friend," he broke in, "don't be surprised that we have come[2] to renew our friendship; we haven't seen you for[8] so long. At first Marie, poor child, hesitated to accompany me, but I insisted on[9] her coming."

"I am afraid you are[10] mistaken," said Pertuis coldly, "I regret that you have[10] . . ."

"Let her come[11] and talk to you herself," said Louche, jumping up. "Wait for me to[12] bring her in!" He ran out.[13]

A moment later he came back, holding Marie by the hand. She was made up, her hair was nicely done, she was wearing a smart suit. She looked at Pertuis with a smile[14], then she lowered her eyes modestly.

Pertuis made up his mind; he had had enough. He pressed a bell on his desk and as soon as his secretary appeared, he said to her sharply:

"Will you see this young lady[15] out?"

Marie stared at him for a moment with eyes of hate, then she took a step towards him:

"Take that!" she shouted, and she smacked his face.

1 'sighing'; § 8(c). 2 Perfect subjunctive; § 40. 3 'you have succeeded'.
4 Use *on*; § 7(a). 5 Use *il faut que* + subjunctive. 6 Use *devenir*.
7 Agreement? § 55. 8 Construction? § 81(b). 9 *pour que* + subjunctive.
10 Subjunctive; § 40. 11 § 37. 12 Use *attendre que* + subjunctive.
13 § 2. 14 'smiling'. 15 'this young lady', *mademoiselle*.

27 A lonely woman

Although the weather was[1] fine when Philippe had set out, the sky had darkened and it was beginning to rain. The boy had made a long detour and he was wondering how he could[2] get back home. Seeing a house behind some tall trees, he went to it[3] to ask his way.

On approaching the door he passed[4] a window and glanced inside. He saw a large room, in a corner of which[5] a woman was sitting on a low chair. She was no longer young; she might have been[6] fifty.

Philippe rang the bell. Almost immediately the door opened and the woman stood[7] before him.

"Who are you? What do you want?" she asked him in a loud voice.

"I have come from the other side of the hill," stammered Philippe.

"Well, where are you going?"

"I am not going anywhere[8]," Philippe said, "I am out for a walk."

"But you must[9] live somewhere?"

"I live at La Saulaie," answered the boy. "I have lost my way."

The woman glared at him with[10] her hard eyes.

"La Saulaie?" she said at last. "What are you doing at M. Maricourt's?"

"He's my grandfather."

"Yes, yes, I see the likeness," she said thoughtfully, "though you have[11] more delicate features[12]. I have never seen you before[13]. But come in, my boy, you can chat awhile with a poor old woman who is very lonely. Then I will show you the way to get home."

---

1 Subjunctive. 2 Tense of *pouvoir*? § 26. 3 § 61. 4 'passed in front of'. 5 Pronoun? § 66. 6 Tense of *pouvoir*? § 26. 7 Tense? § 12. 8 § 78; *nul.* 9 *il faut bien que* + subjunctive. 10 *de.* 11 Subjunctive after *bien que, quoique.* 12 § 47(a). 13 Unnecessary to translate 'before'.

28 A duel

Two men, very well[1] known in Paris, quarrelled and one of them struck the other. The latter immediately challenged his assailant to a duel, a duel not with pistols, but with swords.

The meeting place was[2] agreed on. The men were to[3] fight in the garden of a house to the west of Paris. No[4] attempt was made[5] to keep the affair secret and, although duelling is[6] forbidden by the law, the authorities did nothing to stop the fight. The Press soon had[7] knowledge of it and numerous reporters were sent[5] to describe and photograph what happened[8]. These[9] hid behind walls or posted themselves at windows overlooking the garden.

At the appointed hour a group came out of the house: the combatants, their seconds, a doctor and a few friends. The preparations were[7] brief, the swords were[2] measured, the two men started the fight. One of them was much younger than the other, but he knew nothing about fencing; he had merely[10] taken a few lessons for the occasion. On the other hand, his opponent, although much older, was a fine swordsman.

The young one[11] attacked from[12] the outset, counting on his dash and agility to penetrate the other's defence, but the latter defended himself skilfully, waiting for his opponent to[13] do something rash, so that he could[14] inflict a slight wound on him[15]. The chance soon[16] came and the old man pierced the other's arm with the point of his sword. It was over.

Meanwhile, all along the walls and from[17] nearby balconies the men of the Press were busy taking countless photographs.

---

1 You need not translate 'well'. 2 Tense? § 6. 3 Tense of *devoir*? § 27. 4 Use *ne . . . aucun*. 5 Better to use *on*. 6 Subjunctive after *bien que, quoique*. 7 Tense? § 12. 8 Means 'what would happen'. 9 Pronoun? § 69(c). 10 For 'only' or 'merely' used with a verb, see § 79. 11 'one' not translated. 12 *dès*. 13 *attendre que* + subjunctive. 14 Subjunctive after *pour que*. 15 'on him', *lui*. 16 Express by *ne pas tarder à*; § 21. 17 Use *du haut de*.

29 On the trail

Although he had slept[1] several hours during the night, Gaston felt exhausted after his long journey. However, he had to[2] find Mourot. He spent the morning going[3] from café to café, showing the photograph and asking each time, "Do you know this man?" The reply was everywhere the same, "No, I have never seen him." But Gaston was persuaded that those who knew Mourot would not[4] admit it.

At last, in a little café in[5] the Rue Doumer, he found the information he was seeking. The proprietor was out, it seemed[6], and it was his wife who was serving.

After ordering a drink, Gaston asked the woman, "Tell me, do you know Mourot?"

"Which one[7]?" she said. "I know two men of that name. They are cousins, it appears[6]."

"I mean[8] the big fellow[9], the one[10] who has a scar on his forehead. Just[11] look at this photo."

Having glanced at the portrait, she said, "Yes, it's Alfred. In the old days he was a good customer, but he doesn't come to our place[12] any more. I'm told[13] he is always at the *Floride*. It's a café-restaurant a bit out of the town; anyone[14] will tell you where it[15] is. But if you go there I advise you to be on your guard. Alfred and his pals are toughs, folk to be feared[16]; I'm sure they are capable of anything[17]. Listen, I don't want you to[18] say it was I who sent you. I'm afraid my husband may think[19] I've been unwise."

"Well, you don't need to tell him," said Gaston. "Nobody will know I've been here."

1 Pluperfect subjunctive. 2 *il fallait que* + imperfect subjunctive. 3 *à* + infinitive. 4 Means 'were not willing to'. 5 *de*. 6 Inversion; § 82(d). 7 Pronoun? § 66. 8 'I wish to speak of'. 9 'fellow' need not be translated. 10 Pronoun? § 69(b). 11 Expressed by *un peu*. 12 Use *chez*. 13 Use *on*; § 7(a). 14 § 77. 15 *cela*. 16 *à* + infinitive; § 21. 17 'everything'. 18 *vouloir que* + subjunctive; § 40. 19 Subjunctive; § 40.

30 An evening walk

That evening Lise stayed at home. She did not know what[1] to do.
She did not feel inclined to read, so after wandering from room to
room for some time, she made up her mind to write to Michel. She
wrote a page, she was[2] dissatisfied with it[3], so she tore up the paper
and began again. She took[4] longer to write the second page than the
first. However, she persisted and at last the letter was[5] finished; she
decided to post it.

When Lise went out, night was already beginning to fall. She
made for the post-office, but hardly had[6] she slipped her letter into
the box, when she felt a great desire to get it back. Why had she
been in such a hurry? She ought to have[7] kept the letter until the
next morning. But she was always in a hurry to do things. Then,
when she imagined Michel reading[8] the letter, she was[2] glad.

She did not go home at once, but walked in the direction of the
sea. At that time the beach was deserted. She sat down on the sand
at the foot of a dune, out of[9] the wind, and looked out over[10] the
sea, listening to the sound of the waves breaking[11] on the shore.

A little later, in the half-light, she saw a man walking[12] along the
beach. He was taking his dog for a walk. The animal spotted her and
ran towards her, barking. The man called it back and moved away.
But Lise suddenly felt[2] frightened. Having looked at her watch,
she realized it was later than she thought[13], so she got up hurriedly
and returned home.

1 § 70. 2 Tense? § 12. 3 'dissatisfied with' = *mécontent de*; what will
the pronoun be? 4 'to take time to (do)', *mettre du temps à (faire)*.
5 Tense? § 6. 6 Tense? § 14. 7 Tense of *devoir*? § 27. 8 'who was
reading'. 9 *à l'abri de*. 10 Use *promener les yeux (le regard) sur*. 11
'which were breaking'. 12 'who was walking'. 13 § 81(b).

31 Salmon fishing

It was cold. Several times, in the course of the afternoon, it had snowed. The sky had darkened, the wind had risen, the flakes had begun to fall, so thick at times that we could hardly make out the opposite bank.

I was smoking my pipe, watching Paul spinning[1]. Standing in the water, he cast[2] his bait across the river, wound[2] in his line and began[2] again. He had been fishing[3] for nearly three hours.

Then, at a certain moment, he turned round and said to me, "I am sure a fish has just touched my bait." He cast again. Suddenly his rod bent and began jerking violently[4]. The salmon was hooked. It was now a question of not[5] losing him.

Without hurrying, I got up, took off my raincoat, entered the water with[6] the gaff in my hand and stood a[7] yard or two behind Paul. The struggle lasted about twenty minutes. The salmon was strong. Again and again he dashed off, but each time Paul managed to bring him back. At last I saw the great silvery fish near the surface before he dived[8] again. Although he wasn't[8] huge he was[9] a lovely salmon; he might have[10] weighed twelve or fourteen pounds[11].

All this went on in silence. There was nothing to say. Paul needed all his strength and concentration; as for me, I knew I must[12] make no[13] sudden movement to alarm the fish when he was[14] within our reach.

At last the salmon, quite exhausted, was wallowing on the surface. Paul was bringing him in slowly. I cautiously moved forward, reached out my arm, then with[15] a quick movement I gaffed the fish, lifted him out of the water and carried him to the bank.

---

1 'who was spinning'. 2 These are repeated actions. Tense? 3 Tense? § 17(b). 4 'to give violent jerks'. 5 Negative with infinitive; § 80(b). 6 § 47(a). 7 'at a metre or two'. 8 Subjunctive; § 38. 9 *il était* or *c'était*? § 67(a). 10 Tense of *pouvoir*? § 26. 11 'from twelve to fourteen pounds'. 12 Imperfect of *devoir*. 13 Use *ne . . . aucun*. 14 Means 'when he would be'. 15 *de*.

32 Where is that cheque?

"What a life!" said Gredon, throwing himself into his armchair. "What a life! Let's see, what have I got to do now? By the way, when I think of it[1], we haven't yet received a cheque from Blondin Brothers. I'm surprised they haven't[2] sent it. When we get[3] it we shall be able to settle Menier's account. I must mention it to Potier. But where is Potier? I haven't seen him yet this morning."

"He must be in his office," said the secretary. "If you like, I will go and ask[4] him to come and see[4] you, unless you want[5] to go and see him yourself."

"No," replied Gredon, "ask him to come here a moment."

A minute later the secretary brought in Potier.

"Good morning, Potier," Gredon said to him, "please sit down. We were talking about Blondin Brothers. We carried out a big order for them some time ago, didn't we? They promised to pay as soon as they had[6] received the goods. That's what they always say, but they keep us waiting for months."

Potier raised his[7] eyebrows. "But, sir," he said, "they've already paid!"

"What!" exclaimed Gredon, "you say they've paid? Well, where's the cheque?"

"It's in a drawer in[8] my desk," Potier replied, looking[9] guilty.

"Bless my soul!" shouted Gredon. "I had been expecting[10] that cheque for weeks and all that time it was lying in your desk!"

"No, sir," protested Potier, "it didn't arrive until[11] yesterday. Shall I[12] take it to the bank?"

"Why, of course! But before you go[5] there I want you to[13] sign a letter. Here it is. Just[14] sign, don't trouble to read it."

1 Pronoun? § 29; *penser*. 2 Subjunctive; § 40. 3 Means 'we shall receive'. 4 § 22(b). 5 Subjunctive; § 38. 6 Tense? § 15. 7 Not *ses*; § 47(b). 8 'of my desk'. 9 Cp. *il entra, l'air las*. 10 Tense? § 17(b). 11 'it arrived only yesterday'. 12 § 15, Note 3. 13 Expressed by subjunctive; § 40. 14 Expressed by *simplement* or *seulement*.

33 How to smuggle a watch

As soon as he had[1] taken his seat in the plane, Martin began to worry about the watch he had bought. He thought of all the ways in which[2] people manage to smuggle watches. There are those who hide the watch in their shoe, those who slip the watch down their wives' busts[3], those who stick the watch to their stomachs[4].

He imagined himself in all those situations. If he had the watch in his shoe, the Customs-officer, seeing him hobble away, would call him back and say to him, "Why are you walking like that, sir?"

Then how could[5] he say to a woman passenger, "Excuse me, madam, will you allow me to slip this watch down[6] your bust?" On arrival they[7] would call the police.

Perhaps[8] he could[5] stick the watch to his stomach. But when he was[9] in front of the Customs-officer the watch might[5] come unstuck, it would fall down[6] his trouser leg, it would be seen[10] and he would be arrested.

In his agitation he was groaning quietly. The passenger sitting next to him turned and said to him, "You seemed worried, sir. What's the matter?"

Martin told him his trouble. The man said, shaking his head, "I'm very much afraid you'll be[11] caught. The first thing a Customs-officer does is to[12] look you in the eye. If you look guilty, he knows you've something to hide. Look here[13], take my watch, it's old and cheap; give me yours[14]. I shan't have any difficulty. When we have gone[15] through the Customs, I'll give you back your watch."

The plane landed. In the crowd Martin soon lost sight of his man and he never saw him again[16].

---

1 Tense? § 14. 2 'in a way', *d'une manière*. What pronoun translates 'in which'? 3 'in the bust of their wife'. 4 Singular; § 47(b). 5 Tense of *pouvoir*? § 26. 6 *dans*. 7 Use *on*. 8 Inversion after *peut-être*. 9 Means 'would be'. 10 'one would see it'. 11 Subjunctive; § 40. 12 *c'est de ...* 13 *Tenez*. 14 Pronoun? § 71. 15 Means 'will have gone'. 16 Use *ne ... plus jamais*.

34 Gloomy thoughts

Georges put on his slippers and dressing-gown, went down the stairs and into[1] the little kitchen. He wondered if he should make tea for himself and his parents. But, from their room, he had heard no[2] movement, no[2] sound of voices, although it was[3] nearly nine o'clock. Perhaps[4] they were still asleep.

Not knowing what[5] to do, he sat down on a chair. It was Sunday morning; everything was quiet. He looked round the humble room. It was all[6] just the same as when he was a little boy; the same table, the same chairs, the same gas-cooker. On the wall hung a little print representing a cottage shaded by[7] a large tree. It[8] was, so to speak, a part of the familiar furniture and he had never troubled to look at it closely before[9].

Memories of childhood came back to his[10] mind. He remembered the time when[11] his mother was a comely, rosy-cheeked[12] young woman. When he was about ten, he had been tortured by the thought that one day she would grow old and die. He would calculate the number of days she still had[13] to live, perhaps ten or twelve thousand. But, almost without his noticing[14] it, most of those days had gone by, and now his parents were old, sick and tired. They didn't get up early because they had nothing to do. Life offered them no more[15] pleasure, no more hope.

But suddenly a ray of sunshine came in through the window. Georges got up, telling himself that he must shake off these sombre thoughts. He picked up the kettle.

---

1 'and entered'. 2 Use *ne ... aucun*. 3 Subjunctive; § 38. 4 Inversion after *peut-être*. 5 § 70. 6 'All was ...' 7 'which a large tree shaded'; § 82(e). 8 *Cela*. 9 Unnecessary to translate 'before'. 10 Not *son*. 11 Not *quand*; § 88. 12 'with rosy cheeks'; § 47(a). 13 'which remained to her'. 14 Expressed by *sans que* + imperfect subjunctive. 15 Combined negative: *ne ... plus aucun*.

35 A man of mystery

"Don't look," Madame Bourchier said quietly. "There's Madame Vadin going by[1] on the other pavement. What a woman! It[2] doesn't surprise me that her husband is[3] unhappy at home. I have been told that whatever[4] he says, whatever he does, she goes for him. And yet he is a most[5] likeable man; it's a pity he married[3] such a woman."

"Yes," replied Madame Dupont, "you're right. He is one of the nicest men I know[6]. But let me tell you something in confidence. As regards Vadin there's some mystery. One day last week[7] I went to Paris to buy a coat. As I walked through the Tuileries, I thought I saw[8] Vadin sitting on a bench. It was eleven in the morning. What could a man like him be doing sitting on a bench at that time? And what is more, he was wearing brown shoes and a gaudy tie."

"What! But M. Vadin is not a man[9] to dress like that! It's possible you were mistaken[10]."

"No, I'm sure it was he, and I think he recognized me, because just as I spotted him he looked away. But for that I should have gone and spoken[11] to him."

"Good heavens!" exclaimed Madame Bourchier, "I should never have believed it. I see that man go by every day and I've never seen him wearing[12] brown shoes and a gaudy tie; they're things men like to put on when they're on holiday."

"Well," continued Madame Dupont, "it seems he has[13] left his job or been sacked, without his wife knowing[14] it. Then he must change his shoes and his tie somewhere in Paris. But where and why?"

1 'who is going by'. 2 *Cela*; § 68. 3 Subjunctive; § 40. 4 § 44. 5 § 58(a). 6 Subjunctive after a superlative; § 42. 7 'One day of last week'. 8 Use an infinitive; § 22(c). 9 'the man'. 10 Perfect subjunctive. 11 'to speak to him'. 12 Infinitive. 13 Subjunctive after *il semble que* 14 *sans que* + subjunctive.

36 After the christening

When the ceremony was[1] over, they waited in front of the church for[2] the priest to take off his surplice, then they set off at a good pace for the house, for everybody was thinking of the dinner.

The priest was walking beside the good woman who was carrying the child which had just been christened. After a while she turned to the curé and said to him, "I'm beginning to get tired. Won't[3] you carry the baby a bit of the way?"

He took the child in his arms and kissed it, but then he was[1] embarrassed, for he was clumsy and did not know how to hold it. People began to laugh. One of the men called out, "You know very well, Reverend, that you'll never be a dad yourself!"

The priest made no reply, but strode on, looking intently at the blue-eyed[4] child.

They reached the house. Soon they were all sitting at table and the meal began. They[5] ate, they drank, they swore, they made coarse jokes. But the priest took no notice. He sat[6] quiet, eating little, drinking only water, his eyes fixed on the baby lying in a corner of the room.

Finally, scared by the growing din, the child began to squall. The mother got up and carried it into the next room, where it soon[7] went to sleep in its cradle.

The dinner went on, noisier[8] and noisier. In the end all the men and some[9] of the women were drunk. The priest had long since disappeared, without anybody noticing[10] his absence. But when the young mother went[11] next door to see if her baby was still asleep, she nearly[12] called out in surprise, for the priest was on his knees by the cradle, with[13] his forehead on the pillow where[14] the child's head lay.

1 Tense? § 6. 2 *attendre que* + subjunctive. 3 Use *vouloir*. 4 'with blue eyes'; § 47(a). 5 Use *on*. 6 Use *rester* or *demeurer*. 7 Use *ne pas tarder à (faire)*; § 21. 8 § 57. 9 Pronoun? § 72. 10 *sans que* + subjunctive. 11 Use *passer*. 12 Express with *faillir*; § 22(e). 13 § 47(a). 14 Invert: 'where lay the child's head'.

37 What is progress?

When anybody[1] began to talk of progress, my father would[2] exclaim, "Progress? What sort of progress? Progress towards what?"

"Where do your scientific discoveries lead us?" he would[2] ask. "Nations live in fear[3] of mass extermination; the planet itself is no longer safe; they[1] don't even leave the moon in peace! Then consider the lives[4] people lead today. Wages are enormous, working hours are shorter[5] and shorter; everybody's got money and leisure[6], yet people are more and more[5] dissatisfied with their existence. There's no more struggle, no more discipline, no more faith. Everybody relies on the State, which levies heavier[5] and heavier taxes. Most people spend the evening watching[7] third-rate programmes on the telly. Everybody has a car, so there is no more room on the roads. Yet people aren't satisfied, they never will be[8]. The more[9] they have the more they want."

"But, Father," I would[2] object, "in this age you[1] can't stop technological progress[10]!"

"Progress!" he would[2] scoff. "Do you think we are making[11] progress because kitchens are everywhere full of electrical gadgets? And then do you think young people enjoy themselves better today? You waste endless hours listening[7] to idiotic music. You don't even dance!"

"Oh yes, Father, we do[13]," I would object.

"What do you call dancing[14]? I've watched it. The partners, if there are any, make a few monkey-like movements which anybody[15] can do straight off; there's nothing to learn!"

And so he went on. All this became a sort of joke, which Father himself secretly shared.

1 *on*. 2 Tense? 3 'the fear'. 4 French would use the singular. 5 § 57. 6 Plural. 7 *à* + infinitive. 8 Complete with *le*; § 60(c). 9 § 57. 10 *les progrès*. 11 Subjunctive; § 41. 12 'an idiotic music'. 13 Not *faire*, of course. Either leave out, or say 'Yes, we dance'. 14 Infinitive. 15 Pronoun? § 77.

38 Love and Death

That evening I told her that a man had come to ask me about her health. She was[1] deeply affected and told me the whole story of her alarming adventure.

"This man," she added with a sigh[2], "now follows me like my shadow. I meet him whenever I go out. I have spoken to him only once, yet it seems to me that I have known[3] him for twenty years."

After thinking for a few seconds, she said, getting up, "It's possible that he's[4] under my windows at this very moment."

She moved the curtain aside, and indeed a man was there, sitting on a bench, looking up at[5] the hotel. I recognized him as the one[6] who had come to see me.

It was evident that he loved her with tender and grateful devotion[7], since she had undoubtedly saved his life[8]. I felt, too, that this woman, although she knew she was going to die, was happy to be loved thus with unfailing respect[7] and constancy; yet she obstinately refused to receive him, even to know his name.

"No," she would say, "I don't want to. That would spoil our unavowed friendship. It is better that we remain[9] strangers to each other[10]."

She died one morning about ten o'clock. As I was leaving the hotel, the man came to me[11], his eyes moist with tears.

"I should like to see her, doctor," he said to me.

I took him up to the room. He stood[12] for a few moments, gazing[13] at the dead woman's face, then he took her cold hand and kissed it. After that, without saying a word, he went away, and I have never seen[14] him since.

1 Tense? § 6.   2 'sighing'.   3 Tense? § 17(a)   4 Subjunctive; § 41.   5 'his eyes raised towards ...'   6 Pronoun? § 69(b).   7 Article required; § 46(a).   8 Cp. *Vous m'avez sauvé la vie.*   9 Subjunctive; § 40.   10 'the one to the other'.   11 Disjunctive pronoun; § 63(c).   12 Use *rester* or *demeurer*.   13 *à* + infinitive.   14 Use *revoir.*

39 A worried father

Ledru couldn't keep still. He walked up and down, looking[1] gloomy. Every two or three minutes he went back into the café to look at the clock. At last Charpin said to him:

"What's the matter with you, old chap? You look worried. Are you waiting for somebody by any chance?"

"Why do you expect me to[2] be waiting for somebody?" snapped Ledru. "Anyway, is it your business?"

"Oh," said Charpin gently, "I'm sorry I spoke[3]. I thought that you were perhaps waiting for the postman. Haven't you had any news of your son?"

"There you are!" burst out Ledru. "You want to know everything[4], but you'll know nothing. Mind your own business, unless[5] you want me to say[6] things we shall both regret!"

"Listen, old chap," went on Charpin. "We all[7] know what happened. You quarrelled with your son, didn't you, because he wanted to go abroad. You forget that he is of age, he could do as[8] he liked, you couldn't stop[9] him. If that man wanted to go abroad, he had the right to[9]."

"You say that man. What man? Do you think Jean is[10] a man?"

"Of course. At twenty-two you were married, weren't you, and at that age I suppose you considered yourself as a man?"

"Yes, I did, but I wasn't my son."

"So what's true for you isn't true for him?"

"Oh, you're talking nonsense! All the same I should like to have[11] seen him before he went[12]. He ought to have[13] written to his old dad."

1 Cp. *Il restait là, l'air abattu.* 2 Use *vouloir que* + subjunctive. 3 Use an infinitive: 'I regret having spoken'. 4 Position of *tout*? § 73. 5 § 38; *à moins que.* 6 *vouloir que* + subjunctive. 7 Position of *tous*? § 73. 8 'what'. 9 *en* required; § 62. 10 Subjunctive; § 41. 11 Form of *vouloir*? § 25. 12 § 38; Special Note 2. 13 Form of *devoir*? § 27.

40 Lying

Is there any[1] man who can[2] say the he has never lied? People cite the case of George Washington who claimed never to have lied in[3] his life, but can we believe it?

Although both may be guilty of lying[4], there is a great difference between the man who is a real liar and the one who is not[5]. The real liar lies shamelessly, he sees nothing in it[6], he laughs about it, whereas the fundamentally honest man is worried by it[7], his conscience accuses him. The one lies out of[8] habit, the other out of weakness or necessity.

I remember the first big lie of my life. At school the teacher was distributing some books. He had some old, rather dirty copies, and he had a few beautiful new copies. I had[9] no luck: I received an old book. But I very much wanted a new one, so I hid my book at the back of my desk and told the teacher I had lost it. He gave me a new one[10].

That evening I showed my new book to my parents and I repeated the lie to them. However, when I had[11] gone to bed, I had[9] difficulty in getting to sleep. I couldn't drive out of my mind the idea that I had cheated.

The next day I had[9] no pleasure in[12] using my new book. The following day I was[9] no happier. On the morning of the third day I went to see the teacher, with my book in my hand.

"I've found the old[13] one, sir," I explained to him. "My father told me to return this one[14] to you."

The teacher's look was kindly, but I guessed that he had understood. "I'm glad you've[15] found it," he said, smiling.

1 'a man'. 2 Subjunctive; § 43. 3 *de*. 4 Use the noun, *le mensonge*. 5 Complete with *le*; § 60(c). 6 'attaches no importance to it'. 7 'worried by', *tourmenté de*; so which pronoun represents 'by it'? 8 'out of', *par*. 9 Tense? § 12. 10 *en* required. Cp. *J'en ai un autre*. 11 Tense? § 14. 12 *à* + infinitive. 13 Use *ancien*. 14 Pronoun? § 69(c). 15 Subjunctive; § 40.

41 I give evidence

I was taken[1] into the court-room and told to[2] stand behind a piece of furniture on the right[3]; this was the witness-box. On a platform three important-looking[4] gentlemen were sitting behind a long table; they were obviously the magistrates. In the room there were about thirty people: officials[5], lawyers[5], police officers, reporters.

A young man stood up and asked me:

"Is it[6] true that on August 12th last, at about noon, you were in the High Street of this town?"—"Yes."

"Did you witness an incident involving[7] a pedestrian and a yellow van?"—"Yes."

"Now will you tell the court exactly what you saw?"

I described the incident as briefly as I could[8]. The van had nearly[9] knocked me down, then it had mounted the pavement and one of its sidelights had struck a pedestrian in the back.

When I had[10] finished speaking, another man got up. He must have been[11] about forty. I guessed that he was counsel for[12] the defence. After staring at me for some seconds, he asked me:

"Did you speak to the driver?"

I began to explain that I had gone to the injured pedestrian and had told him that he ought to have[13] the police called, because he might[14] be more seriously hurt than he thought[15]. But the barrister cut me short. He said to me sharply:

"I don't want you to[16] tell the court all that! Will you answer my question: did you speak to the driver? Yes or no?"

"I beg your pardon," I said. "No, I did not speak to the driver."

"That's all," he said, and sat down again.

1 Use *faire entrer* or *introduire*. 2 Construction? § 7(a). 3 Better to say 'which was on the right'. 4 Cp. *un garçon à l'air insolent*. 5 In enumerations one can dispense with the article. 6 *est-ce* or *est-il*? § 67(b). 7 'which concerned'. 8 Tense? § 12. 9 Express with *faillir*; § 22(e). 10 Tense? § 14. 11 Tense of *devoir*? § 27. 12 'of the defence'. 13 *faire* + infinitive; § 24(c). 14 Tense of *pouvoir*? § 26. 15 *ne* required; §81(b). 16 *vouloir que* + subjunctive.

42 The umbrella

For old Perrin there was one glimmer of hope. A girl who worked in the office had agreed to[1] go out with him once or twice. Very likely[2] she was bored and put up with his company because she had nothing better to do.

Then young Tremblet came. He was jolly, he was liked by everybody. It wasn't long before[3] he invited this girl to go out with him, which[4] she did readily. Old Perrin hated the newcomer. Sooner or later a row was bound to[5] break out between them, and this is how it[6] happened.

One November evening[7], as Perrin was about to leave the office, he went into the cloakroom to get his umbrella; it wasn't[8] there. Perrin was[9] annoyed, because it was raining in torrents.

The next morning he saw Tremblet arrive with an umbrella in his hand. He looked at this umbrella and saw it was his[10]. He was[11] furious.

"Excuse me, Mr. Tremblet," he said frowning, "will you tell me why you took my umbrella last night?"

"Oh, I'm sorry I took[12] it," replied Tremblet. "I picked up this one, thinking it was mine. Please forgive me."

"You knew very well it wasn't yours!" shouted Perrin. "It's time you learnt[13] to respect other people's property!"

"But I tell you I didn't know it was yours!" retorted Tremblet, his eyes ablaze with anger. "How could I know which[14] was yours among half a dozen umbrellas?"

"You did it to spite me, didn't you?" went on Perrin, breathing hard. "Come on, give me my umbrella! Give it to me at once!" And he snatched the umbrella from Tremblet's hand.

1 Use *accepter de*. 2 Inversion after *sans doute*. 3 Express by *ne pas tarder à (faire)*; § 21. 4 § 65. 5 Expressed by imperfect of *devoir*. 6 *cela*. 7 'One evening of November'. 8 Use *ne ... plus*. 9 Tense? § 6. 10 Pronoun? § 71. 11 Tense? § 12. 12 Use an infinitive: 'I regret having taken it'. 13 Present subjunctive. 14 Pronoun? § 66.

43 The Frenchman's beer

We went in and sat down at our usual table. The dining room was full. There were obviously a lot of tourists who had noticed this attractive hotel and had stopped[1] for lunch. Among them there were quite a few foreigners, some of whom[2] spoke English pretty well, while others had difficulty in[3] making themselves understood[4].

At the next table there was a French couple. When they ordered their meal, I heard the husband ask for a pint of beer. When their meal was finally served, the poor man still hadn't his beer. However, without waiting any more[5], they began to eat. The wife didn't like her steak. From[6] the way[7] she occasionally shrugged her shoulders and nodded her head, looking meaningfully at her husband, I guessed that she found the meat tough. I noticed, too, that the Frenchman looked repeatedly towards the door, waiting for[8] his beer to be brought. Once he beckoned the waitress, but she merely[9] said, "One moment, please," and disappeared.

They went on eating, looking rather glum. When they had[10] nearly finished, the waitress came in hurriedly, carrying a large glass of beer on a tray.

"Your beer, sir," she said to the Frenchman. "I'm sorry it wasn't[11] brought earlier."

But the Frenchman shook his head, saying, "I'm afraid it's[12] too late. I prefer my drink to be[13] served at the beginning of the meal."

The waitress explained that there was a wine-waiter who looked after the drinks, but it was his day off. The Frenchman looked at her coldly and said to her, "Zat is not my problem."

---

1 'had stopped there'. 2 Order: 'of whom some . . .' 3 à + infinitive
4 Construction? § 24(c). 5 Cp. *sans plus discuter*. 6 à. 7 'the way in which'. 8 *attendre que* + subjunctive. 9 § 79. 10 Tense? § 14. 11 'that one did not bring . . .' (subjunctive). 12 Subjunctive; § 40. 13 Subjunctive: 'I prefer that one should serve . . .'

44 The World Cup

At first we wondered how such a[1] stupid thing could have[2] happened. It appears that the Cup was being exhibited somewhere in[3] London. At the week-end, instead of being deposited[4] in a bank, the Cup had been left in its place at the exhibition. Safety measures had certainly been taken[5]; everything had been locked up and I believe there was even a watchman. In spite of all the precautions the Cup was[6] stolen.

After the event it is easy to blame those who were responsible. Nevertheless it[7] amazes one[8] that anyone[9] could have thought that the Cup was safe because the premises were locked. Nowadays thieves get in anywhere[10] and they manage somehow or other[11] to get in without being seen. They have all the necessary apparatus and they surmount all obstacles. And once they are in[12] they feel so safe that they often spend long hours drinking and enjoying themselves. I think we were all a little ashamed that the Cup had been[13] stolen in London.

But the way in which the Cup was recovered was quite extraordinary. A young workman came out of his house one evening to take his dog for a walk. Instead of running ahead of his master, the dog went into the little garden to sniff at a parcel hidden behind a bush. The man, intrigued, went and picked up this parcel, took it into the house and opened it. It contained the World Cup!

Asked by[14] a journalist sent to interview him if he was pleased, the young man answered, "Yes, of course I'm pleased, but I shall be more so[15] when I get[16] the reward."

---

1 § 74.   2 Real meaning: 'had been able to happen'.   3 *dans* in this case.
4 Turn: 'instead of depositing it ... one had ...'   5 Use *on*.   6 Tense? § 6.
7 *cela*; § 68.   8 'one', as the object, is *vous*.   9 Express as: 'one had been able to think that ...'; subjunctive after *étonner*.   10 § 77.   11 'one does not know how'; § 77.   12 Use *entrer*.   13 Subjunctive; § 40.
14 Turn: 'When a journalist ... asked him ...'   15 § 57; *davantage*.
16 Tense?

45 The camper

One morning the phone bell rang. Mrs. Barnard picked up the receiver.

"Hello!" she said, "Mrs. Barnard here. Who is speaking[1]?"

"It's me, Tom."

She was[2] annoyed. Tom had been a friend of her son at the University and had often been to the house. Although John was now abroad, Tom continued his visits. He wasn't amusing. He claimed he was[3] a[4] poet. With[5] his eyes half-closed he would wander about the house and garden without speaking to anybody. This had finally[6] exasperated Mrs. Barnard and she was resolved to put an end to these visits.

"Ah, it's you, Tom!" she said gaily. "How are you? You would like to come and spend a few days here, I suppose? Well, I'm sorry we can't[7] offer you a room for the moment, they're all occupied."

Then she added, jokingly[8], "You'll have to[9] bring a tent and camp on the lawn!" She thought she had got rid[10] of him.

What was[11] her surprise when, the next day, Tom arrived in his old car, bringing a tent, which he proceeded to put up on the lawn. She let him get on with it[12].

But that night, about eleven o'clock, a thunderstorm broke out, with great flashes of lightning, ear-splitting claps of thunder and torrential rain. Mrs. Barnard, who was terrified by thunderstorms, thought of Tom all alone in[13] his little tent. She rang for the butler and told him to go and ask Tom to come into the house.

Tom did so[14] readily. He stayed three weeks.

1 The phrase used in France is: *Qui est à l'appareil?*   2 Tense?   3 Use an infinitive.   4 No article required in these cases.   5 § 47(a).   6 'This had finished by exasperating ...'   7 Subjunctive; § 40.   8 'joking'.   9 Express by *il faudra que*.   10 You could use the infinitive: 'She thought to have got rid of ...'   11 French uses the negative in such cases: 'What was not her surprise ...'   12 Use *laisser faire*, e.g. *je les laisse faire*.   13 *sous*.   14 § 60(a).

46 Departure for Scandinavia

There were five of us[1]. We had already made several journeys together, but this one was the longest we had[2] ever undertaken. We were proposing to drive through Sweden, Finland and Norway; we hoped we should reach[3] the North Cape. For this expedition we had bought a second-hand van; we had had it overhauled[4] and we had had new tyres fitted[4].

On the day of the departure, as was agreed[5], my four friends came to our house, for we live only twenty miles from the port. When we saw the amount of baggage we had to carry, we wondered how we were going to find room for all this in the van. We got to work and after half-an-hour we had got everything aboard. Then it was a question of knowing how the vehicle would go when laden[6] with five men and the baggage. We all got in and drove round the block. The van went all right, so we said good-bye and set off for the port.

When we got there[7] we still had several hours to wait. We were told[8] to leave the van on the quay until they were[9] ready to take it aboard.

As we were drinking a cup of tea, Roger said to me, "I suppose you've got the spare keys?". No, I hadn't, I must have[10] left them at home. However careful you are[11] you always forget something. I went and telephoned in haste to my parents, telling them that I might have[12] left the keys in my bedroom. Half-an-hour later they arrived with the keys.

Then we had[13] another moment of agony. We went to see our van being shipped[14]. When the crane began to lift it, the back was so heavy that the vehicle nearly[15] tipped up!

1 'We were five'. 2 Subjunctive after superlative; § 42. 3 Use an infinitive; § 22(c). 4 The construction is *faire* + infinitive; § 24(c). 5 'as it was agreed'. 6 'when it would be laden'. 7 You could say: 'Arrived there . . .' 8 Use *on*; § 7(a). 9 Subjunctive after *jusqu'à ce que*. 10 Tense of *devoir*? § 27. 11 § 44. 12 Tense of *pouvoir*? § 26. 13 Tense? § 12. 14 Expressed by *voir* + infinitive, e.g. *nous avons vu démolir la maison.* 15 Use *faillir*; § 22(e).

47 A Christmas concert

This concert took place one Sunday in December, a few days before Christmas. Although I had reached the church early, it was already nearly full and soon there was not a single vacant chair left[1]. There was less room than usual for the congregation, for part of the nave was occupied by the choir and the orchestra.

Before the concert began[2], there was a hum of conversation and a certain confusion. Members of the choir were arriving in groups, talking quietly among themselves; musicians were tuning their instruments. At last everybody was[3] in his place and a hush fell. Then the conductor mounted the platform and, having glanced round the congregation, he raised his baton and the concert began.

For two hours I sat there, listening[4] with deep contentment[5] to the noble and solemn music. As[6] the concert went on, you[7] could[8] see that, outside, the short winter afternoon was drawing to its close. Gradually the windows of the nave grew darker, while[9] inside the church the gold and silver-gilt in the chancel seemed to glow with ever-increasing brilliance. Finally the windows were[3] black and it was night.

When the concert was over[10], I went out with the crowd into the lamp-lit street, where the pavements glittered with rain. It was cold.

As I listen to the recording of that concert, these distant scenes come back to my memory. But now it is no longer winter. Before me I see the flowers in[11] the garden, and away there the wooded hills bathed in summer sun.

1 Use the impersonal form *il reste*; § 9.   2 You could use *le commencement*.   3 Tense? § 12.   4 *à* + infinitive.   5 Article necessary; § 46(a). 6 *A mesure que*.   7 Use *on*.   8 Unnecessary to use *pouvoir*; § 26, Note 1. 9 *pendant que* or *tandis que*? 10 You could say: 'The concert ended, ...'; § 6.   11 'of'.

48 The Duke's suits

Although he was a rich man, the Duke did not greatly bother about[1]
clothes. One day, when[2] his tailor was mentioned[3], he exclaimed,
"Gracious me, I'd almost forgotten the poor man; I haven't seen
him for years[4]. What's become of him[5]? I'm afraid he may have[6]
gone bankrupt." Then, unbuttoning his jacket, he looked at the
little label sewn inside the pocket and discovered that the suit he
was wearing had been made fifteen years before!

As a matter of fact he was comfortable in old suits, he loved them
and went on wearing them until they were quite old-fashioned. One
day, in London, he met a friend much younger than himself. The
latter, having glanced at the Duke's suit, exclaimed, "Bless my soul,
you can't wear a suit like that in London!" The Duke replied,
"Why not? Nobody knows me here, I can wear anything[7]." A few
weeks later this same friend met the Duke in the little town near
which his estate was situated. The latter was wearing another outdated suit. "Good heavens!" said the man, "you can't wear a suit
like that here!" "What does it matter?" said the Duke. "Everybody
knows me here."

He liked to make jokes about clothes. "Let me give you a tip,"
he would say. "You should always have two suits made[8] at once;
they last twice as long." What did he mean?

It was the same with[9] his footwear. "Do you know," he said
one day, "the night before[10] a ceremony I was to[11] attend, I told
my valet to polish my boots. He discovered that the boots were older
than he was. He couldn't get over it[12]!"

1 Could be expressed as: 'did not attach great importance to . . .' 2 § 88.
3 'when one spoke to him'. 4 Construction? § 81(b). 5 § 70. 6 Subjunctive; § 40. 7 § 77. 8 The construction is *faire* + infinitive; § 24(c).
9 'it is the same with', *il en est de même de*. 10 'the eve of'. 11 Tense
of *devoir*? § 27. 12. 'I can't get over it', *je n'en reviens pas*.

49 Passengers alarmed

The train was due[1] to leave at 6.10. Having nothing to do, I was standing on the platform near the open door of my compartment. At exactly[2] six o'clock I heard a whistle and porters began running along the train, shutting the doors. I wondered what was going to happen. Was the train going to leave before time? No, it was impossible that everybody had made[3] a mistake. However, as a[4] precaution, I hastened to get in.

There was[5] a jolt, and the train began to slide slowly along the platform. Then something very funny happened[6]. My compartment was opposite the buffet. As soon as the train started to move, men rushed to the buffet door, glass in hand[7], their mouths[8] open, their eyebrows raised, their eyes popping out. They had left all their things in the train and were taking advantage of the last minutes to drink a glass of beer. And the train was going without them, taking their hats[8], their cases, their umbrellas[8]!

At first they couldn't believe their eyes, but as soon as they had[9] recovered from their amazement, they hastily put down their glasses, ran out and made a dash for the train, hoping to get in before it gathered[10] speed. The young ones[11] bounded along like stags, the old ones[11] galloped heavily, red in the face, breathing hard.

Seeing them coming, the porters shouted to them to stop and grabbed those who tried to get aboard. There were quite a dozen porters struggling with angry passengers. It was like a rugby match!

Actually there was no reason for alarm[12]. The train was going out merely to come back and stand[13] at the next platform. Perhaps passengers ought to have been[14] warned.

1 Use *devoir*. 2 § 88. 3 Subjunctive after *impossible que*; § 41. 4 *par*. 5 Tense? § 12. 6 Use the impersonal *il arrive* or *il se passe*. 7 § 47(a). 8 Singular. 9 Tense? § 14. 10. Subjunctive. 11 'ones' not translated. 12 Use *s'inquiéter*. 13 Use *se ranger*. 14 Use *on*.

50 On the phone

—Hello! Who's on the line[1]? Besson? Oh good! How are you, old chap? What's the weather like down there? Hot, do you say? Here it's raining. I feel like taking a trip to the South[2] myself. . . . Listen. I should like you to[3] try and get some information about a certain Mme de Lannieu. She must be over fifty. It appears that formerly she was very beautiful; she is probably less so[4] now. She was wealthy and was often seen[5] in the casinos. All we know is[6] that she hasn't been heard of[5] for some time and it's possible she's no[7] longer in the district. If she isn't[8], try to find somebody who can[9] inform you as to her movements. Being rich, she must have had[10] servants. From[11] what I have heard, she must have had[10] plenty, for she wasn't the sort of woman at whose house servants would want to stay long. Then there are the tradespeople, the dress-makers, the milliners she must have had[10] dealings with. Perhaps, if she's gone, she left debts. If this is so, you may be sure that those she owed money to have done their best to discover her where-abouts[12]. If you don't find anybody in that direction who can[9] inform you, try the casinos. Perhaps you'll find somebody who remembers[9] her. In a word, find out all you can[13]. Whatever you do[14], don't let yourself[15] be suspected of making an investigation. If you are asked[5] why you want to know, say anything; say you are a relative come back from abroad. Very well, good-bye, old chap. Ring me when you've[16] something to tell me.

1 The expression used is: *Qui est à l'appareil?* 2 *le Midi.* 3 Express by *vouloir que* + present subjunctive. 4 § 60(c). 5 Use *on.* 6 'it is that'. 7 Subjunctive after *possible que.* 8 Complete with *y.* 9 Subjunctive; § 43. 10 Really means 'was bound to have'; tense of *devoir?* 11 *à.* 12 'where she is'. 13 Tense of *pouvoir?* § 26. 14 § 44. 15 Cp. *se laisser voler,* 'to let oneself be robbed' 16 Tense? § 15

51 A distant memory

When the political meeting was over[1], we were shown[2] into a drawing-room, where wine was served[2]. As soon as I saw that Lord P——— was free for a moment, I took advantage of the opportunity of having a word with him. I went up to him and introduced myself.

"It[3] gives me great pleasure to be invited to your house, sir," I said to him, "all the more so as[4] I have not seen you at close quarters since nineteen twenty-two."

"Nineteen twenty-two!" he exclaimed. "Good heavens, I was then only eight years old."

"Yes, sir, you were very young. May I ask you if the name of Houlgate means[5] anything to you?"

"Why of course. It's a resort on[6] the Normandy coast. We used to go there every summer; my mother used to rent a villa for the season. But you must have a remarkable memory; I find it[7] hard to believe you remember things that happened so long ago. But how is it[8] you met me at Houlgate? I suppose you were another boy on the beach?"

"No, sir," I replied, "I am perhaps older than you think[9]. At that time I was a young schoolmaster; I was with a troop of scouts. You came to our camp. You were with two ladies. One of them asked me if her son could go and see the tents. You came and stayed several hours; I believe you ate a baked potato."

"Well I never[10]!" said Lord P———, looking at me closely. "All this is very interesting; I'm glad you have told me about it[11]. Indeed I do remember vaguely going[12] to a camp, but of course it's hardly possible that I should remember[13] you. . . . Now we ought to drink a glass of wine together, don't you think?"

1 You could express as: 'The political meeting finished, . .'; § 6. 2 Use *on*. 3 *Cela*; § 68. 4 *d'autant plus que*. 5 Use *dire*. 6 *de*. 7 'it' not translated; § 60(b). 8 *comment se fait-il que* + subjunctive. 9 *ne* required § 81(b). 10 *Pas possible*! or *Ce n'est pas possible*! 11 'you have spoken to me of it'; or use *raconter*. 12 Perfect infinitive, 'having gone'; § 23. 13 Present subjunctive.

52 Victory and defeat

The old fisherman was alone in his boat on the wide sea, far from land. After long hours of patient effort[1] he finally[2] hooked a swordfish. He knew[3] at once that it was a very heavy fish, but it was not until[4] the swordfish leapt out of the water that the old man realized that it was the biggest he had[5] ever seen in[6] his life.

The struggle had begun. All day long and through the hours of darkness the man fought this monster of the deep. The huge fish did everything to free itself. Sometimes[7] it dived to incredible depths, threatening to drag the boat under the water; sometimes it rushed to the surface and leapt high into the air; sometimes it sulked, refusing to move. But at last it was[8] defeated. The fisherman dragged the dying monster up to the boat and managed to dispatch it. As the fish was far too heavy for him to[9] get aboard, the old man lashed it alongside, then he made slowly for the distant shore.

But then the sharks, drawn by the taste of blood, came along in[10] shoals. They ravenously attacked the carcase, and the fisherman could do nothing to stop[11] them. In the end there was nothing left[12] of the swordfish but the head and backbone. So the old man came back empty-handed, without any[13] reward. He was calm, stoical, resigned; all he wanted was sleep. Of the great battle of his life, of his greatest victory, there remained nothing but a whitened skeleton abandoned on the foreshore and shown[14] as a curiosity to tourists, who soon[15] forgot about it.

1 Probably better to use the plural. 2 Express by *finir par*; § 8(c). 3 Tense? § 12. 4 Expressed as: 'it was only when'. 5 Subjunctive after superlative; § 42. 6 *de*. 7 Use *tantôt ... tantôt ...*; § 84. 8 Tense? § 6. 9 *pour que* + subjunctive. 10 *par* 11 *en* required; § 62. 12 'there remained of the swordfish only ...' 13 Use *aucun*. 14 'and which one showed'. 15 Express by *ne pas tarder à (faire)*; § 21.

53 Too serious

He was a good fellow, very intelligent, very hard-working. He did an enormous amount of[1] work, which was easy to correct because he made hardly any[2] mistakes. Without any doubt he was the best pupil I have[3] ever had. Nobody was surprised when he won a scholarship to go to a famous University.

He started his studies there. During the vacations he would always come back to see me. He trusted me; I was a sort of confessor to[4] him. He poured out his heart, telling me of his hopes and disappointments, his troubles, his times of distress. While he talked, with his eyes downcast, I could[5] see the sweat standing out on his forehead. He was intensely sincere and earnest. He was too much so[6]. I could see that he was making[7] his own life unbearable. I should like to have[8] told him that it is wrong[9] to be too serious, that to some extent one should be tolerant and accept life and people such as they are. But I was afraid I should disappoint[10] him. He would think I was just[11] another man who had[12] betrayed the enthusiasms of his youth.

Bernard Shaw asserted that every[13] man over forty is a scoundrel. Being over forty, according to him I must be a scoundrel, but I am not aware of it and I'm not often called[14] a scoundrel. But you can[5] see what Shaw was driving at. He thought men ought to strive to change society, instead of letting themselves be bogged down[15] in habit and tradition. But I don't wholly agree with[16] Shaw. I think happiness is important; pleasure and laughter should play a large part in life.

1 *énormément de travail.* 2 Use *ne ... guère*; § 79. 3 Subjunctive after superlative; § 42. 4 *pour.* 5 Unnecessary to use *pouvoir.* 6 § 60(c). 7 Use *rendre.* 8 Form of *vouloir?* § 25. 9 'one is wrong'. 10 Use an infinitive; § 40. 11 *tout simplement.* 12 The supposition is expressed as 'who would have betrayed'. 13 *tout.* 14 Use *traiter de*, e.g. *on m'a traité de lâche.* 15 Cp. *il se laisse voler*, 'he lets himself be robbed'. 16 'I am not wholly of Shaw's opinion'.

54 Morning in France

Guy woke early the next morning. Through the wide-open windows of his room he saw the honey-coloured wall of the next building flooded with bright sunshine. The air was already warm. He could hear in the street the sounds of footsteps and from time to time French voices: people saying[1] good morning to each other and exchanging a few remarks as they went by[2]. Shutters were being[3] opened, dustbins were being[3] dragged on to the pavement.

Then the big bell of the neighbouring church began to ring the angelus, and the nine strokes were repeated by the bells of more distant churches and by the light tinkle of convent bells.

Shortly afterwards, in the room below, there was[4] a noise of chairs being moved[3]: the Sisters were going to hear the first Mass of the day. A few moments' silence, then a monotonous murmur, broken by the voices of the Sisters repeating[5] in chorus "So be it"[6]. When Mass was over[7], there was[4] again a scraping of chairs being replaced[3], then silence: everybody had gone. A few minutes later Guy heard soft footsteps in the yard: one of the Sisters, wearing[8] her winged bonnet, was hanging out washing.

Guy felt how much he loved France; not the France of modern Paris[9], of the great industrial centres and the motorways, but ancient and historic France, the provinces with their old towns, their cathedrals, their chateaux, their vineyards, their rivers. The sound of the bells seemed to him[10] the very voice of history.

1 'who were saying'. 2 'in passing'. 3 Use *on*. 4 Tense? § 12. 5 'who were repeating'. 6 *Ainsi soit-il.* 7 You could express as: 'The Mass finished, . . .'; § 6. 8 'wearing' (on the head), *coiffé de.* 9 'of the modern Paris'. 10 Better to say: 'seemed to him to be . . .'

55 Yvette Guilbert remembers

You ask me if I remember Toulouse-Lautrec? But of course I remember him, though he died[1] many years ago. We were good friends. Perhaps you know that in those days I was a star of the old Moulin Rouge in Montmartre. For years Henri spent most of his evenings there, not to enjoy himself, but to work. He was always drawing. With[2] a bit of pencil in his hand, he would make rapid sketches of the artists, of the people in[3] the audience, of anybody[4]. You may have[5] seen some of the numerous portraits he did[1] of me while I was on the stage, wearing my famous black gloves; but I must tell you that these sketches weren't always flattering!

Poor Henri! I pitied him. As you probably know[6], he was a sort of dwarf; he walked on very short legs. He had fragile bones[7], it seems[8]. In his childhood he broke both legs, and after that the growth stopped. Although he seldom complained, he must have[9] suffered a great deal. It[10] hurt him to walk even a short distance. After a while he would stop, lean on his stick and stare at the ground, as though he were thinking of some problem.

In spite of his troubles, he was often gay. He was very intelligent and he was one of the wittiest men I have[11] known, capable of brilliant, sometimes cruel, rejoinders: you have only to look at his pictures to guess that. But, at bottom, he was profoundly sad, like all those who have viewed life without illusions.

Nowadays he is more famous than he was[12] in his life-time. He sold very little, but now that he is recognized as a great painter, his canvases and sketches sell[13] at enormous prices. I still possess several of his pictures. When you are[14] in Paris, come and see them.

1 Perfect tense. 2 'with' not translated; § 47(a). 3 *de.* 4 Pronoun? § 77. 5 Tense of *pouvoir*? § 26. 6 Complete with *le*; § 60(b). 7 § 47(a). 8 Inversion; § 82(d). 9 Means 'was bound to suffer'; tense of *devoir*? 10 *Cela.* 11 Subjunctive after superlative; § 42. 12 § 81(b). 13 Reflexive, *se revendre.* 14 Tense? § 15.

56 Gimlet

They called him Gimlet because of his piercing look. He was one
of those men who live in a constant state of discontent and exasperation. He had it in for[1] everybody, the rich, the poor, the government, the police, women, especially women.

Gimlet always wanted to be arguing. Often he would ask questions
which he answered himself.

"Why is a man poor?" he would ask vehemently. "Because he's
got no brains!"

"How do the rich get their money? By taking it from[2] other
people![3]"

And so on. It was[4] difficult to know what he thought. Not having
done much[5] in life himself, he seemed at the same time to despise those
who have done no better[6] and to detest those who have succeeded.

"What do you mean[7] by success?" he would ask. "I suppose you
mean by that making[8] your pile? But you can't make a fortune
unless you're[9] a crook! No[10] honest man can make millions by his
own work! I'll tell you one thing. If I were in[11] the government I
would tax the rich until they hadn't a bean left![12] And what
sickens me is the way all the people in high society suck up to the
rich man. Whoever you are[13], whatever you've done[13], you're all
right with them provided you've got[14] the dough."

And then he often got words wrong[15]. When he meant *immaterial*
he said *imperial*; instead of *artisan* he said *artesian*. When you felt
inclined to laugh, you couldn't even permit yourself a smile. If he
had caught[16] you making fun of him, he would have hit you.

1 Idioms you could use: *en vouloir à*, e.g. *je lui en veux*; *s'en prendre à*, e.g.
il s'en prend à moi. 2 Preposition? § 30. 3 'others'. 4 *il était* or
c'était? § 67(b). 5 Use *grand'chose*. 6 Position of *mieux*? § 83(a). 7 Use
tendre. 8 Infinitive. 9 Unnecessary to use a subjunctive; use *à
moins de* + infinitive. 10 *nul ... ne* or *aucun ... ne*. 11 Use *faire
partie de*. 12 Use the impersonal *il reste*. 13 § 44. 14 Subjunctive;
§ 38. 15 'to get (something) wrong', *se tromper de*. 16 'to catch someone
(doing)', *surprendre quelqu'un à (faire)*.

57 The inn across the way

In the little café all was quiet. Having waited a while, Michel rapped the table. A few seconds later he heard soft footsteps and a woman appeared in the doorway. She must have been[1] getting on for fifty. She was thin, her cheeks were sunken, her eyes were red and moist as though she had been crying[2].

"What is it, monsieur?" she asked in[3] a toneless voice.

"Have you any Alsatian beer?"

"Yes. I'll fetch you a bottle."

She brought the bottle and a glass, she poured him out the beer. Then she leaned back against the wall, with her arms folded, gazing at the inn opposite. It was one of those pretentious establishments such as[4] one sees today, painted light blue, ornamented with fake escutcheons; its sign bore the name *Hostelry of the Golden Lion*.

Seeing that she was so[5] interested in this house, Michel tried to get[6] the woman to talk.

"Have they been[7] here long, those who keep the inn opposite?[8]" he asked her.

"About a year," she answered sadly. "It will be a year in September. Since then things have gone badly with us. In the old days everybody came here, but those people, especially the wife, who is a Parisian, have done everything[9] to attract the customers. Now nobody comes to our place."

Just then Michel caught a glimpse of the Parisian, who appeared momentarily at a window. She was good-looking, she was wearing a gaudy dress, her hair was nicely done. Inside the inn you could[10] hear men talking loudly, then one of them began to sing.

"That man's got a fine voice," remarked Michel.

"Yes," said the woman, "that's my husband singing."

1 Tense of *devoir*? § 27. 2 Tense? § 1. 3 *de*. 4 § 62. 5 *tellement*. 6 *faire* + infinitive. 7 Tense? § 17(a). 8 § 56(b). 9 Position of *tout*? § 73. 10 Unnecessary to use *pouvoir*.

58 The saxophone player

That music reminds me of something that happened to me in the train one day when[1] I was going to Nice. At a station, I don't remember which[2], a chap got into the compartment, carrying a long case. He sat down in a corner, he opened his case and took out[3] a saxophone, which[4] he began to play. I think he must have[5] been in a dance orchestra and wanted to practise.

Well, after some time, I'd had enough of it, so I protested. I said to the musician, "Sir, I can't stand this noise any longer. I don't want you to[6] play your saxophone in this compartment."

He looked[7] surprised and said to me, "Why not? I've got my ticket, I've the right to be here and I can do as[8] I like."

I replied, "No, sir, you can't do as you like. You know it's forbidden to disturb other passengers. There's nothing to prevent your staying here provided you don't play[9] your saxophone. If you want to go on playing, I insist on your going[10] elsewhere. You'll have to find an empty compartment where you can[11] play as much as you like[11] without disturbing anybody."

In spite of my protests he started playing again, so I said to him, "Very well, I'll fetch somebody who can[12] settle this question."

I found the ticket inspector, I brought him back to the compartment, thinking he would order the musician out[13]. But not at all! Seeing the saxophone, his eyes lit up and he said, "I'm a saxophone player, too, not professional of course. Let me try your instrument." And he took the saxophone from the musician's hands and began to play—but horribly!

1 § 88. 2 Pronoun? § 66. 3 'took out of it'. 4 One says: *jouer du saxophone*; what, then, will the relative be? 5 Tense of *devoir*? § 27. 6 *vouloir que* + subjunctive. 7 Tense? § 12. 8 'what'. 9 Subjunctive after *pourvu que*. 10 Expressed by *insister pour que* + subjunctive. 11 Tense? § 15. 12 Subjunctive; § 43. 13 'to go out'.

59 The retreat from Russia

Night was falling. Numbed with cold, Fabrice was looking for shelter. Seeing a barn a short distance away, he made his way to it[1], pushed open[2] the door and went in. The building was crammed with men. Fabrice looked around and saw a score of generals and officers of high rank. There were plenty of ordinary soldiers there as well, not one[3] of whom would have given up his bed of straw to a Marshal of France. Some[4], leaning back against the walls, had dropped off to sleep where[5] they stood, because there was no room to lie down. It was a mass of men so packed together for warmth that Fabrice looked in vain for a nook where he could even sit down. He carefully stepped over one body after another. Some[4] of the men growled, but none[6] moved.

He groped his way forward until he saw at the far end of the barn a sort of ledge a[7] few feet from the ground. He clambered up to it[1] and was able[8] to lie down at full length. From[9] his ledge he looked at the men of the Grand Army huddled like sheep below him. It was a pitiful sight.

In a small space left free in the middle of the barn a few pine logs were blazing, lighting up the place with a flickering glow.

"If this building caught fire," thought Fabrice, "it would burn like a torch. How many men would get out of it?"

But he was too weary to[10] worry about such dangers and soon[11] fell asleep.

1 *y*; § 61.   2 Just 'pushed the door'.   3 § 78.   4 Pronoun? § 72.   5 § 84; *où*.   6 Use *aucun ... ne*.   7 'at a few feet'.   8 Tense? § 12.   9 'from' anything high is *du haut de*.   10 Preposition?   11 Express by *ne pas tarder à (faire)*; § 21.

60 His new family

Leroy asked to[1] see the principal. He told her that his newspaper wanted to publish an article about the school. As one can well believe[2], she was[3] delighted and flattered[4].

"We shall of course need photographs," he explained to her. "Will you allow me to take four pupils to our offices, so that we can[5] have them photographed?[6] I have a taxi waiting."

"Certainly," said the principal, "provided I go with you."

When they reached the offices, Leroy took the principal into an unoccupied room, where he asked her to wait while he went[7] with the children to see the chief.

Trembling a little, he went up to the latter's office. "Come in!" He opened the door, pushed two of the children before him into the room and, taking the other two by the hand, one on either side, he went in.

The chief looked up in amazement. "What's the meaning of this?" he said sharply. "I thought I'd fired[8] you?"

"Sir, sir," said Leroy in the most piteous tone, "do what you like[9] with me, but don't doom my poor children to starvation!"[10]

"I didn't know you had any children," said the chief, puzzled.

"Yes, sir, and I have two more[11] at home who are still younger than these."

"That's different," said the chief thoughtfully. "Perhaps I've been unjust. I can't sack a man who has six children. Well, I'll give you your job back. But in the future, be careful. Do you understand?"

1 § 34; *demander*. 2 Complete with *le*; § 60(b). 3 Tense? § 6. 4 Really one should put in *en* ('by it', 'by this'). 5 *pour que* + subjunctive. 6 Construction? § 24(c). 7 Means 'while he would go'. 8 Could be expressed by an infinitive: 'I thought to have fired you.' 9 Future. 10 Use *mourir de faim*. 11 'two others'.

61 Manet when young

On their return to Paris, the first week's model was a woman, Marie la Rousse. Manet painted her with such[1] brilliance and vitality that the whole studio applauded him. Now, surely, Couture would be forced to approve. While awaiting his arrival, they placed the canvas in the best light and decorated the easel with flowers.

When Couture arrived, he saw the canvas as he came in[2] at the door, but turned away as if he had not noticed it.

He corrected the work of all the other students before eventually coming to Manet's[3]. He stood in front of the decorated easel and said, "Won't you ever make up your mind to paint what you see?" Manet was[4] outraged. "I paint what I see, and not what it pleases others to see," he replied bluntly.

"Well, my lad," said Couture, "if you're pretentious enough to set yourself up as the[5] head of a studio, go and start one[6] elsewhere."

Manet walked out.

HENRI PERRUCHOT, La Vie de Manet
(translated)
(*Perpetua Books*)

1 Article required; § 46(a).   2 Use the expression: *franchir la porte*.
3 'that of Manet'; § 69(a).   4 Tense? § 6.   5 In such cases, 'as the' or 'as a' is expressed by *en*, e.g. *je te parle en ami*.   6 *en* required in this sentence.

62 The young gipsy

The two boys lay[1] at the edge of the lake on the other side of the wood, waiting[2] for their friend to arrive.

"If he doesn't come soon, we'll be late for lunch," said Robert, taking his watch out of his pocket and shaking it.

"Gipsies don't pay any attention to time and they don't have lunch," David answered, half asleep.

"But Bill's not a gipsy," protested Robert indignantly.

"Be quiet! Listen!"

The day was so calm that the smallest sound could be heard[3]. Now, as they watched, Bill appeared, walking slowly towards them. He was about fifteen, but he looked older. He wore old trousers which were too big for him and a torn shirt. His mouth was smiling, but his eyes were thoughtful and sad.

"We thought you weren't coming," said Robert. "Hurry up! Let's have a swim!"

The three friends undressed quickly, leapt into the water, and swam together to the opposite bank.

"I had a dream last night," Bill said a little later as they dried themselves in the sunshine. "It was a queer dream," he went on, closing his eyes. "I was taking a walk in the moonlight near that old castle on the hill and suddenly I looked up and saw a tall old man who whispered to me very softly, 'Near this place there is a well and right at the foot you will find—happiness'."

Scottish Certificate of Education
(Higher Grade)

1 Means 'were lying'; § 5. 2 'awaiting the arrival of their friend'.
3 'one heard the smallest sound'.

63 A doctor annoyed

The doctor examined his patient and suddenly exclaimed, "My good woman, it's no use my coming[1] here unless[2] you carry out my instructions. You have been giving[3] him bread, haven't you? You want to kill your husband, I suppose? Listen to me. If after this you give him anything[4] beside my medicine, I will never set foot in this house again, and you can[5] look where you like[5] for another doctor."

"But, doctor, my poor husband was starving, he has eaten nothing for four days—"

"Yes, yes, I know, but I merely tell you this: if you let your husband eat a single mouthful of food before I give you permission to[6], you will kill him, do you hear?"

"He shall not have anything, sir. Is he any better?"

"Why, no. You have worsened his condition by feeding him. It[7] amazes me that he is[8] still alive after what you have given him to eat. You must do exactly as I have told you, you understand?"

"Yes, doctor, I would rather die myself than lose[9] him."

1 Express by: *il est inutile que . . .* or *cela ne sert à rien que . . .* 2 Express by *si* + indicative or by *à moins que* + subjunctive; § 38. 3 Tense? § 1. 4 *quoi que ce soit.* 5 Tense? § 15. 6 § 62. 7 *Cela*; § 68. 8 Subjunctive; § 40. 9 *de* + infinitive.

64 The magistrate and the fowls

We dismounted and were shown[1] into a large room where the magistrate sat[2] at a table on which lay a great number of papers. He was a thin-faced[3] old man with[3] stiff grey whiskers like a cat's[4]. Scarcely had[5] we all entered when a hen, leading her family of a dozen chickens, rushed into the room. The chickens dispersed in search of crumbs, while the mother, more ambitious, perched on the table, tossing the papers right and left.

"Devil take the fowls," cried the magistrate, getting up in a fury[6]. "Antonio, go and fetch your mistress this very instant." The servant went out and returned after two or three minutes, followed by a fat woman who sat down, quite exhausted, on a bench. "What's the matter, Fernando?" she asked, with an amiable smile[7]. "How dare you ask me such a question?" bawled the magistrate. "Take your fowls away before[8] I have[9] them all killed."

While his wife calmly moved forward, he began to hurl books and rulers at the unfortunate birds, and at last they were[10] all driven out. A sentinel stood on guard at the door, with orders to decapitate the first chicken that attempted[11] to approach.

University of London
(Advanced Level)

1 Use the active with *on*; § 7(a).   2 Means 'was seated'.   3 § 47(a).
4 'those of a cat'; § 69(a).   5 Construction? § 14.   6 'furious'.   7 'smiling amiably'.   8 Subjunctive after *avant que*.   9 'to have (something) done' expressed by *faire* + infinitive; § 24(c).   10 Tense? § 6.   11 Means 'would attempt'; § 15.

65 The man on an elephant

It was very dark, for the moon would rise late and a mist hid the stars. Long ago the last child had been hunted from the street, the last villagers had left the seat under the old oak-tree, the cows had been brought into the byres. There was no sound except the far-away murmur of a waterfall. The village was plunged in the deep sleep of those who labour hard, go to bed early, and rise with the dawn. Dick put out his pipe and took the lamp from[1] the table.

Suddenly a voice spoke. It came from outside and it asked in French for a match.

Dick nearly[2] dropped the lamp, then stared out of the open window. There was a face there, suspended in the air—a friendly face with a little yellow beard.

"What are you standing on?" Dick asked in amazement.

"I am sitting," was the reply, "sitting on an elephant, if you want to know."

"If you permit," the voice continued, "I'll come in for a minute. One doesn't often meet an Englishman here and my elephant is never in a hurry. As you have no doubt guessed[3], he and I belong[4] to a circus."

Scottish Certificate of Education
(Higher Grade)

1 Preposition? § 33.   2 Express with *faillir*; § 22(e).   3 *le* required; § 60(b).   4 Person of verb? § 63(b).

66 The doctor and the priest

Adèle had been called to the telephone. She came back into the room with a message for Mouraille.

"Doctor, you're urgently needed[1] for old Mother[2] Boffet. Seems she's no longer conscious."

"I'll go at once," said Mouraille, rising to his feet.

He shook hands with Samothrace, asking if he would still be there in an hour's time. Then, on second thoughts:

"Should I[3] bring the holy oil?"

"I see no other medicine to give her."

"In that case drop me at the presbytery. I'll just[4] collect my gear and come on immediately afterwards. Perhaps you could[5] prepare the dying woman to receive me?"

"She's no longer conscious, you know. . . ."

"Yes, of course. . . . All the same, we ought to be with her, both of us."

"Above all on account of the neighbours. No one will be able to accuse the family of failing[6] to do all that was necessary to enable the poor old thing to die according to the rules."

"We'd better be on our way, then."

GABRIEL CHEVALLIER, Clochemerle-les-Bains
(translated)
Secker & Warburg

1 Use *demander*.   2 'old Mother X', *la mère* X.   3 § 15, Note 3.   4 § 79; *ne . . . que*.   5 Tense? § 26.   6 'of having failed'.

67 The long walk

When I awoke again it was day. Everything was quite still, and I could[1] see nothing on the road. I crawled out of the ditch and set off again. I walked several hours, and then I met a boy on a bicycle riding in the direction from which I had come. He stared at me and stopped when I spoke to him. I asked him to tell me the way to Chalford. He said that it was more than thirty miles away[2]. I thanked him and continued my way.

I don't know how long I was on the road. I remember stopping[3] to sleep now and then, sometimes in the day-time and sometimes at night, and I remember that several people[4] gave me food, and one woman once gave me a cup of milk which did me good. I remember nothing clearly though, except that after I seemed[5] to have been walking for weeks I saw houses which I recognized as[6] Chalford. There were women sitting at the doors[7] of the cottages, but I was a little stronger now and I hurried on to reach home.

University of London
(Advanced Level)

1 Unnecessary to use *pouvoir*; § 26, Note 1.   2 § 87(b).   3 Either: 'I remember that I stopped ...' or 'I remember having stopped ...'   4 *personnes*, not *gens*.   5 'after walking for weeks, it seemed to me, ...'   6 Better to say 'those of Chalford'.   7 Singular; § 47(b).

68 The oral

I have a little reminiscence which will show the way in which[1] the French language is taught[2] in some English schools. I once had to examine in French the boys of a very well-known school. The whole day was devoted to the oral examination of the different classes.

After morning school[3] the headmaster invited me to lunch. We talked about the examination, and he asked me if I was satisfied with the result. "Well," I said, "on the whole I am very pleased indeed, and I think that their knowledge of the language is good. In the top class I found boys who could[4] translate French into English quite easily, who knew their grammar well, and who could[4] put a piece of English into a very respectable piece of French. Of course I find that they have great difficulty in speaking[5], but that is not surprising."

"However, among them I found a boy who spoke with an extremely good accent, and I was astonished to find that he had never been to France." "Oh!" said the headmaster, "who is that boy?" I named him. "Oh, I know," he said, "that boy is full of affectation."

University of London
(Advanced Level)

1 'in a way,' *d'une manière*; what, then, will the relative pronoun be?
2 You could use the passive or the reflexive or *on*. 3 Use *la classe*.
4 *pouvoir* or *savoir*? 5 § 21.

69 The Loire

They ate in a restaurant where there were no cloths on the tables, and there was in particular some goat's milk cheese, hard and dry but very tasty, which he had never eaten before[1].

"Is the Loire far off?"

"By road, Beaugency is two kilometres."

"Aren't there any footpaths?"

"There are several, but it'll take you much longer. . . ."

Why had he[2], who never drank much, encumbered himself with a bottle of local white wine, which weighed down his pocket and bumped against his leg?

He remembered nothing about the footpath. They lost their way. Marcelle's feet hurt her. They ended up amidst reeds, on soft ground, and they were impatient because they could[3] not see the Loire.

Suddenly it was[4] there in front of them, cool and shimmering, with its pebbled sandbanks. From where they were they could[3] see nothing but the opposite bank and a man, very far off, wearing[5] a straw hat, who was fishing, sitting on a camp stool in a punt.

They were thirsty. They drank from[6] the bottle of wine, which was lukewarm. They had already drunk with their meal at the inn. Drowsy with the heat, they lay down on the sand amidst the whispering reeds.

GEORGES SIMENON, The Patient
Hamish Hamilton (Copyright 1963)

1 'before' need not be translated. 2 When the subject is thus separated from the verb by a phrase, one uses the disjunctive pronoun. 3 Unnecessary to use *pouvoir*; § 26, Note 1. 4 Tense? § 12. 5 'wearing' on the head, *coiffé de*. 6 'to drink straight from the bottle', *boire à même la bouteille*.

70 The old manor houses of France

Not a few of[1] these houses have been[2] in the same family since the
14th century. Most have been kept up on barely adequate funds
with a great deal of love, sacrifice and hard work. During the war
they were[3] commandeered for German soldiers, their avenues[4]
felled, their gardens spoiled, and during 1944–45[5] some were
damaged. In one drawing-room I know, a couple of German
bullets ripped through the portrait of a great-grandmother, and the
holes have been allowed to remain[6]—as mementoes, and also
because that particular woman, a general's wife, had been in her day
brave and imperturbable.

Not unnaturally[7], their owners love these houses with that intense
patriotism the French reserve for the soil and stones of *la belle
France*. To visit them[8], especially if it is a member of the family
who shows one round[9], can be moving as well as informative.

VINCENT CRONIN
(Article in 'The Sunday Times')

1 *Bon nombre de.*   2 Tense? § 17(a).   3 Tense? § 6.   4 'the trees of their
avenues'.   5 'during the years'.   6 'have been purposely left'.   7 'It is
natural that' or 'It is not surprising that'.   8 Make use of the noun, *une
visite.*   9 'to show round', *faire les honneurs.*

71 The nurse

The steps halted outside the slightly open door, which opened wider, and through his half-closed eyelids, which gave him the feeling he was cheating, he recognized Mlle Blanche in her smart town clothes.

She made a sign to Joséfa, who followed her out, and both of them, talking in low voices, walked down the passage to the cloakroom, where the nurse changed her dress and put on flat-heeled shoes instead of her high-heeled ones. She probably had a small car, which he pictured in some pale colour, blue or light green.

When she came back she was alone. She took up the thermometer. He had not shut his eyes quickly enough and she noticed that he was awake.

"Good morning." she said gaily. "I hear you've had a good night. If you're good, I shall try and give you a drink of[1] orange juice presently."

Why talk[2] to him as if he were a child? She was intelligent. She knew that he was[3] too. If they had met anywhere else than in a hospital, she would have spoken deferentially to him and would not have dreamed of saying anything as stupid as "If you're good . . ."

GEORGES SIMENON, The Patient
Hamish Hamilton (Copyright 1963)

1 'give you an orange juice to drink', or 'make you drink an orange juice'.
2 § 22(a).   3 *le* required; § 60(c).

72 The early days of the war

A young woman was standing at the kitchen door and looking anxiously out. When she saw the boy, sitting on the bench with[1] the baby in his arms, she looked[2] relieved, and, catching sight of Marie, she smiled. "Hullo, I didn't see[3] you. . . ." She came across the yard and stood in front of her. She had very fair hair, and a sweet, round, stupid face with[1] placid thick lips and red-rimmed blue eyes. "Oh . . ." she let out[4] a long sigh and lowered her head, "isn't it awful . . . I can't believe it now. . . ."

"When did you come?"

"Yesterday. Father came over and fetched us. (By train, he had to come. The roads were terrible. But the train was full of soldiers, too). *I* didn't know what[5] to do. There was a bomb[6] on the house across our street and our apartment was all blown in . . . all over dust . . . and the floor gave way. . . . Thank God, we weren't at home, I'd gone shopping . . . and all my things were ruined . . . I couldn't stop crying . . . 'Pierre', I kept on saying, 'Pierre' . . ."

"Is he still away?" Marie asked. She didn't want to hear about[7] the bombs. Already, after only about three days of it, she had stopped finding[8] this kind of story worth listening to and she wanted to hear a bit of good news.

STELLA GIBBONS, White Sand and Grey Sand
Hodder & Stoughton

1 § 47(a). 2 Tense? § 12. 3 Pluperfect; § 13. 4 'she said, letting out . . . and lowering . . .'. 5 § 70. 6 'A bomb fell'. 7 'hear talk of'. 8 'she no longer found that'.

73 The quarrel

Someone was climbing up the attic stairs. There was a sharp knock[1], and my door was thrown open[2]. Sheila came into the room. With one hand she shut the door behind her, but she was looking at me with a gaze expressionless and fixed. She took two steps into the room, then stopped quite still. Her face was pale, hard, without a smile. Her arms were at her sides. I had jumped up, forgetting everything but that she was here, my arms open for her; but when she stayed still, so did I[3], frozen.

"I've come to see you," she said.

"Yes," I said.

"I haven't seen you since that night. You're thinking about that night." Her voice was louder than usual.

"I'm bound to think of it."

"Listen to this: I did it on purpose."

"Why did you do it?"

"Because you made me angry." Her eyes were steady, hypnotic in[4] their glitter. "I've not come to tell you that I'm sorry."

"You ought to be," I said.

"I'm not sorry." Her voice had risen. "I'm glad I did[5] it."

"What do you mean?" I said in anger.

"I tell you, I'm glad I did it."

We were standing a yard apart. Her arms were still at her sides, and she had not moved.

C. P. SNOW, Time of Hope
Macmillan

1 You must use the verb *frapper*. 2 'my door suddenly opened wide'. 3 'to do likewise', *en faire autant*, *faire de même*. 4 Use *par*. 5 Use an infinitive, not the subjunctive; § 40.

74 The tiger who would be king

"I'll be king of beasts by the time[1] the moon rises," said the tiger. "It will be a yellow moon with black stripes, in my honour."

"Oh sure[2]," said the tigress as she went to look after her young, one of whom, a male, very like his father, had an imaginary thorn in his paw.

The tiger prowled through the jungle till he came to the lion's den. "Come out," he roared, "and greet the king of beasts. The king is dead, long live the king."

Inside the den, the lioness woke her mate. "The king is here to see you," she said.

"What king?" he enquired, sleepily[3].

"The king of beasts," she said.

"I am[4] the king of beasts," roared Leo, and he charged out of the den to defend his crown against the pretender.

It was[5] a terrible fight, and it lasted until the setting of the sun. All the animals of the jungle joined in, some taking the side of the tiger, and others the side of the lion. Every creature from the aardvark to the zebra took part in the struggle to overthrow the lion or repulse the tiger, and some[6] did not know which they were fighting for, and some fought for both, and some fought whoever was nearest, and some fought for the sake of fighting.

JAMES THURBER, Vintage Thurber
Hamish Hamilton (Copyright 1963)

1 Express as 'before'. 2 What is the shade of meaning of this? 3 Use an adjective. 4 Not just *Je suis.* 5 Tense? § 12. 6 For the recurring 'some', you could use: *certaines . . . d'autres . . . d'autres encore. . . .*

75 A question of salary

I sat[1] there staring[2] out of the window, trying to make up my mind.
Beyond Justin's head I could[3] see the sooty front of the building
opposite. Even leaning forward, I couldn't see the sky.

"What will you pay me?" I asked.

"We discussed that last time," said Justin curtly.

"Walker got about four thousand a year, didn't he?"

"He'd been with the firm forty years."

"I don't think we should[4] be mean at this moment, Major," said
Nelson quietly.

Justin turned round and regarded Nelson with surprise. "I wasn't
aware of being mean. But what do you suggest?"

Nelson said, "I thought two thousand would be a reasonable
salary for that work and that responsibility."

For a moment I thought[5] Justin would explode, but he swallowed
it[6] down and said, "Well, you've got the whip hand financially. I
think it's excessive, but if you think we can afford it—."

"I think it would be reasonable," said Nelson. "And there would
be director's fees too."

ANTHONY GLYN, The Ram in the Thicket
Hutchinson

1 Use *rester*. 2 *à* + infinitive. 3 Unnecessary to use *pouvoir*; § 26,
Note 1. 4 Means 'ought to'. 5 Tense? § 12. 6 Say 'his anger'.

76 The hostess

The French family with whom I was to[1] stay was that of a retired infantry officer, Commandant Leroy, who had known my father in Paris at the end of the war. I had never met him, though his description, as a quiet little man dominated by a masterful wife, was[2] already familiar to me; so that I hoped there would be no difficulty in[3] recognizing Madame Leroy on the platform. There was, indeed, small doubt as to her identity as soon as I set eyes on her. Tall and stately, she was dressed in the deepest black. A female companion of mature age accompanied her[4], wearing a cone-shaped hat trimmed with luxuriant artificial flowers. No doubt I was myself equally unmistakable, because, even before descending passengers had cleared away[5], she made towards me with[6] eyebrows raised, and a smile that made me welcome not only to her own house, but to the whole of France.

ANTHONY POWELL, A Question of Upbringing
Heinemann

1 § 27.   2 Subjunctive after *bien que*.   3 *à* + infinitive; § 21.   4 Better to say: 'She was accompanied by . . .'   5 Subjunctive after *avant que*. 6 § 47(a).

77 A vigil

He was now quite alone with the sleeping man till the next morning.
He looked again at the candle, which had been lighted for the first
time to show him the way and of which three parts[1] at least were
already consumed. In another hour[2] he would be without light
unless[3] he called at once for a fresh candle.

He lingered irresolutely[4] by the table, waiting till[5] he could
find enough courage to open the door. He picked up the candle—
too quickly—for in an instant it was[6] out and the room was[6]
plunged into complete darkness. Nothing could be heard in the
room but the familiar sound of the rain beating against the window.

Still a vague distrust possessed him, and kept[7] him in his chair.
He had put his suit-case on the table after entering the room; he
now took the key from[8] his pocket, stretched out his hand gently,
opened the case and tried to find in it[9] a small box of matches which
he remembered he had[10] put there.

As soon as he had lit[11] the candle again, it was the bed his eyes
first sought. Just before the light had gone out, he had seen nothing
unusual there, no disarrangement of the folds of the closely drawn
curtains round the bed, but now there[12] protruded a long white
hand. The man had moved.

Joint Matriculation Board
(Advanced Level)

1 *les trois quarts.* 2 'Another hour and he would be ...' 3 § 38.
4 Use an adjective. 5 You could use *attendre que* + subjunctive, or
attendre de + infinitive. 6 Tense? § 6. 7 You could say: 'made him
remain'. 8 Preposition? § 33. 9 § 61. 10 'having put there'. 11 Tense?
§ 14. 12 Use the impersonal form, *il* ...

78 Broken hearts

She knelt down beside me and stroked my hair gently. "Poor Joe," she said. "Poor Joe is tired."

"I'm sorry," I said.

She took my handkerchief from[1] my breast pocket and wiped my eyes[2].

"Poor Joe," she said. "Being sorry[3] won't help us now." She took my hand[2]. "Come with me while I make[4] the coffee." I let her take me into the kitchen.

Watching her setting out the cups, warming the milk, filling the percolator, there was no need to talk any more. I had even a feeling of contentment: there was nothing left[5] to happen[6] to me.

I finished my second cup of coffee and looked at my watch. "I'll have to go," I said.

She corked the thermos.

"Joe, this is your home. You can stay the night if you want. Or why don't you rest for a while?"

"I can't rest now." I picked up the thermos flask. "I'll write you."

"Phone me. Phone me as soon as you've reached[4] London. Promise[7]."

"All right."

She started to cry. "Take care, Joe. Oh, do[8] take care!"

JOHN BRAINE, Life at the Top
Eyre & Spottiswoode

1 Preposition? § 33.   2 § 47(b).   3 Better to use a noun: *les regrets*. 4 Tense? § 15.   5 § 9.   6 'which could happen to me'; § 43.   7 'Promised?'   8 This 'do' is rendered by *je t'en prie*.

79 Secret departure

The moment for which I had waited[1] so long had arrived, but still I hesitated to take the decisive step. However, I dared delay no longer for with every minute I felt my courage fading away. I put out the light and gently drew back the curtains. My room was beside the staircase and I thought that the dim light which now came from the window might[2] help me as I went[3] downstairs. I picked up my suitcase, felt in my pocket for the box of matches, and walked cautiously towards the door. It opened easily and pushing it wide I tiptoed out. All was silent. I waited for a moment, hoping that my eyes would become accustomed to the darkness, and then I made for the stairs. The carpet was thick and soft; I made no sound. Overjoyed, I proceeded to go down.

The first step creaked and my heart began to beat violently. However, I reached the bottom of the stairs without further difficulty. Putting down the suitcase, I took out the matches. Suddenly I thought[4] I heard[5] a voice. I listened, but I could hear nothing and was about to go on when I heard the voice again—an indistinct murmur. There was someone talking in the drawing-room. Then I realized it was only the parrot chattering away. With a sigh of relief I turned the key in the lock, and a moment later I was standing outside in the fresh morning air. I was free!

Scottish Certificate of Education
(Higher Grade)

1 Tense? § 17(b).   2 Form of *pouvoir*? § 26.   3 Tense? § 15.   4 Tense? § 12.   5 Use an infinitive; § 22(c).

80 Where was the kitchen?

"It's not a question of liking or not liking[1]," she added. "The child will eat anything, as you know, but I'm not going to risk making her ill. The heat wave is trying enough without that, I'm sure. You ought to have[2] smelt the cheese, that's all I say. Now dear, please go and get us something plain."

"All right," Grace said. "I don't know where the kitchen is, but I'll do my best." She went off slowly, wondering how she was going to find the first-floor rooms in that big, complicated house built at so many different periods. When at last she had[3] done so[4], she looked first into the drawing-room.

She was[5] almost relieved to find nobody there. Her mission seemed to her so absurd, and really so impolite, that she would have liked to[6] give it up. She was convinced that all the servants would already be asleep and regretted that[7] she was not asleep too. She could hear voices coming from the library but the rest of the house was plunged in silence.

She lingered for a moment by the library door but did not dare to open it, thinking that Charles would be furious at such an interruption. The dining-room was empty. She went through it and found a dark passage which she followed, until she came to a heavy oak door. Hoping that this led to[8] the kitchen, she opened it timidly.

Joint Matriculation Board
(Advanced Level)

1 § 80(b).   2 § 27.   3 Tense? § 14.   4 Probably better to say: 'had found them'.   5 Tense? § 6.   6 § 25.   7 Use the infinitive: 'regretted not to . . .'; § 40.   8 Use *donner accès à*.

81 In Canada

I remained three weeks in this inexpensive hotel, and decided to travel on the following Monday, although the snow was still deep in Montreal, and although[1], too, I knew it would be deeper in the country. I had a small room to sleep in, at a cost of 15 cents per night. There were several others of the same kind, each divided one from the other by a thin wooden partition, which was high enough to ensure privacy, but[2] did not prevent curious lodgers from standing tiptoe on their beds[3], and peering into another's room.

Going to bed early on Sunday night, in view of the fact that I was to continue my journey on the following day, I was[4] somewhat startled on entering my room to hear a gentle knock[5] on the partition.

"Hallo," I cried, "what do you want?"

Whatever[6] the man may have wanted, he remained silent, seemingly frightened at my loud tone, which would most certainly draw the attention of others.

"I want a match, if you have one."

Of course, smoking was not allowed[7] in the bedrooms, but in this respect we were nearly all breakers of the law. Taking a few matches from my pocket, I threw them over the partition. After hearing the sound they made in falling, I heard him[8] groping[9] in the semi-darkness.

Cambridge Local Examinations
(Advanced Level)

---

1 When 'although' is repeated, one uses just *que*, not the full *bien que*.
2 'but which did not'. 3 Singular; § 47(b). 4 Tense? §6. 5 Make use of *frapper*. 6 § 44. 7 § 7(a). 8 to avoid ambiguity, say: 'I heard the man ...' 9 'who was groping.'

82 The examiner and his scripts

Later, as we were walking home, I suddenly realized that I was without[1] my parcel of scripts. It must[2] have been left in the park. I had heard enough[3] to guess that it was a dreadful offence to lose examination scripts and I insisted that[4] we must go back at once for[5] them.

The park was closed, with the gates locked, and it was nearly dark.

"Can't you wait until tomorrow, when the park opens[6]?" asked Betty.

"No," I said unreasonably. "I must get them back before anyone finds them. It's really serious to lose examination scripts!"

I decided to climb into[7] the park, and after choosing a good spot, asked Betty to wait. She looked[8] amused. As I walked around[9] slowly, trying to see my way to[10] the point where we had been sitting, I felt utterly isolated. I was, at that moment, the only person in the whole universe looking for a parcel of examination scripts in a dark, locked park. But I soon[11] found them, and a few minutes later had climbed out.[12] When I saw Betty I held up the parcel and we both laughed with joy.

G. O. JONES, The Catalyst
Faber & Faber

1 'I no longer had'. 2 'I must have left . . .' 3 'enough of it'. 4 *insister pour que* . . . 5 'to get them'. 6 Tense? § 15. 7 'to enter the park by climbing over the railings'. 8 Tense? § 12. 9 Use *errer*. 10 You could use *s'orienter vers*. 11 Use *ne pas tarder à*; § 21. 12 'I had got out of the park'.

83 Police operations

Campion came out of the front door noiselessly. He crossed the path to[1] the lawn and stood[2] waiting. The Inspector's figure emerged from the black shadows round the house and approached him. He did not say anything, but taking Campion's arm led him into the narrow band of darkness below the row of poplars which lined one side of the path. He walked very fast and in complete silence[3] until[4] they were some two hundred yards from the window. Then he sighed.

"Very nicely done, sir," he said enthusiastically. "I didn't know you were here before I caught[5] a glimpse of you a moment ago. We'll have to be careful, though. It would be silly to invent some explanation. Once you do[6], you have to go on remembering what you've said for years afterwards."

Campion did not reply; he walked steadily on towards the gateway.

As he had hoped[7], the inspector went on talking, showing himself a friendly person[8] who was—not without reason—proud of the high rank he had reached in the police force.

"That's why I am doing this job myself," he remarked. "It's not that I haven't got[9] half a dozen men I could trust, but I don't want them to[10] take the risk, you see."

Cambridge Local Examinations
(Advanced Level)

1 Meaning? 2 Use *rester à (faire)*. 3 Article required; § 46(a). 4 § 38. 5 Unnecessary to use the subjunctive; § 40. 6 'you do it (that)'. 7 *le* required; § 60(b). 8 Use *homme*; this avoids trouble with gender. 9 Subjunctive. 10 § 40.

84 Explorers

The king added politely that though it was customary[1] to examine
the baggage of every traveller passing through his country, yet, in
the present instance, he would dispense with that ceremony; adding
I was at liberty to[2] depart when I pleased[3].

Accordingly on the morning of the 23rd, we left Fatteconda, and
about eleven o'clock came to a small village, where we determined
to stop for the rest of the day. In the afternoon my fellow-travellers
informed me that as this was the boundary between Bondou and
Kajaaga, and dangerous for travellers, it would be necessary to
continue our journey by night, until we should reach[4] a more
hospitable part of the country. I agreed to the proposal, and hired
two people for guides[5] through the woods; and as soon as the people
of the village were gone to sleep[6] (the moon shining bright), we set
out. The stillness of the air, the howling of the wild beasts, and the
deep solitude of the forest, made[7] the scene solemn and impressive.
Not a word was uttered by any of us[8] but in a whisper; all were
attentive and every one anxious to[9] show his sagacity, by pointing
out to me the wolves as they glided like shadows from thicket to
thicket. Towards morning we arrived at a village called Kimmoo,
where our guides awakened one of their acquaintances, and we
stopped to give the asses some corn.

Mungo Park

1 'the custom'.   2 'free to'.   3 Tense? § 15.   4 Avoid the imperfect
subjunctive by using *en attendant de* + infinitive.   5 'to guide us'.   6
Tense? § 14.   7 *rendre*, not *faire*.   8 'Not one of us uttered ...'   9 'to
be anxious to (do)', *tenir à (faire)*.

85 Mr. Pepys is jealous

One day in the middle of May Samuel came home in the afternoon to join Elizabeth at her lesson—but no sound of music came from the dancing room.

Samuel went up the steps puzzled and perplexed. He was sure that this was Pemberton's afternoon. He had told Elizabeth at dinner that he had arranged to postpone a trip to Deptford so that he could[1] join her in her lesson, and Elizabeth had not replied. He hurried up the steps quietly, expecting to hear voices when he got to[2] the top.

But there were no voices. He started towards the door, ready to surprise the dancers; but at the threshold he stopped. Someone was whispering.

He moved around[3] silently so that he could[1] see into the room without being seen. Ashwell was not at the spinet; but in the far corner of the room, holding hands and talking in muffled voices, stood Elizabeth and Pemberton. *Ashwell was not in the room.*

A cramp seized Samuel in the pit of the stomach. His heart seemed to stop beating, and he could not catch his breath[4]. He tiptoed back down the steps and looked for one of the servants. He could find no one but Susan, cooking a shoulder of mutton in the kitchen. No one else was there, Susan told him. Mrs. Ashwell had gone to see her mother and Mary, the chambermaid, was out on an errand.

CECIL ABERNETHY, Mr. Pepys of Seething Lane
W. H. Allen

---

1 Unnecessary to use the subjunctive; § 38, Special Note 1. 2 Tense? § 15. 3 Use *se déplacer.* 4 You could use: *avoir le souffle coupé*, or *avoir l'haleine (la respiration) coupée.*

86 The fugitive

As[1] the car approached the frontier, Jack became increasingly sad
and weary. He regretted having left home, he was afraid his family
would not understand[2] his reasons for leaving without a word. Why
had he not simply hidden in the teacher's house, where the police
would never think of looking for him? For a moment he had[3] the
wild idea of throwing himself on the mercy of the police, but,
before he could[4] do so, the car entered the last French town before
the frontier. It was an overgrown village rather than a town, but
the long narrow street was a pleasure to the eye: the plane trees
along[5] either side met overhead to form a tunnel of green, while the
pavements, despite the war, were alive with cheerful, gaily-dressed
crowds.

By the church, he had to stop to ask the way of a passer-by and,
while he was listening to the directions, his heart nearly[6] stopped.
From across the road a policeman was watching him suspiciously.
Jack scarcely dared to breathe, but, hoping that he had not been
recognized, he started off for the colonel's. "What will become of
me," he said to himself, "if I am caught at this late hour? But
there[7], why face[8] dangers that do not yet exist? I have been[9] in
daily peril for six months and will be until the war ends[10]. And
when that happy day arrives, perhaps I shall be able to start living
again without being constantly afraid."

Welsh General Certificate of Education
(Advanced Level)

1 *A mesure que.* 2 Subjunctive; § 40. 3 Tense? § 12. 4 Subjunctive;
§ 38. 5 'which lined it on either side'. 6 Use *faillir*; § 22(e). 7 *Mais
voyons.* 8 Infinitive; § 22(a). 9 Tense? § 17(a). 10 'until the end of
the war'.

87 A memory of childhood

It was one of the long afternoons of childhood. I was nearly nine years old, and it was the June of 1914. It was an afternoon I should not have remembered, except for what happened to me on the way home.

It was getting late when we left the stream, climbed the bank, found ourselves back in the suburb, beside the tramlines. Down in the reeds we could make-believe that we were isolated, camping in the wilds; but in fact, the tramlines ran by[1] parallel to the stream, for[2] another mile. I went home alone, tired and happy after the day in[3] the sun. I was not in a hurry, and walked along[4], basking in[5] the warm evening. The scent of the lime trees hung over the suburban street; lights were coming on in some of the houses; the red brick of the new church was roseate in the sunset glow.

At the church the street forked; to the right[6] past the butcher's, past a row of little houses whose front doors opened on to the pavement; to the left[7] past the public library along[8] the familiar road towards home.

C. P. SNOW, Time of Hope
Macmillan

1 Use *passer à côté*. 2 *pendant*. 3 'spent in'. 4 Use the expression *suivre son chemin*. 5 'enjoying the warmth of the evening'. 6 'going to the right, one passed . . .' 7 'going to the left, one passed . . .' 8 'following'.

88 A homecoming

I opened the gate and went through into the back garden; once again I could look at Sindram Grange through Barbara's eyes, once again I could see it as the magic castle on the top of the hill over-looking the river. Norah had nothing to do with it[1], I wouldn't let her spoil it[2] for me; or for Barbara.

She would be sleeping now under the dark blue ceiling with the silver stars, not knowing that I was standing out here in the moon-light. And when she saw[3] me she would say she was glad to see me first and ask me what I had brought back for her later; if indeed she asked me at all[4]. She wasn't a greedy child.

I took out my packet of cigarettes and then put them back in my pocket again. The smell of tobacco would spoil the smell of the night. The striking of a match would disturb its silence. I leaned back against the wall and let[5] the night and the silence take over. My future was clear at last; I'd stopped being frightened.

JOHN BRAINE, Life at the Top
Eyre & Spottiswoode

1 The phrase to use is: *n'y était pour rien.*   2 Probably best to say 'this' or 'all this'.   3 Tense? § 15.   4 You could say: 'even if she asked me that question'.   5 Express as: 'I gave myself up entirely to . . .', using *se livrer.*

89 Churchill prefers to play cards

WINSTON: "You need not talk so loud, it must be[1] a great effort. I can hear quite well."

ARI (lowering his voice): "I'm sorry, Sir Winston. If people have to work very hard for subsistence[2], if they have to rub their hands[3] to keep warm, they have no time for leisure. They cannot attend to the arts. Things of the spirit, things of the soul are left out of[4] their lives[5]. You told me, Sir Winston, your father died very young; if he had lived to your age you might not have had to[6] struggle so hard. Your life would have been easier, and you might not have done[7] what you did."

Winston, who did not appear to be listening very attentively, broke in:

"No, we were very different people."

ARI: "Yes, of course, you were different, but you would not have been driven on by necessity. My mother died when I was six. If she had lived I might not have[8] worked as hard as I have done ."

WINSTON: "Would you like to play a little cards[10] instead of talking philosophy?"

ARI: "Not philosophy, but history."

LORD MORAN, Winston Churchill: The Struggle for Survival
Constable

1 'that must cost you'. 2 'to live'. 3 § 47(b). 4 'have no place in'.
5 Singular; § 47(b). 6 'perhaps you would not have had to'. 7 'perhaps you would not have done'. 8 'perhaps I should not have worked'.
9 *le* required; § 60(b). 10 'play cards a little'.

90 A Frenchman who knew his worth

Monsieur Dubuisson had been walking up and down one[1] of the paths, studying a newspaper. Now he came across the withered grass and sat down beside me, at the same time taking from the pocket of his black alpaca coat his pipe, of which—like Peter Templer—he was, for some[2] reason, immensely proud. As usual he cleared his throat several times before speaking, and then, leaning backwards, spat sideways over the seat. In[3] his slow, disapproving voice he said: "I think it would be a—a little absurd if I talked French to you in view of our—our relative mastery of each other's tongue. Do you agree[4], Jenkins, yes?"

"Absolutely."

One had to admit that he spoke English remarkably well, in spite of the hesitations made necessary by the subtlety of his processes[5] of thought. There could be no doubt that every sentence was intended to knock you down by its penetrative brilliance[6]. Smiling quietly to[7] himself, as if at some essentially witty conception that he was inwardly playing with, and withheld[8] only because its discernment was not for everybody, he began slowly to fill his pipe with tobacco—again like Peter's—that smelt peculiarly abominable

ANTHONY POWELL, A Question of Upbringing
Heinemann

1 'in one of the paths'. 2 Use *je ne sais quelle*; § 77. 3 *de*. 4 'Are you of this opinion'. 5 'of the processes of his thought'. 6 Better to say 'brilliant penetration'. 7 *pour*. 8 A hard sentence. One could express it thus: 'and which he refrained from expressing only because it would not be given to everybody to understand it'.

91 The cabin companion

I almost[1] asked him what the matter was but I decided not to bother. He went out leaving the lights on[2]. I wondered whether to get up[3] and turn them out, but laziness and politeness prevented me[4]. I was shamming sleep when he returned and went sluggishly and clatteringly back to bed. He seemed[5] to be asleep immediately.

I am one[6] of those people who cannot easily go to sleep again if[7] they are once awakened. I lay for hours listening to his breathing, which was deep enough to irritate me and not quite stertorous enough to justify me in[8] throwing a shoe at him. I had, so it seemed[9], just fallen asleep again, when all the lights went on and he was hunting for his slippers again.

This time I shammed sleep throughout, wondering if the purser could find me another cabin. What had Justin said his name was? Oldham? Oldfield? Perhaps the contact might be useful after all.

I had just struggled back[10] to sleep for the third time when I was[11] awakened by a bell shrilling through[12] the cabin. The lights went on again and with bleary furious eyes[13] I saw Warner sitting on the edge of his bed, stretching[14].

ANTHONY GLYN, The Ram in the Thicket
Hutchinson

1 Use *faillir*; § 22(e). 2 'the lamps alight'. 3 'whether I should get up'. 4 *en* required; § 62. 5 Tense? § 12. 6 'I am of those who'. 7 One could simply say 'once awakened', omitting 'if they are'. 8 Use *me mettre en droit de*. 9 'I had just fallen asleep again, it seemed to me . . .' 10 'I had just got to sleep again with difficulty'. 11 Tense? § 6. 12 'by the shrill noise of a bell resounding in . . .' 13 'with my . . .' 14 'and who was stretching'.

92 The manager

It seemed to me that above all I must[1] remain calm, obviously in control of the situation, and must[1] not expose to anyone the fact that I had no idea of what I was expected to do[2]. I did not know my terms of reference, my powers, or my duties.

It soon appeared[3] to me that since there was practically no situation, I was in control of it, at least for the time being. I must however take account of the possibility that a situation might[4] develop. As soon as there was[5] any sign of one I would act decisively[6] and positively.

Meanwhile, I must behave as if all was clear to me. My staff— of three, as far as I could ascertain—must imagine that, behind my closed doors, I was busy with some manager-like activity: making[7] a plan, writing a report, or, perhaps, assessing a situation.

I wondered whether my staff would ask to be given[8] instructions or whether perhaps I should[9] explain to them that, in the present lull, they could take things easily.

G. O. JONES, The Catalyst
Faber & Faber

1 Tense of *devoir*? 2 'what one expected of me'. 3 Tense? § 12. 4 Tense of *pouvoir*? § 26. 5 Tense? § 15. 6 'in a decisive and positive manner'. 7 'that I was making . . .' 8 'that one (or I) should give them'; use the present subjunctive. 9 Use *devoir*.

93 Mr. Pepys finds his hoard

But getting the gold was Samuel's principal business in Brampton. As soon as it was dark at the end of his first day there, he lit a dark lantern and went into the garden with Elizabeth and his father. When they[1] had pointed out[2] the spot where they were sure they had buried[3] the sacks, he took an iron spit and poked around[4] in the loose earth. But the spit did not strike cloth bags or anything else. Samuel looked at them enquiringly.

They had put the bags in a wooden box, they explained, so that[5] the bags would not rot and lose their coins.

Samuel probed again—and again. But his iron found nothing whatever[6] under the ground. In growing excitement, Samuel jabbed the spit all over the area[7], not only in the hidden place behind the hedge, but also out in the open, in the centre of the garden where any[8] passer-by on the road could have[9] seen if it had been light. Elizabeth and her father-in-law stood by helplessly, protesting that they were sure they had not buried[10] it out so far from the hedge, while Samuel jabbed and sweated and swore. Just as he was about to lose his temper, the iron spit made a dull sound as it hit[11] something solid. Samuel jabbed two or three times more to make sure, and then he snatched the spade from his father's hand and began to dig. In two scoops[12] of the shovel, the blade hit wood. Samuel fell to his knees and pulled away the earth like a dog digging a hole for a bone.

CECIL ABERNETHY, Mr. Pepys of Seething Lane
W. H. Allen

1 Better to say 'these'. 2 Tense? § 14. 3 'certain of having buried'. 4 Use *piquer çà et là*. 5 'so that the bags, in rotting, would not lose . . .' 6 'absolutely nothing'. 7 Use *un peu partout*. 8 § 77. 9 § 26. 10 'certain of not having buried'. 11 'in hitting'. 12 'Two scoops of the shovel, and the blade . . .'

94 Churchill arrives unexpectedly

The Nairns (the Consul-General and his wife), who had heard of
our plight, met us at Tangier, and a little procession of cars carried
off our party to their house on the outskirts of the town. The guests
for a dinner party[1] were already arriving, their spruce evening
clothes made us feel battered and dishevelled, and, perhaps, a little
in the way. T. S. Eliot, one of the guests, said it[2] would make a
wonderful scene for a play. I took him over to Winston, who gazed
at him in an uncomprehending way; his name evidently meant[3]
nothing to him. Eliot drifted away, and Winston was left sitting
apart, looking at the carpet, a little puzzled perhaps about what it
all meant. He could not understand why they did not announce
dinner. "I am very hungry, Charles." Raising his voice, he repeated
this, so that I was afraid Mrs Nairn would hear.[4] I tried to explain
that dinner was waiting for us at the Rif Hotel. He seemed too
tired to make a move; sunk in his chair, he took no notice of the
guests who were sitting about. They had given up making conversation, though[5] one of them said to me that they would talk about
this[6] for a long time.

LORD MORAN, Winston Churchill: The Struggle for Survival
Constable

1 'People invited to dinner'.   2 'this' or 'all this'.   3 Use *dire*.   4 § 40.
5 'One of them said to me, however, that . . .'   6 'this event'.

95 Evening in the hills

Though I saw a hamlet or two below me in the vale, and many lone houses of farmers, it was[1] a very solitary march all the afternoon; and the evening began slowly under the trees. But I heard the voice of a woman singing some sad, old, endless song not far off. It seemed to be[2] about love and a lover, her handsome sweetheart; and I wished I could have[3] taken up[4] the tune and answered her, as I went upon my invisible woodland way.

We came at last into a wide white high-road carpeted with noiseless dust. The night had come; the moon had been shining[5] for a long while upon the opposite mountain, when, on turning a corner, my donkey and I came into her light. The road wound[6] and descended swiftly among masses of chestnut trees. Hot dust[7] rose from our feet and flowed away. Our two shadows lay before us[8] clearly outlined on the road, and now, as we turned a corner, went off into the misty distance and sailed along the mountain like clouds. From time to time a warm wind rustled down the valley, the air was filled with whispering music and the shadows seemed to dance in tune.

ROBERT LOUIS STEVENSON, Travels with a Donkey

1 Tense? § 12. 2 'It was, so it seemed, about . . .' 3 'I should have liked to be able'; § 25. 4 You could say: 'to answer her by taking up the tune'. 5 Tense? § 17(b). 6 You could say: 'the road descended swiftly, winding . . .' 7 'A hot dust'. 8 'preceded us'.

Part Two

Practice Sentences

1 Compound Tenses · The Passive

p. 112 §*1*
1. You have been sleeping.
2. I saw that she had been crying.
3. He will have finished. We should have understood.

p. 112 §*2*
4. She had gone out. I shall have gone. They would have stayed.
5. They had gone to bed. She will have rested. I should have got up.

p. 113 §*4*
6. She had wiped her eyes and rubbed her cheeks.
7. They had wondered if he would come back.

p. 114 §*6*
8. I was awakened the next morning by the same noise.
9. As soon as the door was opened he went in.

p. 115 §*7*
10. We had been told that you were here.
11. I have been asked for my opinion.
12. They are not permitted to leave the country.
13. He will be advised to confess.
14. We were shown a picture.
15. No questions will be asked.

2 Present Participle · Impersonal Verbs

p. 115 §*8*
1. What do you earn by writing articles?
2. While washing up, she had broken a plate.
3. On seeing me he gave a start.
4. In doing this he damaged the machine.
5. While talking he took some papers out of a drawer.
6. While drinking my coffee, I was observing these people.

p. 116 §*9*
7. She had little money left.
8. We have only a few left.
9. They had nothing left.
10. It would be better to take a taxi.

11   It was a question of finding a suitable place.
12   It is not enough to apologize.
13   It seems to me that I have seen them before.
14   There exist several problems to resolve.

3 Imperfect and Past Historic

p. 118 § 12

1   We knew you wanted to see them.
2   He thought we were on the beach.
3   Suddenly he was ashamed of his weakness.
4   He was again enthusiastic.
5   This time he could not resist the temptation.
6   They had the courage to go on to the end.
7   Then I thought I heard the sound of a key in the lock.
8   For a few seconds I had the conviction that he was lying.
9   The next moment I knew that I had been mistaken.
10   As soon as it was known that he was there, a crowd gathered.
11   The house seemed suddenly to become quiet.
12   There were a few moments of strained silence.
13   The door closed and that was all.
14   At first it was impossible to see what was going on.

4 Pluperfect and Past Anterior

p. 119 § 13

1   We told him what would happen.
2   You haven't returned the books I lent you.
3   Here is the letter you asked for.
4   I warned you that it would be difficult.

p. 119 § 14

5   As soon as he had had lunch he went back to the office.
6   As soon as she had recovered from her surprise, she began to think.
7   Scarcely had he reached his destination when he received an urgent message.
8   When the rain had stopped the sun shone again.
9   As soon as I had said this I knew I had made a mistake.
10   When they had gone I resumed my work.

5 Futures · Tenses used with *si*

p. 119 §15
1 When we arrive we will phone you.
2 The first time you hear it, do nothing.
3 May I come back later?—As you like.
4 She said she would call on us when she was in London.
5 Tomorrow you will tell me what you have decided.
6 I knew he would come as soon as he had received my message.
7 We asked him his name but he wouldn't tell us.
8 She was about to close the shop.
9 Shall I write my address?

p. 120 §16
10 If I find it, I will send it to you.
11 If he saw this letter he would recognize your writing.
12 If I had wanted to stay I should have stayed.
13 If he hadn't seen it himself he would never have believed it.
14 I don't know whether they will accept.
15 We were wondering what you would do.

6 Tenses used with *depuis. Venir de (faire)*

p. 121 §17
1 How long have you been learning French?
2 I have been thinking about it for a long time.
3 This question has worried me for a fortnight.
4 We have known them for years.
5 I had been expecting this scene for a long time.
6 They had been travelling for three days.
7 He had been there for several weeks.
8 I had been observing them for some minutes.

p. 121 §18
9 I have just posted some letters.
10 We have just bought a new car.
11 They had just begun playing.
12 Michel had just told me what had happened.

7 Infinitive used with *à*

p. 123 § 20

1 Have you anything to say?—No, I have nothing to say.
2 I should be the first to admit it.

p. 123 § 21

3 My signature is difficult to imitate.
4 Such men are easy to recognize.
5 You will have difficulty in finding a room.
6 I shall have a few minutes to wait.
7 He has several letters to dictate.
8 If you want to go there, you have only to say so.
9 He soon realized his mistake. (Use *ne pas tarder à*)
10 Have you a boat for hire?
11 It's a situation to be avoided.
12 He is a man to dare everything.

8 Certain Constructions with the Infinitive Perfect Infinitive

p. 124 § 22

1 The train has gone. What are we to do?
2 Why complicate things?
3 How are we to explain this silence?
4 What is the good of trying to help them?
5 I am going into town.—What for?
6 I think I must warn you.
7 Who were the people you say you met?
8 We hope we have acted wisely.
9 The child nearly fell out of the train.

p. 125 § 23

10 After going up to his room he came down again.
11 After resting a while we set off again.
12 He doesn't seem to have done much in life.
13 We thank you for coming.
14 I apologize for not writing sooner.
15 Do you remember spending the night in this hotel?

9 *Faire* with the Infinitive

p. 125 § 24

1 This made him hesitate.
2 I try to make her forget her troubles.
3 You have made him miss a fine opportunity.
4 I gave them to understand that I was opposed to it.
5 They have had the house rebuilt.
6 We will have the police called.
7 I have had a meal prepared.
8 We get this work done by the mechanics.
9 He wants to make himself known.
10 A certain excitement makes itself felt.
11 He would not let himself be insulted.
12 I saw it taken away by several workmen.

10 *Vouloir, pouvoir, devoir*

p. 126 § 25

1 I shouldn't like to have been in your place.
2 We should have liked to stay longer.

p. 126 § 26

3 You can do that later.
4 I looked for him, but I couldn't find him.
5 Could you tell me where the post office is, please?
6 You might think before speaking.
7 They might at least have sent us a card.
8 If you had come earlier, I could have given you a room.
9 This young man might have been eighteen or nineteen.
10 I may have looked disappointed, but I wasn't.
11 He might have forgotten the number.

p. 127 § 27

12 I want to know what I must do.
13 They were to take the 6.30 train.
14 I was to have met him here.
15 We must have passed them without seeing them.

16 He wasn't there; he must have gone out.
17 You ought to go to bed earlier.
18 We ought to have asked permission.
19 She must have been at least sixty.
20 I couldn't have looked very pleased.

11 Constructions with certain verbs

p. 128 § 29
1 I have already thought of it.
2 Were you expecting this result?—Yes, I was expecting it.
3 We shall resist all these measures.
4 Ask her for a chair.

p. 129 § 30
5 I have borrowed a tent from Charles.
6 We bought this house from them.
7 He wanted to conceal this secret from them.
8 I took the papers from her.
9 These men had stolen all his money from him.

p. 129 § 31
10 Tell them to come at once.
11 I will ask him to lend me his umbrella.
12 Allow me to ask you a question.
13 We have forbidden them to leave their cars here.
14 He advised them not to do it.
15 Her mother had taught her to play the piano.

p. 129 § 32
16 I use this soap. I use it. This is the soap I use.
17 We remember that match. We remember it. It is a match we shall all remember.
18 I distrust that man. I distrust him. He is a man I distrust.
19 We suspected his complicity. We suspected it.
20 He must have mistaken the room.

12 Subjunctive expressing Imperative
Subjunctive after certain Conjunctions

p. 134 § *37*

1 Let him tell us what he knows.
2 If she doesn't like this frock, let her take the other.
3 Let everything be ready at noon.
4 If they want to do that, let them do it.

p. 134 § *38*

5 Although he doesn't know the town, he will find the street without difficulty.
6 Although they were discreet, he guessed that they knew everything.
7 These people labour so that the world may become better.
8 Try to see him before he goes out.
9 This happened before he could pronounce a word.
10 I can't make a movement without his seeing me.
11 He will go on until he can work no longer.
12 You are satisfied, provided you have your little pleasures.
13 She would marry any man, provided he was rich.
14 We will go for a walk, unless you prefer to rest.
15 We don't encourage him to talk, for fear he may say something unwise.
16 Let us wait until everybody is ready.
17 We must finish this job before we go out.
18 I shall take a taxi so that I can get there quicker.

13 Subjunctive after expressions of
necessity, wish, feeling, possibility, doubt

p. 135 § *39*

1 Must you leave at once?
2 Is it necessary that I should receive him?
3 It will be necessary for you to book a room.

p. 135 § *40*

4 What do you want me to do?
5 The director wanted him to go to Paris.
6 We prefer you to tell us the truth.
7 I am sorry you have been ill.

8   We are surprised that they haven't come to see us.
9   I am glad that he has succeeded.
10 It is a pity you are in a hurry.
11 It is better for you to go to a bank.
12 I am afraid you never think of me.
13 We are sorry we can't come this evening.
14 We are afraid we may get there too late.

p. 136 § 41
15 It is possible that they have already returned?
16 I don't think it is necessary.
17 Do you think those things are possible?
18 It seems that he has done something dishonest.

14 Subjunctive after Superlative, after Indefinite or Negative Antecedent ▪ Other standard examples

p. 136 § 42
1   He is the best doctor I know.
2   It's the easiest job one can have.
3   She was one of the prettiest girls he had ever seen.
4   You are the only one who can reassure me.

p. 136 § 43
5   We need someone who can type.
6   Show me a man who has never cheated.
7   There is nobody else we can consult.
8   I know no woman who is harder to please.
9   There is nothing that can console them.

p. 137 § 44
10 Whoever he is, we can't refuse to help him.
11 Whatever I say, you seem to think I am wrong.
12 Whatever his faults may be, I'm sure he is honest.
13 Whatever his subject, he finds interesting things to say.
14 However busy he is, he always finds time to come and see us.
15 However intelligent you may be, there are plenty of things you don't know.

15 The Article

p. 137 § 46
1. A question of great importance; a man of infinite patience.
2. He has absolute trust in me.
3. His father is a chemist.
4. She is a widow.
5. You're a Frenchman?—No, I'm an Englishman.
6. She is an American.

p. 138 § 47
7. You have very small ears.
8. He had a scar on his chin.
9. She came towards me with hands outstretched.
10. He was sitting there, with his head between his hands, his brow wrinkled.
11. A boy with a thin, narrow face.
12. It is the gentleman with white hair.
13. He shook his head sadly.
14. She wiped her hands on her apron.
15. I shook hands with the doctor.
16. They are words that touch men's hearts.

16 Comparison

p. 142 § 57
1. The situation is becoming more and more serious.
2. For us life is harder and harder.
3. This question is less and less urgent.
4. The less I work, the less I want to work.
5. The more he thought about it, the more certain he was that he was right.
6. I am three years older than my brother.
7. You ought to give more.
8. He was more bored at home.
9. Our taxes are heavy, but I hear that yours are more so.
10. If Louise is smart, Solange is more so.

17 Special uses of *le*

p. 144 § 60
1 He told me so himself.
2 Will you be at home this evening?—I suppose so.
3 Do you think you will be able to come?—I hope so.
4 You know, but you won't tell me.
5 I am not so ignorant as you wish to believe.
6 We found it necessary to dismiss them.
7 He thought it wise to refuse.
8 I find it impossible to believe you.
9 Formerly she was slim, but she isn't now.
10 Most of the men were coarse, but Dorval wasn't.

18 *Y - en - lequel*

p. 144 § 61
1 I daren't think of it.
2 That's all you see in it?
3 Are you determined to do this?—Yes, I am determined.
4 He wanted to become a Minister and he has succeeded.

p. 144 § 62
5 If I have offended you, I didn't intend to.
6 If you want to protest, you have the right to.
7 She wanted to go abroad and we couldn't prevent her.

p. 147 § 66
8 There are things one can't get used to.
9 It is a little garden in the middle of which there is a statue.
10 We know the tricks by means of which he has succeeded.
11 It was the café to which they went every evening.
12 Which of these hats is yours?
13 One of the daughters, I don't remember which, is married.
14 Which of these two watches do you prefer?

19 Ce - il est (possible), c'est (possible) - cela

p. 147 § 67
1 He is a very intelligent young man.
2 They are fairly wealthy people.
3 They are things without importance.
4 It is absolutely certain that they will do it.
5 Is it difficult to obtain tickets?—No, it's easy.
6 It will be impossible to go there today.

p. 148 § 68
7 It surprises me that you don't know him.
8 It amuses me to listen to their arguments.

20 Indefinites

(Quelques-uns, tout, tel, autre, etc.)

p. 149 § 72
1 Some of our clients owe us money.
2 Are there any trout in the river?—Yes, there are a few.

p. 149 § 73
3 He decided to abandon everything.
4 They have sold everything.
5 We all know what has happened.
6 I despise them all.

p. 150 § 74
7 That's life, such as it is.
8 I don't believe such stories.
9 She has such a pretty face, such lovely hair.
10 It was impossible to foresee such important events.

p. 150 § 75
11 We have two cars, but they are both at the garage.
12 I have two good dictionaries; you may borrow either.
13 My son is expecting two friends, but neither has arrived.
14 You ought to help each other.

p. 150 § 77
15 Anybody can do that.
16 Write anything.

17 You can buy that in any grocer's.
18 Which table, please?—Any one.
19 People camp anywhere.
20 He mumbled something or other and went off.

21 Negatives

p. 151 § *78*
 1 She walked through the room without looking at anybody.
 2 You stay there without doing anything.
 3 No sound broke the silence.
 4 They have no hope of winning.
 5 Without any doubt you will be recognized.
 6 What difference does that make?—None at all.
 7 I didn't see that anywhere.
 8 She wasn't in any way envious.

p. 151 § *79*
 9 We had never been there before.
10 They were only teasing him.

p. 153 § *81*
11 Louis didn't know it.—Neither did I.
12 I haven't seen her for three weeks.
13 It is more dangerous than you think.
14 He earns less than I supposed.
15 The town is larger than it was ten years ago.

22 Inversion ▪ Adverbs

p. 153 § *82*
 1 At what time did your friends arrive?
 2 How did these people get in?
 3 When did your son leave for Italy?
 4 Perhaps he has already written.
 5 He had hardly arrived when he was urgently recalled.
 6 Very likely he thought you were joking.
 7 Her father, it appears, is a famous musician.

8   The captain, so it seems, was asleep in his cabin.
9   Did you understand what that man was saying?
10   Can you tell me where M. Serre lives?

p. 154 § 83
11   They played well.
12   It seems to me that you have spent a great deal.
13   I think I have eaten too much.
14   To see better, he had got on to a chair.

p. 155 § 84
15   She opened her mouth as though to say something.
16   In spite of his success, he went on working as though by force of
     habit.

Verbs

§ 1 Compound tenses with *avoir*

J'ai pris	*I have taken*
J'avais pris	*I had taken*
J'aurai pris	*I shall have taken*
J'aurais pris	*I should have taken*

Note these examples:

Regardez! Il a neigé.	*Look! It has been snowing.*
Qu'est-ce que tu as fait?	J'ai travaillé.

What have you been doing? I have been working.

Il avait plu, car les trottoirs étaient mouillés.
It had been raining, for the pavements were wet.

The past participle agrees with a preceding direct object:
Où sont tes gants? Je les ai perdus.
Montre-moi les cadeaux que tu as reçus.
Combien de cartes as-tu achetées?

But no agreement with **en**:
Avez-vous reçu des lettres?—Oui, j'en ai reçu.

§ 2 Verbs conjugated with *être*

aller	*to go*	entrer	*to enter*
venir	*to come*	rentrer	*to go (come) home*
revenir	*to come back*	descendre	*to descend*
devenir	*to become*	monter	*to go (come) up*
arriver	*to arrive*	tomber	*to fall*
partir	*to depart*	retourner	*to return, go back*
sortir	*to go (come) out*	naître	*to be born* (e.g. elle est née)
rester	*to remain, stay*	mourir	*to die* (e.g. elle est morte)

Examples of compound tenses:

ils sont arrivés	*they (have) arrived*
ils étaient arrivés	*they had arrived*
ils seront arrivés	*they will have arrived*
ils seraient arrivés	*they would have arrived*

The past participle agrees with the subject:
elle est partie; ils sont sortis.

a) Transitive use of **sortir, descendre, monter, rentrer**
Used transitively, these verbs are conjugated with **avoir**:

J'ai monté (descendu) les bagages.
I have taken up (brought down) the luggage.

Elle avait sorti son mouchoir.
She had taken out her handkerchief.

J'ai rentré la voiture.   *I have put the car in.*

Useful idioms:
Il monta (descendit) les marches en courant.
He ran up (ran down) the steps.

Un homme sortit de (entra dans) la maison en courant.
A man ran out of (ran into) the house.

§ 3   Reflexive Verbs

a) Examples showing some uses of the reflexive verb:

La porte s'ouvre (se ferme).   *The door opens (closes).*
L'église se vide.   *The church empties.*
Ils se rencontrent à Paris.   *They meet in Paris.*
Nous nous connaissons.   *We know each other (one another).*
Nous nous écrivons.   *We write to each other.*
Comment cela se dit-il?   *How is that said?*
Vous savez comment cela se fait.   *You know how that is done.*

b) Examples of Imperative:
lève-toi!   ne te lève pas!
levons-nous!   ne nous levons pas!
levez-vous!   ne vous levez pas!

§ 4   Reflexive Verbs: Compound Tenses

je me suis arrêté(e)   *I (have) stopped*
je m'étais arrêté(e)   *I had stopped*
je me serai arrêté(e)   *I shall have stopped*
je me serais arrêté(e)   *I should have stopped*

Agreement of the Past Participle:

The fundamental rule of the agreement of the past participle with a preceding direct object applies here. In the majority of cases the reflexive pronoun is the direct object (i.e. is in the accusative case), therefore the past participle agrees:

elle s'est levée   ils se sont habillés

In somewhat rarer cases, the reflexive pronoun is the indirect object (i.e. is in the dative case); consequently the past participle does not agree:

Nous nous sommes écrit   *We have written to each other.*
Elle s'est acheté un manteau.   (se = *for herself*)
Elle s'est essuyé les yeux.
Ils se sont adressé un signe de tête.
Nous nous sommes demandé s'il viendrait.   (demander à)
Elle s'était rappelé le numéro.   (se = *to herself*)
Ils s'étaient procuré une échelle.   (se = *for themselves*)

§ 5 *S'asseoir, être assis,* and similar cases

Je m'assieds.	*I sit down.*	Je suis assis.	*I am sitting.*
Je m'assis.	*I sat down.*	J'étais assis.	*I was sitting.*
Il se coucha.	{ *He lay down.* / *He went to bed.*	Il était couché.	*He was in bed.*
Il s'étendit.	*He lay down.*	Il était étendu.	*He was lying.*
Il se réveilla.	*He woke up.*	Il était réveillé.	*He was awake.*
Elle se leva.	*She got up.*	Elle était levée.	*She was up.*
Il s'agenouilla.	*He knelt down.*	Il était agenouillé.	*He was kneeling.*

NOTE To translate things like *he stood silent, he lay still,* etc., one uses **rester** or **demeurer**:

Il demeura immobile.   *He stood (lay, sat) motionless.*
Elle resta silencieuse.   *She stood (sat) silent.*
Ils restèrent interdits.   *They stood amazed.*

§ 6 Forms of the Passive

The passive is made up of **être** + the past participle, which agrees with the subject. In other words, the past participle is just used as an adjective.

Nous sommes suivis.	*We are (being) followed.*
Nous étions suivis.	*We were (being) followed.*
Nous fûmes suivis.	*We were followed.* (event)
Nous serons suivis.	*We shall be followed.*
Nous serions suivis.	*We should be followed.*
Nous avons été suivis.	*We have been followed.*
Nous avions été suivis.	*We had been followed.*
Nous aurions été suivis.	*We should have been followed.*

One must distinguish between the imperfect and the past historic:
Il fut enfin retrouvé;   il était gravement blessé.

In this example, **il fut retrouvé** records the event of his being found; **il était blessé** describes his state when found.

Le bâtiment fut démoli.   (event)
Dès que ce travail fut fini ...   (completed action)

Instead of a clause containing a passive, the French sometimes use a construction analogous to the Latin ablative absolute:
When this was done ...   Cela fait, ...
As soon as this task was accomplished ...   Cette tâche accomplie, ...

§7 The Passive avoided

a) By using **on**:
On les a vus ce matin.   *They were seen this morning.*
On a retrouvé votre appareil.   *Your camera has been found.*
On dit (sait, croit) que ...   *It is said (known, thought) that ...*

The construction with **on** must be used in cases like the following:

On m'a dit d'attendre.	*I have been told to wait.*
On nous permet d'entrer.	*We are allowed to go in.*
Il nous est permis d'entrer.	
On leur défend de courir.	*They are forbidden to run.*
Il leur est défendu de courir.	
On m'a conseillé de me reposer.	*I have been advised to rest.*
On nous a montré une photo.	*We were shown a photo.*
On m'a donné un permis.	*I was given a permit.*
On vous posera des questions.	*You will be asked questions.*

b) By using the reflexive:
Cela se dit (se fait, s'emploie).   *That is said (done, used).*
Cela se voit (se remarque, se sait).   *That is seen (noticed, known).*
Les cigarettes se vendent au café.   *Cigarettes are sold at the café.*

§8 The Present Participle

a) Agreement:
The present participle is invariable except when used purely as an adjective:
Ne voulant pas le déranger, nous sommes partis.
Sachant qu'il n'y avait personne à la maison, elle ne se pressa pas.
Ayant regardé la photographie, elle hocha la tête.

As an adjective: une femme charmante; des mots touchants.

b) Where in English we should use a present participle, the French often prefer a relative clause:

Une voiture qui traversait le village ...
A car passing through the village ...

Je les entendais qui parlaient dans la cuisine.
I could hear them talking in the kitchen.

un bruit de pas qui s'éloignaient
a sound of receding footsteps

c) En (faisant)

«Très bien», dit-il en se levant.
"Very well," he said, getting up.

«Merci beaucoup», dit-elle en souriant.
"Thank you very much," she said, smiling (with a smile).

«Il va pleuvoir», dit-il en regardant le ciel.
"It is going to rain," he said, looking at the sky.

On (doing), by (doing), while (doing), when (doing) are all expressed by **en (faisant)**:
Elle avait fait du bruit en fermant la porte. (*when shutting*)
En me voyant, il poussa une exclamation. (*on seeing*)
En prenant ce chemin, vous y arriverez plus vite. (*by taking*)
En travaillant dans ma chambre, j'ai entendu un bruit curieux. (*while working*)

Tout en (faisant) conveys the idea of simultaneous action:
Il parlait lentement, tout en bourrant sa pipe.
Tout en mangeant, il parcourait le journal.

NOTE **Par** + infinitive is used only after **commencer** and **finir**:
Il commença par me dire que . . .
Ils finirent par accepter. $\left\{\begin{array}{l}\textit{They finished by accepting.} \\ \textit{In the end they accepted.}\end{array}\right.$

§9 Impersonal Verbs

Il reste,   *there remains*

Il me reste 20 francs.	*I have 20 francs left.*
Il ne m'en reste que trois.	*I have only three left.*
Il ne me reste plus rien.	*I have nothing left.*

Il vaut mieux,   *it is better*
Il vaut (vaudrait) mieux rester ici.
It is (would be) better to stay here.

Il s'agit de,   *it is a question (matter) of*
De quoi s'agit-il?   *What is it all about?*
Il s'agissait d'une auto volée.
It was a question of a stolen car.

Il suffit de,   *it is sufficient (enough) to*
Il suffit de payer. $\begin{cases} \textit{It is sufficient to pay.} \\ \textit{You just have to pay.} \end{cases}$

Il me semble que,   *it seems to me that*
Il nous semblait qu'ils hésitaient.
It seemed to us that they were hesitating.

Other examples:
Il paraît qu'ils doivent de l'argent.
It appears that they owe money.

Il y arrive des accidents.
Accidents happen there.

Il se passe des choses graves.
Serious things are happening.

Il existait une autre possibilité.
There existed another possibility.

Use of tenses

§ 10   The Imperfect

When the English simple past tense is used in description, or with the underlying meaning of *was (doing)* or *used to (do)*, it must be translated by the French imperfect:
Il faisait un temps splendide.
It was lovely weather.

L'hôtel se trouvait en face de la gare.
The hotel was opposite the station.

Le monument se dressait sur une colline.
The monument stood on a hill.

Il posait toujours les mêmes questions.
He always asked (=used to ask) the same questions.

When *would (do)* expresses habit or custom, translate by the imperfect:
Le soir il faisait un petit tour.
In the evening he would go for a short stroll.

Après dîner, mon père fumait un cigare.
After dinner my father would smoke a cigar.

§ 11 The Past Historic

In a regular narrative, the past historic records the definite happenings, the successive events, the things people did.

Example:

A quatre heures M. Vattier ouvrit sa porte, traversa le couloir, jeta un coup d'œil dans le bureau des employés et parut sur le point de parler. Mais il changea d'idée, regagna sans mot dire son propre bureau, et la porte se referma derrière lui.

When dialogue is introduced, the characters use the Perfect:

«Avez-vous vu M. Thomas ce soir?» demanda Bourdet à la concierge.
«Oui, répondit celle-ci. Il est rentré vers sept heures. Il est monté dans son appartement, il y est resté un quart d'heure, puis il est redescendu et il est sorti.»

Bourdet remercia la concierge, puis il sortit dans la rue et se dirigea vers le métro.

The past historic is used for any event which is considered as *finished*, no matter what its duration:

La guerre dura six ans.
Ils y restèrent trois mois.
Il travailla ferme pendant deux heures, puis il alla déjeuner.

§ 12 More Difficult Points of Tense Usage

Take these examples:
Je croyais qu'il était ici.
Il savait que je voulais le voir.
Elle voulait rentrer chez elle.

In these cases we use the imperfect because we are expressing what the person was thinking, what was going on in his mind.

Now study these examples:
D'abord je crus qu'il dormait.
At first I thought he was asleep.

Alors je sus que c'était vrai.
Then I knew (realized) that it was true.

Il fut soudain découragé.
Suddenly he was (felt) discouraged.

Alors il eut peur.
Then he got frightened.

In these cases we use the past historic because we are recording a new idea or feeling, something which happened in the person's mind.

Here are other examples of the past historic used for recording things which occurred at a particular moment, which are sharply delimited in time:

Il y eut un moment de silence.

Sa porte se referma et ce fut tout.

Enfin il put sortir.

Le soleil brilla de nouveau.

Le lendemain il plut à verse.

Tout fut si confus, d'abord, qu'il fut impossible de savoir ce qui se passait.

§ 13 The Pluperfect

Examples: j'avais pris; il était arrivé; elle s'était couchée.

Note the use of the pluperfect in cases like these:

Nous les avions avertis du danger.
We warned them of the danger.

Je lui avais bien dit qu'il se trompait.
I told him he was mistaken.

Ah! pardon, je ne vous avais pas reconnu.
Oh, sorry, I didn't recognise you.

The implication is that something further has happened or has been said.

§ 14 The Past Anterior

Examples: il eut compris; il fut parti; il se fut arrêté.

This form is used after conjunctions of time (quand, lorsque, dès que, aussitôt que, après que) when the main verb is in the past historic; in other words it records one event occurring immediately before another.

Dès qu'il eut parlé, il comprit qu'il se trompait.

Aussitôt qu'ils furent partis, je fermai la porte à clef.

Quand il se fut éloigné des maisons, il s'assit pour se reposer.

A peine eut-il prononcé ces mots, qu'un coup de feu retentit.

§ 15 Future Tenses

After conjunctions of time, the future must be used when future time is meant:

Je le ferai quand j'aurai le temps.
I will do it when I have (=will have) time.

Faites ce que vous voudrez.
Do what you (will) like.

Ils ne feront rien tant que vous serez là.
They won't do anything as long as you are (=will be) here.

Il a dit qu'il le ferait quand il aurait le temps.
He said he would do it when he had (=would have) time.

Quand j'aurai lu ce roman, je vous le prêterai.
When I have (=will have) read this novel, I will lend it to you.

Il a dit qu'il me rendrait ce livre dès qu'il l'aurait lu.
He said he would return that book to me as soon as he had (=would have) read it.

NOTES

1 *Will, would,* expressing willingness, are rendered by **vouloir**:
Il a de l'argent, mais il ne veut pas payer.   (*will not pay*)
Jean était fatigué; il ne voulait pas jouer.   (*would not play*)

2 *To be about to (do)* is expressed by **être sur le point de (faire)** or by **aller (faire)**:
J'étais sur le point de protester.
J'allais protester.

3 *Shall I (do),* asking for instructions, is translated thus:
Shall I write to them? { Voulez-vous que je leur écrive?
{ Faut-il leur écrire?
Shall we wait here? { Voulez-vous que nous attendions ici?
{ Faut-il attendre ici?

§ 16   Tenses used with *si* (=*if*)

Si vous êtes en retard, je vous attendrai.
Si vous étiez en retard, je vous attendrais.
Si vous aviez été en retard, je vous aurais attendu.

Note that *if* + the simple past tense is regularly translated by **si**+ imperfect:
If I knew . . .   Si je savais . . .
If we went . . .   Si nous allions . . .

Si may be followed by the future or the conditional only in indirect questions, i.e. when it means *whether*:
Je me demande s'il viendra.
Je me demandais s'il viendrait.

§ 17 Idiomatic constructions with *depuis*

a) **Depuis** + present tense:
{ Depuis quand habitez-vous Lille?
{ Depuis combien de temps habitez-vous Lille?
How long have you been living in Lille?

J'habite Lille depuis cinq ans.
I have been living in Lille for five years.

These forms are also used:
Il y a cinq ans que j'habite Lille.
Voilà cinq ans que j'habite Lille.

b) **Depuis** + imperfect:
{ Depuis quand attendait-il?
{ Depuis combien de temps attendait-il?
How long had he been waiting?

{ Il attendait depuis une heure.
{ Il y avait une heure qu'il attendait.
He had been waiting for an hour.

§ 18 Venir de (faire)

Mon ami vient d'arriver.	*My friend has just arrived.*
Mon ami venait d'arriver.	*My friend had just arrived.*

The infinitive
§ 19 Construction of some common Verbs with the Infinitive

(Abbreviations used: qn = quelqu'un; s.o. = someone)

accuser de faire	*to accuse of doing*
alder à faire	*to help to do*
aimer faire	*to like to do*
aimer mieux faire	*to prefer to do*
ailer faire	*to go to do, to go and do*
s'amuser à faire	*to amuse oneself (by) doing*
apprendre à faire	*to learn to do*
s'arrêter de faire	*to stop doing*
arriver à faire	*to manage to do*
s'attendre à faire	*to expect to do*
avoir besoin de faire	*to need to do*
avoir peur de faire	*to be afraid to do (of doing)*
cesser de faire	*to cease doing*
chercher à faire	*to attempt to do*

commencer à faire	*to begin to do*
compter faire	*to reckon (expect) to do*
conseiller à qn de faire	*to advise s.o. to do*
continuer à faire	*to continue to do*
craindre de faire	*to fear to do*
décider de faire	*to decide to do*
se décider à faire	*to make up one's mind to do*
défendre à qn de faire	*to forbid s.o. to do*
demander à qn de faire	*to ask s.o. to do*
se dépêcher de faire	*to hurry to do*
désirer faire	*to desire to do*
devoir faire	*to have to do*
dire à qn de faire	*to tell s.o. to do*
empêcher qn de faire	*to prevent s.o. from doing*
encourager à faire	*to encourage to do*
entreprendre de faire	*to undertake to do*
espérer faire	*to hope to do*
essayer de faire	*to try to do*
s'étonner de faire	*to be surprised to do*
éviter de faire	*to avoid doing*
s'excuser de faire	*to apologize for doing*
faire semblant de faire	*to pretend to do*
finir de faire	*to finish doing*
se hâter de faire	*to hasten to do*
hésiter à faire	*to hesitate to do*
inviter à faire	*to invite to do*
laisser faire	*to let (allow to) do*
menacer de faire	*to threaten to do*
mériter de faire	*to deserve to do*
se mettre à faire	*to start to do*
offrir de faire	*to offer to do*
oser faire	*to dare to do*
oublier de faire	*to forget to do*
passer son temps à faire	*to spend one's time doing*
perdre son temps à faire	*to waste one's time doing*
permettre à qn de faire	*to permit s.o. to do*
pouvoir faire	*to be able to do*
préférer faire	*to prefer to do*
se préparer à faire	*to prepare to do*
prétendre faire	*to claim to do*
prier qn de faire	*to ask (beg) s.o. to do*
promettre de faire	*to promise to do*

proposer de faire	*to propose to do*
refuser de faire	*to refuse to do*
regretter de faire	*to regret to do*
renoncer à faire	*to give up doing*
réussir à faire	*to succeed in doing*
savoir faire	*to know how to do*
sembler faire	*to seem to do*
tâcher de faire	*to try to do*
tenter de faire	*to attempt to do*
il vaut mieux faire	*it is better to do*
venir faire	*to come to do, to come and do*
vouloir faire	*to wish (want) to do*

§ 20 Construction of other common words with the Infinitive

certain de faire	*certain to do (of doing)*
charmé de faire	*charmed to do*
content de faire	*pleased (glad) to do*
étonné de faire	*astonished to do*
heureux de faire	*happy to do*
obligé de faire	*obliged to do*
surpris de faire	*surprised to do*
le droit de faire	*the right to do*
l'occasion de faire	*the opportunity (chance) to do*
la permission de faire	*(the) permission to do*
le temps de faire	*(the) time to do*
prêt à faire	*ready to do*
le premier à faire	*the first to do*
le dernier à faire	*the last to do*
beaucoup à faire	*much (a lot) to do*
rien à faire	*nothing to do*
quelque chose à faire	*something to do*

§ 21 Examples involving *à* + Infinitive

C'est facile à comprendre.
C'est impossible à décrire.
J'ai eu de la difficulté à trouver la maison

Nous avons une heure à attendre.
Vous n'avez qu'à demander.
J'ai plusieurs clients à voir.

Il ne tardera pas à revenir.
{ *He won't be long coming back.*
{ *He will soon come (be coming) back.*

un homme à plaindre   *a man to be pitied*
un ennemi à craindre   *an enemy to be feared*
un appartement à louer   *a flat to (be) let*

un bruit à réveiller les morts
a noise enough to wake the dead

Ce n'était pas l'homme à hésiter.
He wasn't the man to hesitate.

§ 22   Other Infinitive constructions

a) J'ai perdu la clef! Que faire?   *What am I (are we) to do?*
Pourquoi le faire?   *Why do it?*
A quoi bon attendre?   *What is the use of waiting?*
Je vais en ville.—Pourquoi faire?   *I am going to town.—What for?*
Comment sortir de cette situation?
How am I (are we, etc.) to get out of this situation?

The infinitive may express instructions:
S'adresser au concierge.   *Apply to the caretaker.*
Ne pas se pencher au dehors.   *Do not lean out.*

b) The second verb of expressions such as *go and tell, come and see*, is
translated by an infinitive:
Va dire à ta mère que . . .   *Go and tell your mother that . . .*
Venez voir cette bête!   *Come and see this creature!*

c) Typical cases of the infinitive used instead of a noun clause:
Je crois le connaître.   *I think I know him.*

Nous espérons vous revoir l'an prochain.
We hope we shall see you again next year.

Je regrette de ne pas pouvoir vous aider.
I am sorry that I can't help you.

d) **Pour** must be used with the infinitive after **trop** and **assez**:
Il était trop fatigué pour courir.
Vous êtes assez intelligent pour le comprendre.

e) Important idioms:
J'étais en train d'astiquer ma voiture.
I was just cleaning my car.

J'ai failli tomber à l'eau.
I nearly fell into the water.

Il faillit renverser un piéton.
He nearly knocked down a pedestrian.

Vous avez beau protester . . .
It's no use (good) your protesting . . .

§ 23 The Perfect Infinitive

After (doing) is always expressed by the perfect infinitive:
Après avoir fumé une cigarette, il reprit son travail.
Après être sortie chercher du bois, elle alluma du feu.
Après nous être reposés, nous avons recommencé.

Other examples:
Je pensais l'avoir déjà vu.
I thought I had seen him before.

Je suis content d'avoir vu cela.
I am glad to have seen (that I saw) that.

Il regrettait d'être venu.
He regretted having come (that he had come).

Je les remerciai d'avoir envoyé mes affaires.
I thanked them for sending (having sent) my things.

Il partit sans avoir vu son frère.
He went off without seeing (having seen) his brother.

§ 24 Use of *faire* with the Infinitive

a) faire attendre, *to keep waiting.*   Je vous ai fait attendre.
faire entrer, *to bring (take) in.*   Faites entrer ce monsieur.
faire monter, *to bring (take) up.*   Il fit monter le visiteur.
faire voir, *to show.*   Faites voir votre passeport.
faire venir, *to bring.*   Elle fit venir le curé.

b) Vous me faites rire.   *You make me laugh.*
Cela la fit trembler.   *This made her tremble.*

When the infinitive depending on **faire** has a direct object or is followed by **que** + a noun clause (which counts as a direct object), the person is made dative (i.e. is used with **à**):
Le douanier lui fit ouvrir sa valise.
Je leur ai fait perdre une belle occasion.
Je lui ai fait comprendre que j'avais besoin d'essence.

c) **Faire** + infinitive renders the English form *to have a thing* (*done*):
Nous faisons construire une maison.
We are having a house built.

Je ferai réparer ce fauteuil.
I shall have this armchair repaired.

Vous ferez signer cette lettre par le directeur.
You will have (get) this letter signed by the director.

Note this form:
se faire comprendre, *to make oneself understood.*
se faire respecter, *to make (get) oneself respected.*
Vous vous faites comprendre.   *You make yourself understood.*
Elle se fit photographier.   *She had herself photographed.*

Laisser is used in the same sort of construction:
Il se laissa prendre.   *He allowed himself to be caught.*
Vous vous laissez voler. *You allow yourself to be robbed.*

Also **voir**:
Nous l'avons vu arrêter.   *We saw him arrested.*

Modal verbs

§ 25 Vouloir

Voulez-vous signer, s'il vous plaît?
Will you sign, please?

Je voudrais connaître leur adresse.
I should like to know their address.

J'aurais voulu les voir.
{ *I should like to have seen them.*
{ *I should have liked to see them.*

Veuillez nous informer si ...   *Please (Kindly) inform us whether ...*
Que veut dire cette phrase?   *What does this sentence mean?*
Nous voulons bien vous aider.   *We are (quite) willing to help you.*

§ 26 Pouvoir

In the idiomatic uses of **pouvoir**, the tense used will be better understood if one expresses *could*, *might*, *may*, etc., in terms of *to be able.*

Can or *may* sometimes refers to the future:
Je pourrai faire cela demain.
I can (=*shall be able*) *to do that tomorrow.*

Could, meaning *was able,* is translated by the imperfect:
Je ne pouvais pas le faire.
I could not (=was not able to) do it.

Could, or *might,* meaning *would be able,* is translated by the conditional:
Il a dit qu'il pourrait venir demain.
He said he could (might) come tomorrow.

Could have or *might have* is rendered by the conditional perfect:
Vous auriez pu venir plus tôt.
You could have (might have) come earlier.

Rarer examples:
Il pouvait avoir vingt ans.
He might have been twenty.

Nous pouvions être à cinq kilomètres de la ville.
We might have been five kilometres from the town.

Ils ont pu partir dans l'autre direction.
They may have gone off in the other direction.

{ Il avait pu téléphoner en notre absence.
{ Il pouvait avoir téléphoné en notre absence.
He might have telephoned in our absence.

NOTES

1 *Can, could* need not always be translated.
Je ne les vois pas. *I can't see them.*
Il ne comprenait pas pourquoi ... *He could not understand why ...*
Je les entendais chanter. *I could hear them singing.*

2 When *can* means *know(s) how to,* use **savoir**:
Je sais nager (conduire, danser, jouer du piano, etc.).

§27 Devoir

Je dois écrire.	*I must write. I have to write.*
J'ai dû écrire.	{ *I (have) had to write.* { *I must have written.*

In a past narrative, *must have* is often to be rendered by **avait dû**:
Sa chambre était en désordre. Il avait dû partir en hâte.

Je devais écrire.	{ *I had to (used to have to) write.* { *I was to write (to have written).*
Je dus écrire.	*I had to write.*
Je devrais écrire.	*I ought to write.*
J'aurais dû écrire.	*I ought to have written.*

In these rarer examples, the tense used will be better understood if **devoir** is taken as meaning *to be bound to*:

Il devait être très vieux.
He must have been very old.

Elle ne devait pas avoir plus de vingt ans.
She couldn't have been more than twenty.

Ils ne devaient pas avoir passé la frontière.
They could not have crossed the frontier.

§ 28 Falloir

Il faut, il fallait, etc. may be followed by an infinitive or by **que** + subjunctive:

{ Il me faut partir.
{ Il faut que je parte.

{ Il lui fallut (fallait) attendre.
{ Il fallut (fallait) qu'il attendît.

The pronoun (me, lui, leur, etc.) is often omitted:
Voyons, il faut rentrer.   *Come now, we must go home.*
Il faut profiter de votre liberté.   *You must take advantage of your liberty.*

Il faudrait may translate *ought*:
Pour y arriver à midi, il faudrait partir à huit heures.
To get there at twelve, you ought to start at eight o'clock.

Il aurait fallu may express *ought to have*:
Monsieur, il aurait fallu appeler la police.
Sir, you ought to have called the police.

Avoir à (faire), *to have to (do)*
J'ai à repondre à quelques lettres.
Vous n'avez qu'à signer ce papier.

Government of verbs

§ 29   Verbs governing the dative (i.e. requiring *à* before their object):

penser à, *to think about*	Je pensais à mon frère. Je pensais à lui.
	Je pense à mon travail. J'y pense.
réfléchir à, *to reflect on, to think about*	Il réfléchissait à sa situation.
	Il y réfléchissait.

s'attendre à, *to expect*	Je ne m'attendais pas à ce résultat.
	Je ne m'y attendais pas.
ressembler à, *to resemble, to be like.*	Tu ressembles à ta mère.
plaire à, *to please*	Il ne plaît pas à mes parents.
résister à, *to resist*	Il résiste à tous nos efforts.
	Il y résiste.
renoncer à, *to renounce, to give up*	J'ai renoncé au tabac.
	J'y ai renoncé.
succéder à, *to succeed, to follow*	Une belle journée succéda à cette nuit d'orage.
obéir à, *to obey*	Il faut obéir aux ordres.
pardonner à, *to forgive*	Je lui ai pardonné.

§ 30 'From' is translated by *à* after a few verbs all expressing some idea of 'getting from':

demander, *to ask*	Demandez le numéro à l'employé.
acheter, *to buy*	J'achète des œufs à cette bonne femme.
emprunter, *to borrow*	Il emprunta une bicyclette à un ami.
cacher, *to hide, conceal*	Je leur cachai mon inquiétude.
prendre, *to take*	L'homme lui prit son passeport.
voler, *to steal*	Quelqu'un lui vola son portefeuille.
arracher, *to snatch*	Le policier lui arracha le couteau.

§ 31 Construction with *dire, demander,* etc.

Je dirai à ce monsieur d'attendre.
Il demanda au jardinier de couper la branche.
Nous leur permettons de jouer ici.
Son père lui défendit d'y aller.
Je lui ai conseillé de se reposer.
Il leur ordonna de sortir.

§ 32 Verbs followed by *de*

se souvenir de	*to remember*	se douter de	*to suspect*
se servir de	*to use, make use of*	rire de	*to laugh at*
s'approcher de	*to approach*	dépendre de	*to depend on*
se moquer de	*to make fun of*	se méfier de	*to distrust*
remercier de	*to thank for*	se passer de	*to do without*
s'apercevoir de	*to perceive*	s'excuser de	*to apologize for*
		s'emparer de	*to get possession of*

EXAMPLES:

Je me souviens de mon oncle. Je me souviens de lui.
Je me souviens de cet incident. Je m'en souviens.
C'est une personne (une chose) dont je me souviens.

Notice how **se tromper** (*to mistake*) is used:
Je me suis trompé de porte.   *I mistook the door.*

Note also the difference between **se souvenir de** and **se rappeler** (lit. *to recall to oneself*):
Je me souviens du numéro.   Je m'en souviens.
Je me rappelle le numéro.   Je me le rappelle.

§ 33   Useful examples

Je passe devant leur maison.
I pass their house.

Il prit dans sa poche une vieille pipe.
He took an old pipe out of his pocket.

Elle ramassa un verre sur la table.
She picked up a glass from the table.

Ils buvaient du café dans de grandes tasses.
They were drinking coffee out of large cups.

§ 34   Notes on some common verbs

apercevoir = *to perceive, see* (with the eye):
  Dans la foule, j'ai aperçu Georges.

  s'apercevoir de = to perceive mentally, to perceive a fact:
  Je m'aperçus de sa présence.
  Je m'aperçus qu'elle tremblait.

approcher: Nous approchons de Paris.   *We are getting near Paris.*
  s'approcher de has more idea of purpose:
  Je m'approchai pour mieux voir.

attendre: J'attends un ami.
  s'attendre à, to expect:

  Je ne m'attendais pas à ce refus.
  Je ne m'y attendais pas.
  Je m'attendais à les trouver ici.

changer: Ils ont changé l'heure du train.   *They have changed*
(altered) the time of the train.
changer de = to exchange one thing for another:
Je vais changer de robe, de souliers.

décider: Nous avons décidé de rester.
se décider à = *to make up one's mind:*
Il se décida à demander une augmentation (*a rise*).

demander:

Je lui demandai de m'indiquer le chemin.
Le policier demanda à voir mes papiers.

échapper à = *to escape*, in the sense of not to fall into:
échapper à la punition, échapper à la mort.
s'échapper de = *to escape out of, to break free from:*
Ils s'échappèrent de leur prison.

entendre:

J'ai entendu parler de lui.
I have heard of him.

J'ai entendu dire qu'ils sont revenus.
I have heard that they have come back.

Entendre is sometimes used with the sense of *to mean* or *to intend*:
Qu'entendez-vous par cette phrase?
What do you mean by this sentence?

Je n'entends pas qu'il me voie.
I don't intend him to see me.

jouer: Ils jouent au football (au tennis).
Elle joue du piano (du violon).

manquer:

J'ai manqué le train.   *I missed the train.*
Il manque de courage.   *He lacks courage.*
Je ne manquerai pas de vous informer.
I shall not fail to inform you.

marier = *to give in marriage, to marry off:*
L'an dernier ils ont marié leur fille.
to marry = se marier avec *or* épouser:
Elle s'est mariée avec un Anglais.
Elle a épousé un Anglais.

obliger: Je suis obligé de payer.

Ils m'obligèrent à descendre de la voiture.

penser: Il pensait à ce qui s'était passé.

penser de = *to think of*, in the sense of to have an opinion of:

Que penses-tu de leur appartement?

répondre: Répondez à ma question.

Je ne réponds pas de votre sûreté.

I do not answer for your safety.

servir de = *to serve as:*

Ce hangar servira de garage.

This shed will serve (do) as a garage.

servir à (faire) = *to serve to (do):*

Ces poteaux servent à amarrer les bateaux.

These posts serve for (are used for) mooring the boats.

se servir de = *to make use of, to use:*

Je me sers d'un petit marteau.   *I use a small hammer.*

tenir à = *to think (make) much of:*

Elle tient à sa bague.   *She thinks (makes) a lot of her ring.*

tenir à (faire) = *to be anxious to (do):*

Je ne tiens pas à dormir dans la voiture.

Je n'y tiens pas.

The subjunctive

§ 35 Form of the present subjunctive

In most cases the stem is provided by the 3rd person plural of the present indicative:

		SUBJUNCTIVE
finir	ils finissent	je finisse
mettre	ils mettent	je mette

The endings are:

–e	je finisse	je mette
–es	tu finisses	tu mettes
–e	il finisse	il mette
–ions	nous finissions	nous mettions
–iez	vous finissiez	vous mettiez
–ent	ils finissent	ils mettent

Irregular:

aller	aille, ailles, aille, allions, alliez, aillent.
avoir	aie, aies, ait, ayons, ayez, aient.
être	sois, sois, soit, soyons, soyez, soient.
faire	fasse, fasses, fasse, fassions, fassiez, fassent.
pouvoir	puisse, puisses, puisse, puissions, puissiez, puissent.
savoir	sache, saches, sache, sachions, sachiez, sachent.
vouloir	veuille, veuilles, veuille, voulions, vouliez, veuillent.

There are a few verbs which revert in the 1st and 2nd plural to a form identical with the imperfect indicative:

prendre:	je prenne	nous prenions
	tu prennes	vous preniez
	il prenne	ils prennent
appeler:	j' appelle	nous appelions
jeter:	je jette	nous jetions
envoyer:	j' envoie	nous envoyions
croire:	je croie	nous croyions
voir:	je voie	nous voyions
boire:	je boive	nous buvions
devoir:	je doive	nous devions
venir:	je vienne	nous venions
tenir:	je tienne	nous tenions
recevoir:	je reçoive	nous recevions

§ 36 Form of the Imperfect Subjunctive

Always one of three types, according as the past historic ends in **–ai**, **–is** or **–us**:

je donnai	je vendis	je reçus
je donnasse	je vendisse	je reçusse
tu donnasses	tu vendisses	tu reçusses
il donnât	il vendît	il reçut
nous donnassions	nous vendissions	nous reçussions
vous donnassiez	vous vendissiez	vous reçussiez
ils donnassent	ils vendissent	ils reçussent

Exceptions:

venir:	vinsse, vinsses, vînt, vinssions, vinssiez, vinssent.
tenir:	tinsse, tinsses, tînt, tinssions, tinssiez, tinssent.

NB. Most of these long forms have fallen into disuse, though in literary style the 3rd person (il vînt, il allât, il fût, etc.) is still used.

Perfect and Pluperfect Subjunctive

Just use the subjunctive form of the auxiliary:

il a dit	bien qu'il ait dit
elle est descendue	avant qu'elle soit descendue
il avait pris	quoiqu'il eût pris
il était descendu	avant qu'il fût descendu

§ 37 Present Subjunctive expressing the Imperative (3rd person)

Qu'il vienne me le dire.
Let him come and tell me.

Qu'elle dise ce qu'elle pense.
Let her say what she thinks.

Qu'ils fassent ce qu'ils veulent.
Let them do what they like.

The rarer first person of the imperative is similarly expressed:
Que je voie comme tu es beau!
Let me see how handsome you are!

§ 38 Subjunctive after certain Conjunctions

bien qu'il soit	*although he is*
quoiqu'il fût	*although he was*
pour que vous sachiez	*so that you may know*
avant qu'il sorte	*before he comes out*
sans que j'entende	*without my hearing*
jusqu'à ce que je voie	*until I see*
pourvu que vous preniez	*provided (that) you take*
à condition que je reçoive	*on condition that I receive*

A moins que (*unless*) and **de peur que** (*for fear that*, *lest*) also require **ne** before the subjunctive verb:

à moins que vous ne préfériez sortir
unless you prefer to go out

de peur que nous ne refusions
for fear that we may refuse

To wait until is simply **attendre que**:
Attendons qu'ils soient prêts.

NB The idea of *not until* is expressed as *only when*:
Nous ne partirons que lorsque tout le monde sera prêt.
We shall not start until everybody is ready.

SPECIAL NOTES

1 Use an infinitive, not the subjunctive, when principal and subordinate clauses have the same subject:

Je vous verrai avant de partir.
I shall see you before I go.

Il se lèvera à cinq heures, pour pouvoir partir à six heures.
He will get up at five so that he can start at six.

Je ne suis pas entré, de peur de le déranger.
I didn't go in for fear I might disturb him.

2 Occasionally we can dispense with the subjunctive by using a noun:

avant mon départ	*before I leave (left)*
avant son arrivée	*before he arrives (arrived)*
avant leur retour	*before they return (returned)*
avant (jusqu'à) sa mort	*before (until) he died*

§ 39 Subjunctive after *il faut que, il est nécessaire que:*

Il faut que j'y aille.
Il est nécessaire que vous veniez ici.

§ 40 Subjunctive after expressions of *wishing* and *feeling*, such as:

vouloir que	*to wish that*
désirer que	*to desire that*
préférer que aimer mieux que }	*to prefer that*
regretter que	*to regret (be sorry) that*
s'étonner que	*to be surprised that*
être content (heureux) que	*to be glad (happy) that*
avoir honte que	*to be ashamed that*
c'est dommage que	*it is a pity that*
il vaut mieux que	*it is better that*
il est temps que	*it is time that*

EXAMPLES:

Je veux que vous restiez ici.
I want you to stay here.

Nous regrettons que votre femme soit souffrante.
We are sorry that your wife is unwell.

Je m'étonne qu'il ne le sache pas.
I am surprised that he doesn't know it.

Avoir peur que also requires **ne** before the verb:

J'ai peur qu'il ne fasse quelque chose d'imprudent.
I am afraid he may do something unwise.

Note again that when both clauses have the same subject, one uses an infinitive:

Je regrette d'être si occupé.
I'm sorry I'm so busy.

Il regrettait d'être venu.
He was sorry that he had come.

J'ai peur de perdre la clef.
I'm afraid I may lose the key.

§ 41 Subjunctive after expressions of *possibility* and *doubt*:

il est possible que ⎱
il se peut que   ⎰   *it is possible that*

il est impossible que   *it is impossible that*

je ne dis (pense, crois) pas   *I do not say (think) that*
  que

douter que   *to doubt that*

il semble que   *it seems that*

EXAMPLES:

Il est possible que ⎱
Il se peut que   ⎰   vous vous trompiez.

Je ne pense pas qu'il soit encore arrivé.

Je doute qu'il puisse le faire tout seul.

Il semble que vous ayez eu des difficultés.

But note that **il me semble que** takes the indicative:
Il me semble que vous avez raison.

§ 42 Subjunctive in clauses depending on a *Superlative*:

C'est l'homme le plus habile que je connaisse.
C'est le film le plus amusant que j'aie jamais vu.

Also after the virtual superlatives **seul, premier, dernier**:
C'est le seul homme qui puisse le faire.

§ 43 Subjunctive in clauses depending on a *negative* or *indefinite antecedent*:

Nous n'avons trouvé personne qui les connaisse.
Je ne dirai rien qui puisse l'offenser.

Je cherche quelqu'un qui puisse réparer la machine.
Il faut trouver un endroit où nous puissions laisser la voiture.

§ 44 Other standard examples

Qui que vous soyez . . .	*Whoever you are . . .*
Quoi que je fasse . . .	*Whatever I do . . .*
Quelles que soient les difficultés . . .	*Whatever the difficulties may be . . .*
Quelque forts qu'ils soient . . . Si forts qu'ils soient . . . }	*However strong they are (may be) . . .*
Où que vous soyez . . .	*Wherever you are . . .*

§ 45 The Tense of the Subjunctive to use

After conjunctions, the tense to use is obvious:

Although he is . . .	Bien qu'il soit . . .
Although he was . . .	Bien qu'il fût . . .
Although he had been . . .	Bien qu'il eût été . . .

Strictly speaking, after a principal verb in the past historic, imperfect or conditional, one should use the imperfect subjunctive:

Il fallait qu'elle partît tout de suite.
Ils voulaient qu'il allât les voir.

In actual fact, in conversation and often in narrative, the French habitually use the present subjunctive after past tenses, indeed after any tense:

Il fallait que le client attende.
Elle voulait que je lui écrive.
J'aurais voulu que vous restiez plus longtemps.

The article

§ 46 The Indefinite Article

a) Always used with an abstract noun qualified by an adjective:
un grand courage,   *great courage*
une sincérité parfaite,   *perfect sincerity*
avec une patience remarquable,   *with remarkable patience*

b) Omitted when one is stating a person's occupation, religion or status:

Je suis professeur.	*I am a teacher.*
Sa femme est catholique.	*His wife is a Catholic.*
Son père est pharmacien.	*His father is a chemist.*
Il a été nommé directeur.	*He has been appointed manager.*

But note: Son père est un médecin connu.

So also with nationality:

Je suis Anglais.   *I am an Englishman.*
Sa femme est Française.   *His wife is a Frenchwoman.*

Note the alternatives:

He is a Canadian. $\begin{cases} \text{Il est Canadien.} \\ \text{C'est un Canadien.} \end{cases}$

She is a hairdresser. $\begin{cases} \text{Elle est coiffeuse.} \\ \text{C'est une coiffeuse.} \end{cases}$

§ 47   The Definite Article

a) Used in descriptive expressions:

J'ai les doigts courts.   *I have short fingers.*
Elle a le nez pointu.   *She has a pointed nose.*
Il a une cicatrice au front.   *He has a scar on his forehead.*
Il marchait lentement, les mains dans les poches.
He was walking slowly, with his hands in his pockets.

Elle entra, le sourire aux lèvres.
She came in with a smile on her lips

La dame au chapeau rouge.   *The lady with (in) the red hat.*
La maison à la porte verte.   *The house with the green door.*

b) Used with parts of the body:

Il leva la tête.   Elle ouvrit la bouche.
Elle s'essuya les yeux.   Il se frotta le bras.
Il me saisit le bras.   Je lui pris la main.

NOTE The French usually keep to the singular when speaking of *la tête, la vie*, etc., of which each person possesses only one:

Tous deux hochèrent la tête.   *Both shook their heads.*
Il leur sauva la vie.   *He saved their lives.*
Les hommes enlevèrent leur chapeau.   *The men removed their hats.*

§ 48   Geographical names

Feminine names of countries (the great majority):
Nous allons en Italie.
Leur fille est en Angleterre.
Ils sont revenus d'Espagne.

In titles one uses **de**:
la reine d'Angleterre   Banque de France

138

One says, however:
Le Midi de la France.
Les régions industrielles de l'Angleterre.

Languages:
Vous parlez bien (le) français.
Il connaît bien l'allemand.
Nous apprenons l'espagnol.

§ 49 The Partitive Article

a) After a negative one uses **de** rather than the full partitive article (du, de la, etc.):
Nous n'avons plus d'essence.
Il n'a jamais d'argent.

But note these examples, which do not express absence or lack:
Ce ne sont pas des Anglais, ce sont des Américains.
Elle ne boit que de l'eau minérale.

Not a is normally expressed by **pas de**:
Je n'ai pas de chapeau. Elle n'a pas de parapluie.

Note how **sans** is used:
sans argent,   *without any money.*
sans chapeau,   *without a hat*
sans amis,   *without any friends*

b) When a plural noun is preceded by an adjective, one uses **de**:
de belles maisons   de vieux amis
d'autres villes   de tels hommes

In a few common instances, when adjective + noun form a single idea, the French use **des**:
des jeunes filles; des jeunes gens; des petits enfants; des petits poissons; des grandes personnes.

When the noun is understood, the rule holds good:
Prenez ces allumettes, j'en ai d'autres.
As-tu des poires cette année?—Oui, et j'en ai de très grosses.

§ 50 Quantity

Bien is often used to add emphasis to the partitive and thus gives the meaning of *much* or *many*:
bien de la peine ⎫
beaucoup de peine ⎭ *much trouble*

bien des efforts }
beaucoup d'efforts } *many efforts*
après bien des années, *after many years.*

La plupart (*most*) takes a plural verb:
La plupart des élèves sont sérieux.

Most of, applying to the singular, is **la plus grande partie de**:
J'ai dépensé la plus grande partie de mon argent.
One does say, however: la plupart du temps, *most of the time.*

§ 51   Note the use of *de* in these cases:

quelque chose d'intéressant,   *something interesting*
quelqu'un d'important,   *someone important*
rien de plus facile,   *nothing easier*
personne d'autre,   *nobody else*
Qu'a-t-il fait d'imprudent?   *What foolish thing has he done?*

§ 52   Points regarding certain Nouns

The following are always feminine: la personne, la connaissance, la victime:
Quelle est cette personne?—C'est un homme qui habite en face.
Quel est ce monsieur?—C'est une vieille connaissance de ma famille.
Il fut la victime d'un accident d'automobile.

An adjective used before **gens** (*people, folk*) is feminine; an adjective used after **gens** is masculine:
les bonnes gens; les vieilles gens
les gens instruits; les gens bien élevés
In spite of this, one says: tous les gens.

Surnames do not take the plural *s*:
les Dupont; les Girard; les Morisset.

Adjectives

§ 53   Position of Adjectives

Two adjectives qualifying one noun usually keep their normal position:
une petite ville française
un beau tapis rouge
une grande table ronde

One would say, however:
une grise après-midi d'hiver, *a grey winter afternoon*
une femme remarquablement belle, *a remarkably beautiful woman*
un garçon extrêmement gentil, *an extremely nice lad*

Two adjectives following the noun are usually linked by **et**:
une rue étroite et sombre, *a narrow, dark street*
un visage maigre et pâle, *a thin, pale face*
l'eau profonde et noire, *the deep, dark water*

§ 54 Adjectives are often used as nouns:

un pauvre, *a poor man*
un paresseux, *a lazy man (boy)*
un petit, *a little one, a child*
un malheureux, *an unfortunate (man), a wretch*
un brun, *a dark man (boy)*
une blonde, *a fair woman (girl)*

Note the use of the adjective when the noun is understood:
Quelle robe préfères-tu?—La rouge (*the red one*).
Lequel de ces garçons est ton cousin?—Le grand (*the tall one*).
Quels cahiers, monsieur?—Les bleus (*the blue ones*).
Est-ce le même bateau?—Oui, c'est le même (*the same one*).

§ 55 Agreement of the Adverbial *tout*

Tout (= *quite, all, altogether*) used before an adjective, agrees only when the adjective is feminine and begins with a consonant:

tout seul   toute seule   tout étonnée
tout seuls   toutes seules tout étonnées

§ 56 *a)* Note the use of the adjective (demonstrative, possessive or interrogative) in cases of this sort:
A sa vue, *at the sight of him.*
Avez-vous de ses nouvelles? *Have you any news of him?*

Nous sommes allés à leur rencontre.
We went to meet them.

Que savez-vous à son sujet?
What do you know about him?

Que savez-vous à ce sujet?
What do you know about this?

Il est venu me parler.—A quel sujet?
He came to talk to me.—What about?

b) Adjectival expressions are often made up of **de** + another word:
le moment d'après,   *the next moment*
   but: un moment après,   *a moment later (after)*
nos voisins d'en face,   *our neighbours opposite*
les pattes de devant,   *the forelegs*
le journal d'hier,   *yesterday's newspaper*
le train de midi,   *the midday train.*

§ 57   Examples involving Comparison

Il est aussi avare que son père.   *He is as mean as his father.*
fort comme un bœuf,   *as strong as an ox*
pâle comme la mort,   *as pale as death*
de plus en plus grand,   *bigger and bigger*
de plus en plus difficile,   *more and more difficult*
de moins en moins important,   *less and less important*
Plus on a, plus on désire.   *The more one has, the more one wants.*
Il est plus âgé que moi de deux ans.   *He is two years older than I.*

More (less) than, referring to quantity, is **plus (moins) de**:
plus de cinq cents élèves
plus de cinquante kilomètres
moins de mille francs
   Plus (moins) que is used in actual comparisons:
Tu manges plus que moi.
Je travaille moins que vous.

   Davantage (=*more*) is never followed by **de** or **que**; it usually translates *more* falling as the last word:
Ils ont des chambres, mais nous en avons davantage.
Moi, je gagne davantage.
Il voulait en savoir davantage.   *He wanted to know more.*
Le père était généreux, le fils l'est davantage.
The father was generous, the son is more so.

§ 58   The Superlative

a) Examples of the superlative when the adjective follows the noun:
le moment le plus dangereux
la question la moins importante
les choses les plus stupides
ses amis les plus fidèles

A most + adjective is rendered thus:
un homme des plus intelligents,   *a most intelligent man*
une femme des plus charmantes,   *a most charming woman*

b) **Le (la) moindre** = *the smallest, the slightest, the least considerable*:
Cela n'a pas la moindre importance.
sans la moindre difficulté
Smallest, in size, is **le plus petit**:
Jeannot est le plus petit des enfants.

Pire (*worse*), **le (la) pire** (*the worst*) usually applies to actions or moral
matters:
La guerre est pire.   *War is worse.*
la pire négligence; la pire cruauté
Worst, in the material sense, is **le plus mauvais**:
C'est moi qui ai la plus mauvaise chambre.
Cette chambre est encore plus mauvaise que l'autre.   (*worse*)

c) After a superlative or a virtual superlative (le seul, le premier, le
dernier), *in* is translated by **de**:
le plus grand magasin de la ville
le meilleur élève de la classe
le seul de son groupe
le premier joueur de l'équipe

Pronouns

§ 59   Pronoun Objects

a) Examples showing position:
Je ne les vois pas.
Je les ai vus. Je ne les ai pas vus.
J'y suis allé. Je n'y suis pas allé.
Je veux les voir.
Nous allons leur écrire.
Le voici! Vous voilà!

b) Order of two pronoun objects:
Il me les donne.
Je le leur envoie.
Je vous y ai vu.
Vous m'en avez parlé.

c) Pronoun objects with the imperative:
Apportez-les!   Ne les apportez pas!
Écrivez-lui!   Ne lui écrivez pas!

Allez-y!	N'y allez pas!
Montrez-le-lui!	Ne le lui montrez pas!
Donnez-les-moi!	Ne me les donnez pas!
Mettons-les-y!	Ne les y mettons pas!

§ 60   More special uses of *le*

a) **Le** sometimes renders *so*:

Tu me l'as dit hier.	*You told me so yesterday.*
Oui, je le crois.	*Yes, I think so.*
Si vous le désirez.	*If you so desire.*

b) **Le** is often used where we should not use *it* in English:

Comme vous le savez déjà ...	*As you already know ...*
Comme je vous l'ai déjà dit ...	*As I have already told you ...*
Si vous le savez, dites-le-moi.	*If you know, tell me.*
Combien, je le répète, combien?	*How much, I repeat, how much?*

But note that *it* in expressions like *I find it impossible to ...*, *I think it wise to ...*, has no counterpart in French:

Je trouve impossible de refuser. *I find it impossible to refuse.*
Nous croyons nécessaire de vous avertir.
We think it necessary to warn you.

c) **Le** may be used to replace an adjective:
On le croyait honnête, mais il ne l'était pas.   (*he was not*)
Raymond est fier, Vincent ne l'est point.
Autrefois il était énergique, mais il ne l'est plus.

§ 61   Some uses of *y*

Je vais à Dijon; j'y vais samedi.
Avez-vous pensé à cette question?—Oui, j'y ai pensé.
Je n'y prends aucun plaisir.   (y = *in it*)
Voici des tiroirs. Je peux y mettre mes papiers.   (y = *in them*)
Ils y mirent le feu.   (y = *to it*)

Y sometimes stands for **à** + infinitive:
Avez-vous réussi à le faire?—Oui, j'y ai réussi.
Est-il décidé à y aller?—Oui, il y est décidé.
Vous préparez le déjeuner? Je vais vous y aider.

§ 62   Uses of *en*

En always stands for **de** + something:
As-tu du tabac?—Oui, j'en ai.   (en = *some*)
J'ai du travail; j'en ai trop.   (en = *of it*)

Avez-vous une voiture?—Nous en avons deux.   (en = *of them*)
Comme je passais devant l'église, le curé en sortit.   (en = *of it*)
Je m'en sers.   *I make use of it.*   (se servir de)
Je m'en souviens.   *I remember it.*   (se souvenir de)
Je vous en remercie.   *I thank you for it.*   (remercier de)

Note these idioms:
Nous avons vu ces hommes; ils étaient quatre.
We saw those men; there were four of them.

J'en étais venu à détester ces visites.
I had come to hate these visits.

C'était une robe bon marché, comme on en vend partout.
It was a cheap dress, such as are sold everywhere.

En sometimes stands for **de** + infinitive:
Je voudrais le faire, mais je n'en ai pas le droit.
Il croyait que j'allais payer, mais je n'en avais pas l'intention.
S'il veut le faire, je ne peux pas l'en empêcher.
Je suis allé voir sa mère, ainsi qu'il m'en avait prié.

§ 63   Various uses of the Disjunctive Pronoun

a) With prepositions:
Avec moi, sans toi, loin d'eux.
Chez moi, chez eux, etc.
C'est moi, c'est vous, etc. But one says: ce sont eux (elles).
L'un d'eux, *f.* l'une d'elles,   *one of them.*
Ils parlaient entre eux.   (*among themselves*)
Plusieurs (quelques-uns, beaucoup, certains, la plupart) d'entre eux.
Several (a few, many, certain, most) of them.

b) For emphasis:
Moi, je n'en sais rien.   *I don't know.*
Lui ne fait rien.   *He does nothing.*
Ce n'est pas moi qu'il cherche.   He is not looking for *me*.
    Also when the subject is separated from the verb by another word or expression:
Moi aussi, je les ai vus.   *I saw them too.*
Lui seul le savait.   *He alone knew it.*
Lui, qui avait tant travaillé, a échoué.
He, who worked so hard, has failed.

Composite subject:
Mon ami et moi sommes allés à la pêche.
Toi et ton frère avez bien joué.

c) With reflexive verbs followed by **de** or **à**:

Je me souviens de lui.

Personne ne s'occupe de moi.

Je me fie à lui. Adressez-vous à eux.

Also with verbs of motion, including **penser à**:

Je courus à elle.   Il vint à moi.

Je pensais à toi.

d) **Soi** (*oneself*) is used in association with **on, chacun, personne tout le monde**:

On rentre chez soi.   chacun pour soi

Personne ne reste chez soi.

On est content de ce qu'on fait soi-même.

§ 64   Relative Pronouns

a) **Qui** (*whom*) is used with prepositions in relative clauses and in questions:

les gens avec qui nous sortons   *the people we go out with*

De qui parlez-vous?   *Whom are you talking about?*

Quoi (*what*) is similarly used:

J'ai tout fermé à clef, après quoi je suis sorti.

I locked everything up, after which I went out.

Nous ignorons de quoi ils parlent.

We don't know what they are talking about.

A quoi faisait-il allusion?

What was he alluding to?

b) **Dont** (*of which, of whom, whose*):

l'homme dont vous parlez

la maison dont vous parlez

les choses dont nous avons besoin

Dont is always the first word of the relative clause:

une chambre dont les fenêtres étaient ouvertes

C'est un jeune homme dont je connais les parents.

§ 65   *Ce qui, ce que, ce dont*

Je sais ce qui se passe.   *I know what is going on.*

Je sais ce que vous allez dire.

I know what you are going to say.

Ce qui est certain, c'est qu'il le fera.

What is certain is that he will do it.

146

Ce n'est pas ce dont nous avons besoin.
It isn't what we need.

Je ferai tout ce qui sera nécessaire.
I will do all that is necessary.

J'ai entendu tout ce qu'il disait.
I heard all he was saying.

Ce qui is also used to refer to the sense of a foregoing phrase:
La porte était ouverte, ce qui me parut singulier.
Elle jouait sans cesse du piano, ce qui ennuyait les voisins.

§ 66   *Lequel, laquelle,* etc.

L'auto dans laquelle ils voyageaient.
Le stylo avec lequel j'écris.
Les raisons pour lesquelles nous refusons.
Un bois au milieu duquel se trouvait un étang.
Des questions auxquelles je ne veux pas répondre.

With **parmi** (*among*), **lesquels (lesquelles)** may refer to persons:
les gens parmi lesquels je vivais

In which, on which, etc. are often translated by **où**:
la rue où je demeure   *the street in which I live*
le banc où j'étais assis   *the bench on which I was sitting*

Lequel, lesquels, etc. are used in questions with the sense of *which
one*(s):
Un des enfants est malade.—Lequel?   (*Which one?*)
J'ai brisé une fenêtre.—Laquelle?
Laquelle de ces bicyclettes est la tienne?
Lesquelles de ces valises sont les vôtres?

Demonstrative pronouns

§ 67   *a*) Examples involving **ce**:

C'est un pigeon.	*It is a pigeon.*
Ce sont des pigeons.	*They are pigeons.*
C'est un brave homme.	*He is a good fellow.*
Ce sont des gens charmants.	*They are charming people.*

b) **Il est (difficile) ...** and **c'est (difficile) ...**
Il est leads off when the adjective is followed by **de** + infinitive or by
que + phrase:

Il est difficile (facile, possible, nécessaire, etc.) de . . .
Il est certain (vrai, probable, évident, etc.) que . . .

But **c'est possible** (difficile, etc.) is complete in itself: **c'est** really
means *that* (i.e. what has been mentioned) *is possible* (*difficult*, etc.).
Il est évident qu'ils vont accepter.—Oui, c'est évident.
Il est possible d'y aller?—Oui, c'est possible.

§ 68   **Cela** translates *it* in a number of expressions, chiefly of feeling:

Cela m'amuse de les voir jouer.
Cela me plaît de les écouter.
Cela me fait plaisir de rouler à toute vitesse.
Cela m'ennuie d'aller chez eux.
Cela m'étonne que vous restiez ici.

§ 69   *Celui, ceux; celle, celles*

a) Followed by **de**:

Ce n'est pas mon sac, c'est celui de Nicole.   (*Nicole's*)
Je n'ai pas de bicyclette; je prendrai celle de Jean.   (*John's*)
Voici vos lettres, et voilà celles du directeur.   (*the manager's*)

b) Followed by a relative (**qui, que, dont**):

Quelle dame?—Celle qui vient de sortir.   (*she who, the one who*)
Quel journal?—Celui que vous lisez.   (*the one which*)
Quelles photos?—Celles que je t'ai envoyées.   (*the ones which, those which*)
Je vois tous ceux qui entrent et sortent.
I see all (*those*) *who go in and out.*

c)

MASC.			FEM.		
celui-ci	*this one*		**celle-ci**	*this one*	
celui-là	*that one*		**celle-là**	*that one*	
ceux-ci	*these*		**celles-ci**	*these*	
ceux-là	*those*		**celles-l?**	*those*	

EXAMPLES:

Voici deux chapeaux. Celui-ci est à 39 francs, celui-là à 45.
Quelles assiettes? Celles-ci?—Non, celles-là.
«Qui êtes-vous?» demanda celui-ci.   (*asked the latter*)

§ 70   Useful examples involving **que**:

Qu'arrive-t-il?
Que se passe-t-il?   } *What is happening?*
Que sont ces papiers?   *What are these papers?*

Que vous faut-il? *What do you require?*
Qu'est-il devenu? *What has become of him?*
Que reste-t-il? *What remains? What is left?*
Je ne savais que faire. *I did not know what to do.*
Qu'est-ce que c'est que cette plaisanterie? *What is this joke?*

§ 71 The Possessive Pronoun

	SINGULAR		PLURAL	
mine	le mien	la mienne	les miens	les miennes
yours	le tien	la tienne	les tiens	les tiennes
his, hers	le sien	la sienne	les siens	les siennes
ours	le (la) nôtre		les nôtres	
yours	le (la) vôtre		les vôtres	
theirs	le (la) leur		les leurs	

EXAMPLES:
Voici ta valise. Où est la mienne?
Voici nos bagages. Où sont les vôtres?
J'ai ma voiture, et Jean a la sienne.

NOTE: *A friend of mine,* un de mes amis.
doctor friend of mine, un médecin de mes amis.

Indefinite adjectives and pronouns

§ 72 **Chaque** (adj.), *each*: chaque jour, chaque personne.

   Chacun(e) is a pronoun:
Chacun de ces hommes, *each of these men*
Chacun aura sa part. *Each (one) will have his share.*

   Quelqu'un, *someone, somebody:*
J'attends quelqu'un. Quelqu'un d'important.

   Quelques-un(e)s, *some, a few,* used apart from the noun:
Quelques-uns de mes élèves. Quelques-unes de ces maisons.
As-tu pris des photos?—Oui, j'en ai pris quelques-unes.

§ 73 Tout

Nous voulons tout voir. *We wish to see everything.*
J'ai tout essayé. *I have tried everything.*
Vous le savez tous. *You all know it.*
Je les connais tous. *I know them all.*
Tous (les) deux sont partis. } *Both (of them) have gone.*
Ils sont partis tous (les) deux. }

§ 74   Tel, *such*

un tel homme,   *such a man*   de tels hommes, *such men*
une telle chose, *such a thing*   de telles choses,   *such things*
  But one says:
un si bel homme,   *such a handsome man*
de si jolies villas,   *such pretty villas*
  In this connection, **aussi** is sometimes used instead of **si**, especially when the adjective follows the noun:
Une question aussi importante,   *such an important question.*

§ 75   Autre

Je n'ai que trois verres.   Où sont les autres?   (*the others, the rest*)

NB: *The rest* meaning the remaining portion is **le reste**:
le reste du temps; le reste de son argent.

Tu peux mettre ces gants, j'en ai d'autres.   (*others, some more*)
Choisissons autre chose.   *Let us choose something else.*
Personne d'autre,   *nobody else*;   quelqu'un d'autre,   *somebody else*;
rien d'autre,   *nothing else*
Ses filles sont mariées, l'une et l'autre.   (*both*)
J'ai deux chambres; vous pouvez louer l'une ou l'autre.   (*either*)
Ni l'un ni l'autre n'avait bougé.   (*neither*)
Nous nous aidons l'un l'autre.   (*each other*)
nous autres Français   *we French people.*

§ 76   Quiconque, *whoever*

Quiconque lui résistait perdait sa place.
Whoever resisted him lost his job.
  But *whoever* is often rendered by **celui qui**:
Celui qui ferait cela serait fou.

  Quelconque, *some* (*any*) *sort of*:
Il trouvera une place quelconque.

§ 77   *a*) N'importe qui vous le dira.   *Anybody will tell you.*

Chantez n'importe quoi.   *Sing anything.*
Vous trouverez cela dans n'importe quelle épicerie.   (*any grocer's*)
Quelle carte?—N'importe laquelle.   (*any one*)
Où faut-il le mettre?—N'importe où.   (*anywhere*)

  b) Je ne sais qui me l'a dit.
Somebody or other told me.

Il se plaignait de je ne sais quoi.
He was complaining of something or other.

Je l'ai lu dans je ne sais quel journal.
I read it in some newspaper or other.

J'en suis sorti je ne sais comment.
I got out of it somehow or other.

Negative forms

§ 78 Personne

Personne n'est venu.
Je n'ai vu personne.
Nous ne le dirons à personne.
Qui veut y aller?—Personne.

Rien

Rien ne bouge.
Il n'a rien dit.
Qu'a-t-il fait?—Rien.
Il ne veut rien dire.
Sans rien dire.
Il n'y a rien de plus facile.

Aucun(e) + **ne**, *none, not one*
Il n'y avait aucun bruit, aucun movement.
There was no sound, no movement.

Aucune voiture n'attendait devant la gare.
No car was waiting before the station.

Quelle importance cela a-t-il?—Aucune. (*none, none at all*)
Sans aucun espoir, *without any hope.*

Pas un(e) + **ne**, *not one*
Pas un homme n'hésita.
Pas un ne s'échappa.

Nul (*f.* **nulle**) + **ne**, *none*
Nul ne sait. *None knows.*
Cela n'existe nulle part. *That doesn't exist anywhere.*
Je ne suis nullement coupable. *I am not in any way guilty.*

§ 79 Ne . . . jamais

Je n'y vais jamais.
Nous ne l'avons jamais vu.

Y êtes-vous allé?—Jamais.
C'était quelqu'un que je n'avais jamais vu.
It was somebody I had never seen before.

Jamais means *ever* in sentences like these:
Avez-vous jamais vu cela?
Si jamais il vient ici . . .
Il cria plus fort que jamais.

Ne . . . plus

Je ne leur écris plus. $\left\{\begin{array}{l}\textit{I no longer write to them.} \\ \textit{I do not write to them any more.} \\ \textit{I do not write to them now.}\end{array}\right.$

Ne . . . que, *only, nothing but*
Je n'ai qu'une valise.
I have only one suitcase.

Vous n'avez qu'à attendre.
You have only to wait.

Je n'ai qu'un peu de jambon.
I have nothing but a little ham.

Le car ne part qu'à trois heures.
The bus does not leave until three o'clock.

Only, merely, with a verb is expressed thus:
Il ne fit que hausser les épaules. $\left.\begin{array}{l}\\\end{array}\right\}$ *He only (merely) shrugged his*
Il se contenta de hausser les épaules. $\left.\begin{array}{l}\\\end{array}\right.$ *shoulders.*

Ni . . . ni + ne
Ni le directeur ni ses collègues ne le savaient.
Neither the manager nor his colleagues knew it.

Je n'ai ni imperméable ni parapluie.
I have neither a raincoat nor an umbrella.

Ne . . . guère, *hardly, scarcely*
Ce n'est guère possible.   *It is hardly (scarcely) possible.*

Vous n'avez guère de temps à perdre.
You have scarcely any time to waste.

§ 80   *a*) Two negatives combined:

Il ne fait plus rien.
He no longer does anything.
He does not do anything now.

Ils ne me donnent jamais rien.
They never give me anything.

Il n'y connaît plus personne.
He doesn't know anybody there now.

   b) **Negatives with the Infinitive:**
   Both parts (ne pas, ne rien, etc.) are placed before the infinitive:
Je leur dirai de ne pas attendre.
Il était décidé à ne rien dire.
   But: Elle préfère ne voir personne.

§ 81   *a*) Other Examples involving Affirmation or Negation

Il n'est pas parti?—Si, il est parti.
Je crois que oui.   *I think so.*
Je crois que non.   *I think not, I don't think so.*
Jacques ne viendra pas non plus.   *Jacques won't come either.*
(Ni) moi non plus.   *Nor I (either).   Neither shall I.*
Je croyais trouver des amis, non pas des ennemis.
I thought I should find friends, not enemies.

Elle ne m'a même pas regardé.
She didn't even look at me.

Il ne viendra certainement pas aujourd'hui.

Il me demanda si je n'avais rien entendu.
He asked me if I had heard anything.

Ils voulaient savoir si personne n'était sorti.
They wanted to know if anybody had come out.

   b) Special idioms involving **ne**:
Il y a longtemps que je ne l'ai vu.
It is a long time since I saw him.

Il est plus rusé que vous ne croyez (pensez).
He is more artful than you think.

Il a pris cela mieux que je n'espérais.
He took that better than I hoped.

Elle est moins jolie qu'elle ne l'était il y a deux ans.
She is less pretty than she was two years ago.

§ 82   Cases of Inversion

   a) This case is already well known:
«Non!» répéta-t-il.

«Pourquoi?» lui demanda l'homme.
«Tu l'as fait?» m'a demandé Charles.

b) Note questions of this sort, in which the subject is a noun:
Pourquoi ton ami est-il parti?
Combien Louis a-t-il payé son auto?
Comment vos amis vont-ils trouver la maison?
Quand le garagiste pourra-t-il faire cette réparation?

One may also use **est-ce que** in such cases:
{ A quelle heure ton père va-t-il rentrer?
{ A quelle heure est-ce que ton père va rentrer?

c) Inversion occurs in sentences beginning with **peut-être, aussi** (= *so, therefore*), **à peine** (*scarcely, hardly*), **sans doute** (*very likely*):
{ Peut-être est-il déjà revenu.
{ Peut-être qu'il est déjà revenu.
Aussi décida-t-elle de rester chez elle.
A peine fut-il parti qu'une auto s'arrêta devant la maison.
Sans doute pensez-vous que j'ai tort.

d) Note expressions such as **paraît-il, semble-t-il**, introduced parenthetically:
Ils y ont réussi, paraît-il.
C'est ce que vous devriez faire, me semble-t-il.

e) Inversion often occurs in subordinate clauses, particularly after **où, que, ce que**:
Savez-vous où habitent ses parents?
Il y avait une cour, où jouaient quelques enfants.
As-tu entendu ce que disait Madeleine?
Elle était dans une voiture que conduisait un jeune homme.

Adverbs

§ 83 *a*) Note the position of the adverb in these cases:
Vous avez bien joué.
Elle avait tant souffert.
Il a trop bu.
Nous avons beaucoup voyagé.
Pour bien jouer, il faut s'entraîner.

b) Several words are used both as prepositions and adverbs:
Après vous.   Il est venu après.
Avant lui.   Elle était arrivée deux minutes avant.

Derrière l'église.   Moi, je marchais derrière.
Devant la gare.   L'officier alla devant.

§ 84   Notes on some Adverbs

Comme. Comme il est tard, il faut rentrer.   (*As it is late . . .*)
 Il s'arrêta comme pour me parler.   (*as though to . . .*)
 Tout disparut comme par magie.   (*as if by . . .*)
 Que c'est joli!   }
 Comme c'est joli! } *How pretty it is!*

Plutôt = *rather, if anything*
 Leur maison est plutôt petite.

Assez = *rather* in the sense of to a fair degree:
 Je crois qu'ils sont assez riches.

Au moins, *at least,* expresses a minimum, e.g. au moins cent francs.
 Du moins, *at least,* expresses a reservation:
 Du moins, je le crois.   *At least, I think so.*

Tôt, *early.*   Il se lève tôt.
 Pourquoi est-il revenu si tôt?   (*so soon, so early*)
 Vous devriez partir plus tôt.   (*earlier, sooner*)
 N'y arrivez pas trop tôt.   (*too soon, too early*)

Tantôt . . . tantôt . . ., *sometimes . . . sometimes . . .*
 Tantôt on gagne, tantôt on perd.
 Sometimes you win, sometimes you lose.

Tard = *late,* without reference to a particular time:
 Je me suis couché tard.
 En retard = *late,* in the sense of after time:
 Je devais y arriver à midi. J'étais en retard.

Avant, *before,* e.g. une heure avant
 Auparavant (*before, previously*) tends to be used more in literary
 narrative:
 Son père était mort quelques mois auparavant.

 Note these examples:
 Je ne l'avais jamais vu.
 I had never seen him before.

 Nous sommes déjà venus ici.
 We have been here before.

Jusqu'ici, *up till now*

Jusque-là }
Jusqu'alors } *until then, up till then*

Où is a relative, e.g. l'usine où je travaille.
  Where used without an antecedent is **là où**:
  Là où j'habite, il y a beaucoup de vignes.
  Partout où = *wherever*:
  Partout où je vais, je trouve la même chose.

Dedans, *in, inside*:
  Qu'y a-t-il dedans?—Il y a une bête dedans.
  Que font-ils là-dedans? *What are they doing in there?*

Dessus, *on top, on (over) it*:
  On a versé de l'encre dessus.
  Mets ton chapeau dessus!
  Là-dessus il s'éloigna. *Thereupon he walked away.*

§ 85 Notes on some Prepositions

À: à mon arrivée (retour), *on my arrival (return)*
  à mon avis, *in my opinion*
  Au secours! *Help!* Au voleur! *Stop thief!* Au feu! *Fire!*
  Je l'ai reconnu à sa voix. *I recognised him by his voice.*
  à la lumière d'une lampe, *by the light of a lamp*
  À ce qu'il dit ... *From what he says ...*
  À ce que j'ai entendu dire ... *From what I have heard ...*
  Il ne comprend rien au problème.
  He understands nothing about the problem.

De: La route (le train) de Paris. *The road (train) to Paris.*
  Les arbres du jardin, *the trees in the garden.*
  Sa maison de la rue du Bac. *His house in the Rue du Bac.*
  De nos jours, *in our day.*
  D'un ton naturel, *in a natural tone.*
  D'une main tremblante, *with a trembling hand.*
  De tout mon cœur, *with all my heart.*
  De toutes ses forces, *with all his might (strength).*
  De cette façon (manière), *in this fashion (manner, way).*
  De ce côté, *on this side.* De l'autre côté, *on the other side.*
  Du côté de la gare, *in the direction of the station.*

En: En l'air; en l'absence de; en l'honneur de; en mon nom.
  En l'an 1914, *in the year* 1914.

De maison en maison, *from house to house.*
Je vous parle en ami. *I speak to you as a friend.*

Entre: Entre nous, je crois qu'il est jaloux. (*between ourselves*)
Ils discutaient entre eux. (*among themselves*)
Entre les mains de l'ennemi, *in the hands of the enemy.*

À travers, *through*, *across*: à travers les champs
Au travers de implies resistance: au travers de la jungle
En travers de means *across* (position), *athwart*:
Un arbre était tombé en travers de la route.

Vers, *towards* (direction), e.g. vers le collège
Envers, *towards* (conduct or attitude):
respectueux envers les maîtres

Depuis, *since*: Ils habitent Vichy depuis deux ans.
Je ne les ai pas vus depuis.
Depuis may also mean *from*, in reference to place or price:
depuis l'Arc de Triomphe jusqu'au Louvre
robes depuis 30 francs *dresses from 30 francs*

Sans, *without*: les arbres sans feuilles, *the leafless trees*
Sans vous, nous aurions été battus.
But for you we should have been beaten.

Pendant, *during*, *for*: pendant une heure, pendant deux ans.
Pre-arranged time limit is expressed by **pour**:
Nous sommes ici pour trois jours.
Pendant may be used of distance:
chaussée déformée pendant 3 kilomètres
bad road-surface for 3 kilometres

À partir de, *from* (= starting from), e.g. à partir de demain

Pour: J'en ai pour un quart d'heure.
It will take me a quarter of an hour.

Pour lui, c'est une catastrophe.
To him, it is a catastrophe.

Sur: Marcher sur une route (but: dans une rue).
Sur un signe de ... *At a sign from* ...

Sous:
sous le règne de Louis XIV, *in the reign of Louis XIV*
marcher sous la pluie (la neige), *to walk in the rain* (*the snow*)

Par:
par politesse, *out of politeness*
par nécessité, *out of necessity*

par un temps pluvieux, *in rainy weather*
par ce temps, *in this weather*
Par ici, madame. *This way, madam.*
C'est par là. *It is that way.*

Miscellaneous

§ 86 *a*) Numbers

80   quatre-vingts
81   quatre-vingt-un
600   six cents
620   six cent vingt

une vingtaine de personnes, *about twenty people*
un homme d'une trentaine d'années, *a man about thirty*
cent hommes, 100 *men* (*exactly* 100)
une centaine de personnes, *about* 100 *people*
des centaines de voitures, *hundreds of cars*
un millier d'hommes, *about* 1000 *men*
des milliers d'oiseaux, *thousands of birds*

neuf sur dix, *nine out of ten*
les trois premiers chapitres, *the first three chapters*

b) Fractions

la moitié de mon argent, *half my money*
un quart de litre, *a quarter of a litre*
trois quarts d'heure, *three quarters of an hour*
un tiers, *a third*; les deux tiers, *two thirds*
un cinquième, *a fifth*; un huitième, *an eighth*

§ 87 *a*) Price

2 francs le kilo, 2 *francs a kilo*
5 francs la pièce, 5 *francs each*
35 francs par jour, 35 *francs a day*
Il m'en a pris (demandé) 26 francs.
He charged me 26 francs for it.

Je l'ai vendu 150 francs.
I sold it for 150 francs.

b) Distance

Versailles est à 18 kilomètres. *Versailles is 18 kilometres away.*
Combien (Quelle distance) y a-t-il d'ici à Paris?
How far is it from here to Paris?

Nous roulions à 80 kilomètres à l'heure.
We were travelling at 50 miles an hour.

c) **Dimensions**
Cela a deux mètres de long (de large, de haut).
This is two metres long (wide, high).

Cette table est longue de trois mètres.
{ Ce mur est épais de 25 centimètres.
{ Ce mur a 25 centimètres d'épaisseur.

§ 88   Expressions of Time

Le mercredi, 6 décembre. *Wednesday, December 6th.*
Nous y allons samedi.
We are going there on Saturday (i.e. next Saturday).

Nous y allons toujours le samedi.
We always go there on Saturday(s).

Le 26 août au matin.   *On the morning of August 26th*
la veille, *the day before*;   la veille au soir,   *the evening before*

   La journée, la matinée, la soirée are used when we are thinking of what
goes to fill up the time:
une journée chargée, *a heavy day*
les occupations de la matinée
une soirée tranquille
Je n'ai rien fait de la journée.
I have done nothing all day.

Je n'ai pas fermé l'œil de la nuit.
I haven't slept a wink all night.

à onze heures précises,   *at exactly 11 o'clock*
vers dix heures   }
à dix heures environ   } *at about 10 o'clock*
On peut y aller en deux heures.   (*time taken*)
Ils arriveront dans une heure.   (*in an hour's time*)

One says:
le jour (l'heure, le moment) où . . .
the day (the hour, the moment) when . . .
But:
un jour (un matin, un soir) que . . .
one day (one morning, one evening) when . . .
Un jour, que je rentrais chez moi . . .
Un matin, qu'il se rendait à son travail . . .

INFINITIVE	PARTICIPLES	PRESENT INDICATIVE	IMPERFECT PAST HIST.	FUTURE CONDITIONAL

Avoir, être

INFINITIVE	PARTICIPLES	PRESENT INDICATIVE	IMPERFECT PAST HIST.	FUTURE CONDITIONAL
avoir, *to have*	ayant eu	ai, as, a avons, avez, ont	avais eus	aurai aurais
être, *to be*	étant été	suis, es, est, sommes, êtes, sont	étais fus	serai serais

Donner, finir, vendre

donner, *to give*	donnant donné	donne, –es, –e, donnons, –ez, –ent	donnais donnai	donnerai donnerais
finir *to finish*	finissant fini	finis, –is, –it, finissons, –ez, –ent	finissais finis	finirai finirais
vendre, *to sell*	vendant vendu	vends, –s, vend, vendons, –ez, –ent	vendais vendis	vendrai vendrais

Irregular Verbs

aller, *to go*	allant allé	vais, vas, va, allons, allez, vont	allais allai	irai irais
asseoir (Reflex. s'asseoir, *to sit down*)	asseyant assis	assieds, –s, assied, asseyons, –ez, –ent	asseyais assis	assiérai assiérais
battre, *to beat*	battant battu	bats, –s, bat, battons, –ez, –ent	battais battis	battrai battrais
boire, *to drink*	buvant bu	bois, –s, –t, buvons, –ez, boivent	buvais bus	boirai boirais
conduire, *to lead, drive*	conduisant conduit	conduis, –s, –t, conduisons, –ez, –ent	conduisais conduisis	conduirai conduirais
connaître, *to know*	connaissant connu	connais, –s, connaît, connaissons, –ez, –ent	connaissais connus	connaîtrai connaîtrais
courir, *to run*	courant couru	cours, –s, –t, courons, –ez, –ent	courais courus	courrai courrais
craindre, *to fear*	craignant craint	crains, –s, –t, craignons, –ez, –ent	craignais craignis	craindrai craindrais

PRESENT SUBJUNCTIVE	IMPERATIVE	REMARKS Verbs similarly conjugated
aie, aies, ait ayons, ayez, aient	aie, ayons ayez	
sois, sois, soit, soyons, soyez, soient	sois, soyons, soyez	
donne, –es, –e, donnions, –iez, –ent	donne, donnons, donnez	
finisse, –es, –e, finissions, –iez, –ent	finis, finissons, finissez	
vende, –es, –e, vendions, –iez, –ent	vends, vendons, vendez	
aille, –es, –e, allions, –iez, aillent	va, allons, allez	Conjugated with *être.*
asseye, –es, –e, asseyions, –iez, –ent	assieds, asseyons, asseyez	Used reflexively: s'asseoir, *to sit down*
batte, –es, –e, battions, –iez, –ent	bats, battons, battez	combattre, abattre
boive, –es, –e, buvions, –iez, boivent	bois, buvons, buvez	
conduise, –es, –e, conduisions, –iez, –ent	conduis, conduisons, conduisez	produire, construire, traduire, etc.
connaisse, –es, –e, connaissions, –iez, –ent	connais, connaissons, connaissez	paraître, and compounds of both.
coure, –es, –e, courions, –iez, –ent	cours, courons, courez	accourir, and other compounds
craigne, –es, –e, craignions, –iez, –ent	crains, craignons, craignez	Verbs in –indre, e.g. plaindre, éteindre, joindre.

INFINITIVE	PARTICIPLES	PRESENT INDICATIVE	IMPERFECT PAST HIST.	FUTURE CONDITIONAL
croire, *to* *believe, think*	croyant cru	crois, –s, –t, croyons, –ez, croient	croyais crus	croirai croirais
croître, *to grow*	croissant crû	croîs, croîs, croît, croissons, –ez, –ent	croissais crûs	croîtrai croîtrais
cueillir, *to gather*	cueillant cueilli	cueille, –es, –e, cueillons, –ez, –ent	cueillais cueillis	cueillerai cueillerais
devoir, *to owe*	devant dû (f. due)	dois, –s, –t, devons, –ez, doivent	devais dus	devrai devrais
dire, *to say*	disant dit	dis, –s, –t, disons, dites, disent	disais dis	dirai dirais
dormir, *to sleep*	dormant dormi	dors, –s, –t, dormons, –ez, –ent	dormais dormis	dormirai dormirais
écrire, *to write*	écrivant écrit	écris, –s, –t, écrivons, –ez, –ent	écrivais écrivis	écrirai écrirais
envoyer, *to send*	envoyant envoyé	envoie, –es, –e, envoyons, –ez, envoient	envoyais envoyai	enverrai enverrais
faire, *to do,* *to make*	faisant fait	fais, –s, –t, faisons, faites, font	faisais fis	ferai ferais
falloir, *to be* *necessary*	fallu	il faut	il fallait il fallut	il faudra il faudrait
fuir, *to flee*	fuyant fui	fuis, –s, –t, fuyons, –ez, fuient	fuyais fuis	fuirai fuirais
lire, *to read*	lisant lu	lis, –s, –t, lisons, –ez, –ent	lisais lus	lirai lirais
mettre, *to put*	mettant mis	mets, –s, met, mettons, –ez, –ent	mettais mis	mettrai mettrais
mourir, *to die*	mourant mort	meurs, –s, –t, mourons, –ez, meurent	mourais mourus	mourrai mourrais
naître, *to be born*	naissant né	nais, –s, naît, naissons, –ez, –ent	naissais naquis	naîtrai naîtrais
ouvrir, *to open*	ouvrant ouvert	ouvre, –es, –e, ouvrons, –ez, –ent	ouvrais ouvris	ouvrirai ouvrirais

PRESENT SUBJUNCTIVE	IMPERATIVE	REMARKS Verbs similarly conjugated
croie, −es, −e, croyions, −iez, croient	crois, croyons, croyez	
croisse, −es, −e, croissions, −iez, −ent	croîs, croissons croissez	accroître
cueille, −es, −e, cueillions, −iez, −ent	cueille, cueillons, cueillez	accueillir, recueillir
doive, −es, −e, devions, −iez, doivent	dois, devons, devez	
dise, −es, −e, disions, −iez, −ent	dis, disons, dites	
dorme, −es, −e, dormions, −iez, −ent	dors, dormons, dormez	s'endormir, servir, sentir, mentir
écrive, −es, −e, écrivions, −iez, −ent	écris, écrivons, écrivez	décrire, inscrire
envoie, −es, −e, envoyions, −iez, envoient	envoie, envoyons, envoyez	renvoyer
fasse, −es, −e, fassions, −iez, −ent	fais, faisons, faites	
il faille		
fuie, −es, −e, fuyions, −iez, fuient	fuis, fuyons, fuyez	s'enfuir
lise, −es, −e, lisions, −iez, −ent	lis, lisons, lisez	relire
mette, −es, −e, mettions, −iez, −ent	mets, mettons, mettez	permettre, promettre, remettre, omettre
meure, −es, −e, mourions, −iez, meurent	meurs, mourons, mourez	Conjugated with **être**, e.g. il est mort
naisse, −es, −e, naissions, −iez, −ent	nais, naissons, naissez	Conjugated with **être**, e.g. elle est née
ouvre, −es, −e, ouvrions, −iez, −ent	ouvre, ouvrons, ouvrez	couvrir, découvrir, offrir, souffrir

163

INFINITIVE	PARTICIPLES	PRESENT INDICATIVE	IMPERFECT PAST HIST.	FUTURE CONDITIONAL
partir, to depart	partant parti	pars, −s, −t, partons, −ez, −ent	partais partis	partirai partirais
plaire, to please	plaisant plu	plais, −s, plaît, plaisons, −ez, −ent	plaisais plus	plairai plairais
pleuvoir, to rain	pleuvant plu	il pleut	il pleuvait il plut	il pleuvra il pleuvrait
pouvoir, to be able	pouvant pu	peux, −x, −t, · pouvons, −ez, peuvent	pouvais pus	pourrai pourrais
prendre, to take	prenant pris	prends, −s, prend, prenons, −ez, prennent	prenais pris	prendrai prendrais
recevoir, to receive	recevant reçu	reçois −s, −t, recevons, −ez, reçoivent	recevais reçus	recevrai recevrais
rire, to laugh	riant ri	ris, −s, −t, rions, −ez, −ent	riais ris	rirai rirais
rompre, to break	rompant rompu	romps, −s, −t, rompons, −ez, −ent	rompais rompis	romprai romprais
savoir, to know	sachant su	sais, −s, −t, savons, −ez, −ent	savais sus	saurai saurais
sentir, to feel, to smell	sentant senti	sens, −s, −t, sentons, −ez, −ent	sentais sentis	sentirai sentirais
servir, to serve	servant servi	sers, −s, −t, servons, −ez, −ent	servais servis	servirai servirais
sortir, to go (come) out	sortant sorti	sors, −s, −t, sortons, −ez, −ent	sortais sortis	sortirai sortirais
suffire, to suffice	suffisant suffi	suffis, −s, −t, suffisons, −ez, −ent	suffisais suffis	suffirai suffirais
suivre, to follow	suivant suivi	suis, −s, −t, suivons, −ez, −ent	suivais suivis	suivrai suivrais
taire (reflex. se taire, to be silent)	taisant tu	tais, −s, −t, taisons, −ez, −ent	taisais tus	tairai tairais

PRESENT SUBJUNCTIVE	IMPERATIVE	REMARKS / Verbs similarly conjugated
parte, –es, –e partions, –iez, –ent	pars, partons, partez	Conjugated with **être.** Similar verb: sortir.
plaise, –es, –e, plaisions, –iez, –ent	plais, plaisons, plaisez	
il pleuve		
puisse, –es, –e, puissions, –iez, –ent		
prenne, –es, –e prenions, –iez, prennent	prends, prenons, prenez	apprendre, comprendre, surprendre, reprendre
reçoive, –es, –e, recevions, –iez, reçoivent	reçois, recevons, recevez	apercevoir, décevoir, concevoir
rie, –es, –e, riions, riiez, rient	ris, rions, riez	sourire
rompe, –es, –e, rompions, –iez, –ent	romps, rompons, rompez	interrompre
sache, –es, –e, sachions, –iez, –ent	sache, sachons, sachez	
sente, –es, –e, sentions, –iez, –ent	sens, sentons, sentez	dormir, servir, mentir
serve, –es, –e, servions, –iez, –ent	sers, servons, servez	dormir, sentir, mentir
sorte, –es, –e, sortions, –iez, –ent	sors, sortons, sortez	Conjugated with **être.** Similar verb: partir
suffise, –es, –e, suffisions, –iez, –ent	suffis, suffisons, suffisez	
suive, –es, –e, suivions, –iez, –ent	suis, suivons, suivez	poursuivre
taise, –es, –e, taisions, –iez, –ent	tais, taisons, taisez	Used reflexively: se taire, *to be (become) silent*

INFINITIVE	PARTICIPLES	PRESENT INDICATIVE	IMPERFECT PAST HIST.	FUTURE CONDITIONAL
tenir, *to hold*	tenant tenu	tiens, –s, –t, tenons, –ez, tiennent	tenais tins, –s, –t tînmes, tîntes tinrent	tiendrai tiendrais
valoir, *to be worth*	valant valu	vaux, –x, –t, valons, –ez, –ent	valais valus	vaudrai vaudrais
venir, *to come*	venant venu	viens, –s, –t, venons, –ez, viennent	venais vins, –s, –t vînmes, vîntes vinrent	viendrai viendrais
vivre, *to live*	vivant vécu	vis, –s, –t, vivons, –ez, –ent	vivais vécus	vivrai vivrais
voir, *to see*	voyant vu	vois, –s, –t, voyons, –ez, voient	voyais vis	verrai verrais
vouloir, *to wish, want*	voulant voulu	veux, –x, –t, voulons, –ez, veulent	voulais voulus	voudrai voudrais

Verbs in -er showing slight variations

a) In verbs like **manger** and **commencer**, the g or c must be softened (ge, ç) before o or a, e.g. nous mangeons, nous commençons: je mangeais, il commença.

b) Verbs like **mener, lever, acheter** require è before mute endings. **Appeler** and **jeter** open the e by doubling the consonant.
Répéter, espérer, posséder, etc., change é to è before mute endings, except in the future, where é stands.

je mène	j'appelle	je jette	je répète
tu mènes	tu appelles	tu jettes	tu répètes
il mène	il appelle	il jette	il répète
nous menons	nous appelons	nous jetons	nous répétons
vous menez	vous appelez	vous jetez	vous répétez
il mènent	ils appellent	ils jettent	ils répètent
je mènerai	j'appellerai	je jetterai	je répéterai
je mènerais	j'appellerais	je jetterais	je répéterais

PRESENT SUBJUNCTIVE	IMPERATIVE	REMARKS Verbs similarly conjugated
tienne, –es, –e, tenions, –iez, tiennent	tiens, tenons, tenez	contenir, retenir, appartenir, etc.
vaille, –es, –e, valions, –iez, vaillent	vaux, valons, valez	
vienne, –es, –e, venions, –iez, viennent	viens, venons, venez	devenir, revenir, convenir, parvenir, se souvenir
vive, –es, –e, vivions, –iez, –ent	vis, vivons, vivez	survivre, revivre
voie, –es, –e, voyions, –iez, voient	vois, voyons, voyez	revoir
veuille, –es, –e, voulions, –iez, veuillent	veuille, veuillons, veuillez	

c) Verbs in **–oyer** (e.g. employer, nettoyer) and those in **–uyer** (e.g. ennuyer, appuyer) change **y** to **i** before mute endings.

In the case of **essayer, payer**, etc., the change is optional.

j'emploie	j'appuie	j'essaie or j'essaye, etc.
tu emploies	tu appuies	
il emploie	il appuie	
nous employons	nous appuyons	
vous employez	vous appuyez	
ils emploient	ils appuient	
j'emploierai	j'appuierai	
j'emploierais	j'appuierais	

Index to the Grammar

Vocabulary

(Abbreviations: s.o. = someone; qn = *quelqu'un*)

a
to **abandon,** abandonner
ablaze with, étincelant de, enflammé de
able, to be, pouvoir
aboard; to get (take) aboard, embarquer; **to get aboard,** s'embarquer, monter
abominable, abominable
about (= *approximately*), environ, à peu près; **about 3 o'clock,** vers 3 heures; **about** (= *concerning*), au sujet de, à propos de; **I know nothing about football,** je n'entends rien au football, je ne sais rien du football; **about** (= *round*), à l'entour; **to be about to do,** être sur le point de faire, aller faire
above, au-dessus de; **above all,** surtout
abroad, à l'étranger
absence, l'absence (*f.*)
absolute, absolu; **absolutely,** absolument
absurd, absurde
accent, un accent
to **accept,** accepter
accident, un accident
to **accompany,** accompagner
accomplice, le complice
according to, selon; **accordingly,** donc
account, le compte; **to take account of,** tenir compte de; **on account of,** à cause de
to **accuse,** accuser
accustomed; to get accustomed to, s'accoutumer à, s'habituer à
acquaintance, la connaissance
across, à travers; **to come (go) across,** traverser
to **act,** agir (*conj. like* finir)
activity, une activité

actually, à vrai dire; effectivement
to **add,** ajouter
address, une adresse
adequate, suffisant
administrative, administratif
to **admit,** admettre
advantage; to take advantage of, profiter de
adventure, une aventure
to **advise s.o. to (do),** conseiller à qn de (faire)
affair, une affaire; **it's my affair,** cela me regarde
affectation, l'affectation (*f.*), l'afféterie (*f.*)
affected, affecté, ému
to **afford to (do),** avoir les moyens de (faire), être en mesure de (faire)
afraid; to be afraid, avoir peur, craindre; **to be very much afraid,** avoir bien peur, avoir grand'peur
after, après; **afterwards,** après, par la suite; **after a few minutes,** au bout de quelques minutes
afternoon, un(e) après-midi
again, de nouveau; **again and again,** à plusieurs reprises
against, contre
age, l'âge; (= *period*) le siècle; **of age,** majeur
agility, l'agilité (*f.*)
agitation, l'agitation (*f.*)
ago; a month ago, il y a un mois; **long ago,** depuis longtemps
agony, l'angoisse (*f.*)
to **agree,** être d'accord; **to agree to,** approuver, accepter, consentir à; **it is agreed,** c'est convenu; **to agree on,** convenir (de)
ahead of, en avant de; devant

air, l'air (m.)

alarm, l'alarme (f.); (signal) l'alerte (f.); **to alarm,** alarmer, effràyer

Algerian, algérien

alight, allumé

alive, vivant; **to be alive with,** fourmiller de; être animé de

almost, presque; **I almost protested,** je faillis protester

alone, (tout) seul; **to leave alone,** laisser tranquille

along, le long de; **to walk along the street,** marcher dans la rue, longer la rue

alongside (boats), le long du bord

alpaca, l'alpaga (m.)

Alsatian, alsacien

altar, un autel

although, quoique, bien que (+ subj.)

amazement, l'étonnement (m.); **in amazement,** étonné, avec étonnement

ambitious, ambitieux

ambulance, une ambulance

an American, un(e) Américain(e)

amiable, aimable

amidst, au milieu de

among, parmi, entre

amount, la quantité

amusing, amusant, drôle

anchor, une ancre; **to cast anchor,** mouiller l'ancre

ancient, ancien, –ienne

angelus, l'angélus (m.)

anger, la colère; **in anger,** en colère; **to make angry,** mettre en colère, fâcher

angry, irrité

animal, un animal, une bête

to announce, annoncer

annoyed, fâché, ennuyé, vexé, contrarié; **to get annoyed,** se fâcher

another, un(e) autre

to answer, répondre

to anticipate, prévoir

anyway, de toute façon, en tout cas

anywhere; not . . . anywhere, ne . . . nulle part; **anywhere else,** ailleurs

anxious, anxieux; **to be anxious to (do),** tenir à (faire); **anxiously,** anxieusement, avec inquiétude

apart, à part; à l'écart

apartment, un appartement

aperitive, un apéritif

to apologize, s'excuser, faire des excuses

apparatus, les appareils (m.)

to appear, paraître; **it appears,** il paraît

to applaud, applaudir (conj. like finir)

appointed (= fitted), aménagé; (= agreed) convenu

appointment, le rendez-vous

to approach, s'approcher (de); (= simply to draw near) approcher (de)

to approve, approuver

apron, le tablier

archway, une arche

to argue, discuter

argument, la discussion

arm, le bras

armchair, le fauteuil

armed, armé

army, une armée

around, autour de; **I looked around,** je regardai autour de moi

to arrange to (do), s'arranger pour (faire)

to arrest, arrêter

arrival, l'arrivée (f.); **on arrival,** à l'arrivée

art, l'art (m.)

artesian, artésien

article, un article

artificial, artificiel, –ielle

artisan, un artisan

artist, un(e) artiste; (= painter) le peintre

as, comme; **as to,** quant à; **as for you,** quant à vous; **as soon as,** dès que, aussitôt que; **as though,** comme si; **as though perplexed,** comme perplexe

ascent, une ascension

to ascertain, s'assurer, constater
ashamed, honteux; to be
   ashamed, avoir honte
aside; to move aside, écarter.
to ask, demander; (= to beg,
   request) prier; to ask a
   question, poser une question;
   to ask about, s'informer de;
   to ask s.o. to (do), demander
   à qn de (faire); to ask to (see),
   demander à (voir)
askew, de travers
asleep; to be asleep, dormir;
   to fall asleep, s'endormir; to
   go to sleep again, se
   rendormir; asleep, endormi
ass, un âne
assailant, un agresseur
to assert, affirmer, prétendre (conj.
   like vendre)
to assess, évaluer
to astonish, étonner
atmosphere, une atmosphère
to attach, attacher
to attack, attaquer, s'attaquer à
to attempt to (do), tenter de
   (faire); attempt, la tentative
to attend (= be present), assister (à);
   to attend to, s'occuper de,
   s'appliquer à, s'intéresser à
attention, l'attention (f.); to
   pay attention, faire attention
attentive, attentif; attentively,
   attentivement
attic, la mansarde
to attract, attirer
attractive, attrayant
audience, l'assistance (f.)
authentic, authentique
authorities, les autorités (f.)
avenue, une avenue
to avoid, éviter
to awake, se réveiller, s'éveiller;
   awake, réveillé; to awaken,
   réveiller
aware; to be aware of, avoir
   conscience de, être conscient de
away (= absent), absent; away
   there, là-bas; 10 metres
   away, à 10 mètres; to give
   away (= denounce), dénoncer;
   to go (get) away, s'en aller;

to look away, détourner la
   tête; to move (walk) away,
   s'éloigner
awful, affreux, terrible
awhile, un moment
awning, la tente

b

baby, le bébé
back, le dos; (of a vehicle)
   l'arrière (m.); back garden,
   le jardin de derrière; at the
   back (of), au fond (de); to
   call back, rappeler; to get
   back into, rentrer dans; to get
   back home, rentrer à la maison;
   to get back (= repossess),
   reprendre, reprendre
   possession de; to put back,
   remettre
backbone, l'échine (f.); la
   grande arête
backwards; to lean
   backwards, se pencher en
   arrière, se renverser
bad, mauvais
badly, mal; things are going
   badly with us, les choses
   vont (tournent) mal pour
   nous
bag, le sac
baggage, les bagages (m.)
bait, l'appât (m.)
baked, cuit
balcony, le balcon
ballast, le lest
band (= strip), la bande
bang, la détonation
bank (of river), la rive, (high)
   la berge; bank (= slope), le
   talus
bank (money), la banque; to go
   bankrupt, faire faillite
bar, le bar
to bar, barrer
barely, à peine
to bark, aboyer
barn, la grange
barrister, un avocat
basking, chauffé
bathed in, baigné de

bathing costume, le costume (le maillot) de bain

baton, le bâton

battered, exténué

battle, la bataille

beach, la plage

bean; I haven't a bean left, il ne me reste plus un sou

to **bear,** porter

beard, la barbe

beast, la bête; **the king of beasts,** le roi des animaux

to **beat,** battre

beautiful, beau, *f.* belle

beauty, la beauté

because, parce que; **because of,** à cause de

to **beckon,** faire signe à

to **become,** devenir; **what has become of him?** qu'est-il devenu?

bed, le lit; **to go to bed,** se coucher; **to go back to bed,** se recoucher; **bedroom,** la chambre

beer, la bière

before (*position*), devant; (*time or order*) avant; **before** (*adv.*), avant, auparavant; **before (doing),** avant de (faire)

to **begin to (do),** commencer à (faire), se mettre à (faire); **to begin again,** recommencer

beginning, le commencement

to **behave,** se conduire, se comporter

to **believe,** croire; **I can't believe my eyes,** je ne peux pas en croire mes yeux

bell (*church*), la cloche; (*office, etc.*) le timbre; **phone bell,** la sonnerie du téléphone; **to ring the bell,** sonner

to **belong to,** appartenir à; faire partie de

below (*adv.*), au-dessous; (*prep.*) au-dessous de; **below** (= *under*), sous; **down below,** en bas

bench, le banc

to **bend,** se courber

beside, à côté de; (= *in addition to*) outre, en plus de

besides, d'ailleurs

best (*adj.*), le meilleur; (*adv.*) le mieux; **to do one's best,** faire de son mieux

to **betray,** trahir (*conj. like* finir)

better (*adv.*), mieux; **are you better?** allez-vous mieux? **it is better (to do),** il vaut mieux (faire); **it is better that . . . ,** il vaut mieux que + *subj.*; **you had better stay,** vous feriez mieux de rester

between, entre

bewildered, stupéfait, interdit

beyond, au delà de

bicycle, la bicyclette; **on a bicycle,** à bicyclette, en bicyclette

big, gros, *f.* grosse; important

bird, un oiseau

a **bit** (= *a little*), un peu; **a bit of paper,** un bout de papier

black, noir

blade, la lame; (*of spade*) le fer

to **blame,** blâmer

to **blaze,** flamber

bleary, trouble

bless my soul! nom d'une pipe! tiens, tiens, tiens!

block (*of houses*), le pâté de maisons

blood, le sang

blow, le coup

to **blow,** souffler; **blown in,** défoncé

blue, bleu, *pl.* bleus

bluntly, carrément, sans ménagements

boat, le bateau

body, le corps; (*dead*) le cadavre

to **bog down,** enliser

bomb, la bombe

bone, un os

bonnet; winged bonnet, la cornette

to **book,** retenir

boots (= *top boots*), les bottes (*f.*)

bored, ennuyé; **to be bored,** s'ennuyer

to borrow, emprunter
boss, le patron
both, tous (les) deux, f. toutes
  (les) deux
to bother (oneself), se déranger;
  to bother about, se soucier
  de, s'occuper de; to bother
  to (do), se donner la peine
  de (faire)
bottle, la bouteille
bottom, le fond; at the bottom,
  au fond; bottom (= foot),
  le pied, le bas
boulevard, le boulevard
to bound (along), bondir (conj.
  like finir)
bound to (do), obligé de (faire)
boundary, la limite; la
  frontière, la ligne de
  démarcation
box, la boîte
boy, le garçon; (in school) un
  élève
brains; he has no brains, il
  n'a pas d'intelligence, il
  manque d'intelligence
brave, courageux
to break, briser; rompre; (bones)
  casser; (of waves) se briser;
  to break in (= interrupt),
  interrompre; to break out,
  éclater; to break the law,
  enfreindre la loi
breaker (of law, etc.), le
  violateur
breast-pocket, la poche de
  poitrine
breath, l'haleine (f.), le souffle;
  la respiration; out of breath,
  essoufflé
to breathe, respirer; to breathe
  hard, respirer avec force
breathing, la respiration; deep
  breathing, la respiration
  forte (bruyante)
Breton, breton, f. bretonne
brick, la brique
bridge, le pont
brief, bref, f. brève; briefly,
  brièvement; briefness, la
  brièveté
bright, clair; (colour) vif, f. vive

brightened with, égayé de
brilliance, l'éclat (m.); le
  brillant
brilliant, brillant
to bring (thing), apporter,
  (person) amener; to bring
  back, ramener; to bring in
  (person), faire entrer,
  introduire; to bring in
  (fish), ramener
Brittany, la Bretagne
broad, large
brook, le ruisseau
brother-in-law, le beau-frère
brow, le front
brown, brun; brown shoes,
  les souliers jaunes
brush (artist's), le pinceau
buffet, le buffet
to build, bâtir, construire
  building, le bâtiment, un
  édifice; (= shack, wooden
  building) la bâtisse
bullet, la balle
to bump, buter, battre
burglar, le cambrioleur
to burn, brûler
to burst (out), éclater; to burst
  out laughing, éclater de rire
to bury, enterrer
bush, le buisson
business, les affaires (f.);
  (= piece of business) une
  affaire; (= occupation)
  l'occupation; it is not my
  business, cela ne me regarde
  pas; mind your own
  business, mêlez-vous de ce
  qui vous regarde
bust, le corsage
busy (doing), occupé à (faire);
  to be busy with, s'occuper de
but for, sans
butcher's (shop), la
  boucherie
butler, le maître d'hotel
to buy, acheter
by, par; (= near) près de;
  (= on the edge of) au bord
  de; to go by, passer; by the
  way, à propos
byre, une étable

C

cabin, la cabine
café-restaurant, le
  café-restaurant
to calculate, calculer
to call, appeler; to call back,
  rappeler; to call out, crier;
  to call for, faire apporter; to
  call on, rendre visite à
calm, calme; calmly,
  calmement, avec calme,
  tranquillement
camp, le camp; camp-stool,
  le pliant; to camp, camper;
  camper, le campeur
Canada, le Canada
candle, la bougie
canvas, la toile
capable, capable
capital (city), la capitale;
  (money) les capitaux (m.)
to capsize, chavirer
captain, le capitaine
car, la voiture; car park, le
  parking, le parc à voitures,
  le parc pour autos
carcase, la carcasse
card, la carte; to play cards,
  jouer aux cartes
care, le soin; to take care,
  prendre garde
careful, attentif; soigneux;
  to be careful, prendre garde,
  faire attention; carefully,
  soigneusement
carpet, le tapis; carpeted
  with, tapissé de
to carry, porter; to carry off,
  emporter; to carry out,
  accomplir, commettre;
  (instructions) suivre, exécuter;
  (business) traiter, négocier
case, le cas; (= suitcase) la valise;
  (for instruments, etc.) un étui;
  in that case, en ce cas
casino, le casino
to cast, lancer; to cast anchor,
  mouiller l'ancre
castle, le château
catarrh, le catarrhe
to catch, attraper, prendre; to
  catch sight of, apercevoir,

aviser; to catch in,
  accrocher
cathedral, la cathédrale
cautiously, avec précaution
ceiling, le plafond; la voûte
to celebrate, célébrer, fêter
centre, le centre
century, le siècle
ceremony, la cérémonie
certain, certain; certainly,
  certainement
chain, la chaîne
chair, la chaise
to challenge, défier; to challenge
  someone to a duel, défier
  (provoquer) qn en duel
chambermaid, la femme de
  chambre
chance, une occasion; the
  chance comes, l'occasion se
  présente; by (any) chance,
  par hasard
chancel, le chœur, le sanctuaire
to change, changer; I change my
  shoes, je change de souliers
chap, l'homme, le garçon;
  (slang) le type; old chap,
  mon vieux
to charge (money), prendre; to
  charge out of, s'élancer
  (bondir) hors de; to take
  charge of, se charger de
charm, le charme; to charm,
  charmer; charming, charmant
to chase, poursuivre
to chat, causer, bavarder
to chatter (away), bavarder,
  jacasser
cheap, bon marché
to cheat, tricher
cheek, la joue
cheerful, heureux, allègre;
  cheerfulness, la gaieté
cheese, le fromage
chemist, le pharmacien
cheque, le chèque
chestnut tree, le châtaignier
chicken (small), le poussin;
  (larger) le poulet
chief, le chef; chief inspector,
  le commissaire
childhood, l'enfance (f.)

chilly, frais, *f.* fraîche; froid
chin, le menton
choir, le chœur
to choose, choisir
in chorus, en chœur
to christen, baptiser;
    christening, le baptême
Christmas, (la) Noël
church, une église
cigarette, la cigarette
circus, le cirque
to cite, citer
to claim (to do), prétendre (faire)
to clamber, grimper
clap of thunder, le coup de
    tonnerre
class, la classe; classroom,
    la salle de classe
clatteringly, bruyamment,
    avec bruit
clear, clair; clearly,
    clairement; (= *sharply*)
    nettement
clever, intelligent, habile
client, le client
cliff, la falaise
to climb, grimper; (= *to walk
    up*) gravir (*conj. like*
    finir), monter; to climb
    over, escalader, franchir
    (*conj. like* finir)
climb (= *ascent*), une ascension;
    climber, un alpiniste, un
    ascensionniste
cloakroom, le vestiaire
clock, une horloge
to close, fermer; to close again,
    refermer; closed door, la
    porte close; half-closed,
    mi-clos, à demi fermé; at
    close quarters, de près;
    closely, de près; (*leaving no
    space*) étroitement; close
    (= *end*), la fin
cloth (*for bags, etc.*), la toile;
    (= *table cloth*) la nappe
clothes, les habits (*m.*), le(s)
    vêtement(s); l'habillement (*m.*)
cloud, le nuage; (*of things*)
    la nuée
clumsy, maladroit
coarse, grossier

coast, la côte
coat (= *jacket*), le veston;
    (*overcoat*) le pardessus;
    (*woman's*) le manteau
coffee, le café
coin, la pièce de monnaie
cold, froid; coldly, froidement;
    cold (*ailment*), le rhume
colleague, le collègue
to collect (= *get*), prendre
to collide, entrer en collision
colonel, le colonel
colour, la couleur; coloured,
    de couleur
combatant, le combattant
to come, venir; to come back,
    revenir; to come in, entrer;
    to come out, sortir; to come
    up, monter; (= *approach*)
    s'approcher; to come down,
    descendre; to come down
    again, redescendre; to come
    along, arriver; to come and
    go, aller et venir; come now!
    allons! voyons!
comely, beau, *f.* belle; joli
comfortable (*thing*), confortable;
    (*of persons*) à l'aise, à son aise
to commandeer, réquisitionner
to communicate, communiquer
companion, le compagnon, *f.*
    la compagne
company, la compagnie
compartment, le compartiment
to complain (about), se plaindre (de)
complete, complet, *f.* complète
complexion, le teint
to complicate, compliquer;
    complicated, compliqué
complicity, la complicité
to conceal, cacher
concentration, la concentration,
    l'attention (*f.*)
conception, la conception;
    une idée, la notion
to concern, concerner; regarder
concert, le concert
condition, la condition;
    (= *state*) un état
conductor (*music*), le chef
    d'orchestre
cone-shaped, en forme de cône

to **confess**, avouer
confessor, le confesseur
confidence, la confiance; **in confidence**, en confidence
confusion, la confusion
congenial, sympathique
congregation, l'assistance (*f.*)
conscience, la conscience
conscious; **he is not conscious**, il n'a plus sa connaissance; il a perdu connaissance
to **consider**, considérer; envisager
to **console**, consoler
constable, un agent (de police)
constancy, la constance
constant, constant, continuel; **constantly**, constamment
construction, la construction
consul-general, le consul-général
to **consult**, consulter
consulting-room, le cabinet de consultation
to **consume**, consumer
contact, le contact; (*person*) la relation
to **contain**, contenir
contempt, le mépris
contentment, le contentement
to **continue**, continuer
in control of, maître de
convent, le couvent
conversation, la conversation; **to make conversation**, entretenir la conversation
convinced, convaincu
conviction, la conviction
to **cook**, faire cuire
copy (*of book*), un exemplaire
cordiality, la cordialité
to **cork**, boucher
corn, le blé
corner, le coin; **to corner** (*a person*), acculer
to **correct**, corriger
corridor, le couloir, le corridor
corruption, la corruption
cost, le prix
cottage, la chaumière
councillor; **city councillor**, le conseiller municipal

counsel, le conseil
to **count**, compter
countless, innombrable, sans nombre
country, le pays; **countryside**, la campagne; **(fellow) countryman**, le compatriote
couple, le couple
courage, le courage
of course, bien entendu, évidemment, naturellement; **of course!** parbleu! bien sûr! **of course not!** bien sûr que non! **in the course of**, au cours de
to **court**, faire la cour à
court, le tribunal; **courtroom**, le tribunal, la salle d'audience
cousin, le cousin
to **cover**, couvrir (*conj. like* ouvrir); **covered with**, couvert de
cow, la vache
crack, la fente
cradle, le berceau
crammed with, bondé de
cramp, la crampe
crane, la grue
to **crawl**, se traîner
to **creak**, craquer, émettre un craquement
creature, la bête
crime, le crime
crimson, cramoisi
crook, un escroc, le gredin
to **cross**, traverser
crossroads, le carrefour
crowd, la foule; **crowded**, bondé (de monde)
crown, la couronne
cruel, cruel, *f.* cruelle
crumb, la miette (de pain)
to **cry** (= *weep*), pleurer
cuff; **to give someone a cuff**, flanquer une taloche à qn
cup, la tasse; **the World Cup**, la Coupe du Monde
curiosity, la curiosité
curious, curieux, bizarre, singulier
current, le courant

to curse, jurer
curtain, le rideau
curtly, sèchement
customary; it is customary
to, il est de coutume de
customer, le client
Customs officer, le douanier
to cut, couper; he cut me short,
il me coupa la parole

d

daily, tous les jours,
quotidiennement
to damage, endommager
damp, humide
to dance, danser; dance, la danse;
dancing room, la salle de
danse; dancer, le danseur
danger, le danger; in danger,
en danger; dangerous,
dangereux, périlleux
to dare (to do), oser (faire)
dark, noir, sombre; it is dark
(gloomy), il fait sombre; it
is dark (night), il fait nuit, il
fait noir; it is very (quite)
dark, il fait nuit noire
to darken, grow dark,
s'assombrir (conj. like finir)
darkness, dark (= night),
l'obscurité (f.), la nuit
darling, chéri(e)
dash, la fougue; to dash off,
partir précipitamment; to
make a dash for, s'élancer
vers
to date, dater
daughter, la fille
dawn, l'aube (f.)
day, le jour; day after day,
jour après jour; daybreak,
le point du jour, l'aube (f.);
daylight, le jour; it is day
(daylight), il fait jour; all
day long, toute la journée,
tout le long du jour; in his
day, de son temps, de son
vivant; day off, le jour de
congé
dead, mort

deal; to (have to) deal with,
to have dealings with,
avoir affaire à
death, la mort
debt, la dette
to decapitate, décapiter
to decide to (do), décider de
(faire)
decisive, décisif
to decorate, orner, décorer
deep, profound; deeply,
profondément; deep down,
au fond; the deep (sea),
l'abîme (f.)
defeat, la défaite; to defeat,
vaincre
defence, la défense
to defend, défendre (conj. like
vendre)
deferentially, avec déférence,
d'un ton de déférence
defiance, le défi
dejected, abattu, découragé
to delay (= put things off),
différer les choses
delicate, délicat
delighted, enchanté, ravi
delightful, délicieux
den, un antre, la tanière
to denounce, dénoncer
to depart, partir
department (administrative),
le service
departure, le départ
to depend on, dépendre de
to deposit, déposer, consigner
depressed, triste, abattu
depth, la profondeur
to descend, descendre
to describe, décrire
deserted, désert
desire, le désir, une envie
desk, le bureau; (school) le
pupitre
despair, le désespoir
to despise, mépriser
despite, malgré
destination, la destination
to determine to (do), résoudre
de (faire); p. hist. je résolus;
determined to, résolu à,
décidé à

to **detest**, détester
detour, le détour
to **develop**, se développer
devil take it! que le diable
  l'emporte!
to **devote**, consacrer
devotion, le dévouement
to **dictate**, dicter
dictionary, le dictionnaire
to **die**, mourir
difference, la différence;
  different, différent
difficult, difficile; **difficulty**,
  la difficulté; la peine
to **dig**, creuser; **to dig in**, enfoncer
dim (*light*), faible; **dimly**,
  vaguement
din, le tapage, le vacarme
dinner, le dîner
direction, la direction, le sens;
  in the direction of, du côté
  de; **in that direction**, de ce
  côté; **directions**
  (= *instructions*), les indications,
  les instructions
director, le directeur
dirty, sale
to **disappear**, disparaître
to **disappoint**, décevoir (*conj like*
  recevoir); **disappointed**, déçu;
  disappointment, la déception
disapproving, désapprobateur,
  f. –trice
disarrangement, le dérangement
discernment, le discernement
discipline, la discipline
discontent, le mécontentement
to **discover**, découvrir (*conj. like*
  ouvrir)
discovery, la découverte
discreet, discret, *f*. –ète
to **discuss**, discuter
dishevelled, débraillé
dishonest, malhonnête;
  dishonesty, la malhonnêteté
to **dismiss**, renvoyer, congédier
to **dismount**, mettre pied à terre
to **dispatch**, achever, donner le
  coup de grâce à
to **dispense with**, se passer de
to **disperse**, se disperser
to **displease**, déplaire (à)

dissatisfied (with), mécontent
  (de)
distance, la distance;
  (= *distant view*) le lointain;
  distant, lointain
distinctly, distinctement
distress, la détresse,
  l'angoisse (*f*.)
to **distribute**, distribuer
district, le pays, la région; (*of a
  town*) le quartier
distrust, la méfiance; **to
  distrust**, se méfier de
to **disturb**, déranger; (*sleep,
  silence*) troubler
ditch, le fossé
to **dive**, plonger
to **divide**, diviser; séparer
doctor, le médecin; le docteur
to **dominate**, dominer
donkey, un âne
to **doom**, condamner
door, la porte; (*of vehicle*)
  la portière; **front door**,
  la porte d'entrée; **next door**,
  à côté; **doorway**, l'encadrement
  de la porte
doubt, le doute; **no doubt**,
  doubtless, sans doute
dough, la galette
down below, en bas; **down
  there**, là-bas; **to go
  downstairs**, descendre;
  downcast, baissé
to **doze off**, s'assoupir (*conj. like*
  finir)
dozen, la douzaine; **half a
  dozen**, la demi-douzaine
to **drag**, tirer, traîner; **to drag
  away**, entraîner
to **draw**, tirer; (= *attract*) attirer;
  to draw (*art*), dessiner
drawer, le tiroir
drawing-room, le salon
dreadful, effroyable
dream, le rêve; **to have a
  dream**, faire un rêve; **to
  dream of (doing)**, songer à
  (faire)
dreary, morne, triste
drenched to the skin, trempé
  jusqu'aux os

dress, la robe
to dress, s'habiller; dressed in,
    habillé de, vêtu de;
    dressing-gown, la robe de
    chambre; dressmaker, le
    couturier, f. la couturière
to drift, flotter; drifting, flottant
to drink, boire; to order a drink,
    commander à boire,
    commander une
    consommation; drinks, la
    boisson
to drive, conduire; (= to chase)
    chasser; to drive on (= urge),
    pousser; to drive out,
    chasser; to drive past,
    dépasser; to drive round,
    faire le tour de; to drive
    through, traverser; what are
    you driving at? où
    voulez-vous en venir?
    driver, le chauffeur
to drop, laisser tomber; to drop
    (from a car), déposer; to drop
    off to sleep, s'endormir
    drowned; to be (get) drowned,
    se noyer
    drowsy, assoupi, somnolent;
    engourdi
    drunk, ivre
    dry, sec, f. sèche; to dry
    oneself, se sécher
    duel, le duel; duelling, le duel
    duke, le duc
    dull (sound), sourd
    dumbfounded, stupéfait,
    interdit
    dune, la dune
    during, pendant
    dust, la poussière; dustbin,
    la poubelle
    duty, le devoir; on duty,
    de service
    dwarf, le nain
    dying, mourant

e

    each (adj.) chaque; (pron.)
    chacun(e)
    ear, une oreille; ear-splitting,
    à fendre l'oreille

    early (adv.), de bonne heure,
    tôt; early (adj.), premier;
    earlier, plus tôt
to earn, gagner
    earnest, sérieux
    earth, la terre, le sol
    easel, le chevalet
    Easter, Pâques
    easy, facile; aisé; easily,
    facilement, aisément; to take
    things easy (easily), prendre
    les choses en douceur
to eat, manger
    eavesdropper, l'écouteur
    (f. l'écouteuse) aux portes;
    l'indiscret, l'indiscrète
    edge, le bord; at the edge of,
    au bord de
    effort, un effort
    egg, un œuf
on either side, de chaque côté,
    des deux côtés, de part et
    d'autre
to elect, élire (conj. like lire);
    elected, élu
    electrical, électrique
    elephant, un éléphant
or else, ou bien; nobody else,
    personne d'autre;
    elsewhere, ailleurs
    embarrassed, gêné
to emerge, émerger
    empty, vide; to empty, vider
to enable, permettre
to encounter, rencontrer
to encourage, encourager
to encumber oneself with,
    s'encombrer de
    end, la fin; (of a thing) le bout;
    at the far end, au fond;
    in the end, à la fin; to put
    an end to, mettre fin à; to
    end up, aboutir (conj. like
    finir); endless, interminable,
    sans fin
    engaged, fiancé
    engine, le moteur
    English, anglais; Englishman,
    un Anglais
to enjoy (life, etc.), jouir de; to
    enjoy oneself, s'amuser
    enormous, énorme

enough, assez; **it is enough to,** il suffit de; **we've had enough of it,** nous en avons assez

enquiring, interrogateur

to **ensure,** assurer

enthusiasm, l'enthousiasme (*m.*); **enthusiastic,** enthousiaste

envious, envieux

errand, la commission, la course

escutcheon, un écusson

especially, surtout

essential, essentiel, *f.* –elle; **essentially,** essentiellement

establishment, un établissement

estate, le domaine, la propriété

to **esteem,** estimer

eve, la veille

even, même

evening, le soir; la soirée; **evening clothes,** la tenue de soirée

event, un événement

eventually, enfin

ever, jamais; **ever-increasing,** sans cesse croissant, toujours croissant

everybody, tout le monde; **every month,** tous les mois, chaque mois; **everything,** tout; **everywhere,** partout

evidence; to give evidence, témoigner, déposer

evident, évident; **evidently,** évidemment

exactly, exactement

examination, un examen; to **examine,** examiner; **examiner,** un examinateur

to **exasperate,** exaspérer; **exasperation,** l'exaspération (*f.*)

excellent, excellent

except, sauf, excepté; **except for,** sans

exception, une exception

excessive, excessif; **excessively,** excessivement

to **exchange,** échanger, troquer (On troque une chose contre une autre)

excitedly, avec animation

excitement, l'émoi (*m.*)

to **exclaim,** s'écrier, s'exclamer

excursion, une excursion

excuse me! pardon!

to **exert,** exercer

exhausted, épuisé

to **exhibit,** exhiber, exposer

exhibition, une exposition

to **exist,** exister

existence, l'existence (*f.*)

exit, la sortie

to **expect,** attendre; s'attendre à

expedition, une expédition

experience, une expérience

to **explain,** expliquer

explanation, une explication

to **explode,** éclater

exploit, un exploit

to **explore,** explorer; **explorer,** un explorateur

to **expose,** exposer, révéler

expression, une expression; **expressionless,** sans expression, impassible

extent, une étendue; **to some extent,** dans une certaine mesure

extermination, l'extermination (*f.*)

extraordinary, extraordinaire

eye, un œil, *pl.* des yeux; **to look s.o. in the eye,** regarder qn dans les yeux; **eyebrow,** le sourcil; **eyelid,** la paupière

f

face, le visage, la figure; **north face,** la face nord

to **face,** affronter, envisager

fact, le fait; **in fact,** en effet, à vrai dire; **as a matter of fact,** à vrai dire

factory, une usine

to **fade away** (= *diminish*), diminuer, s'affaiblir

to **fail,** échouer; **to fail to (do),** manquer de (faire)

faint (*sound*), faible

to **faint**, s'évanouir (*conj. like* finir)
fair, blond
fairly, assez
faith, la foi
fake, faux, *f.* fausse
to **fall**, tomber; **to fall back**, retomber
familiar, familier; **familiarly**, familièrement
family, la famille
famous, célèbre, fameux
far (off), loin; **not far (off)**, non loin; **far** (*adj.*), (le plus) éloigné, (le plus) reculé; **far away** (*adj.*), lointain; **far end**, le fond; **as far as I know**, autant que je sache
farmer, le fermier, le paysan
fast, vite, rapidement
fat, gras, *f.* grasse
father-in-law, le beau-père
fault (= *failing*), le défaut
favourite, préféré, favori
fear, la peur, la crainte; **to fear**, avoir peur, craindre
feature, le trait
to **feel**, sentir; (= *experience*), éprouver, ressentir; **to feel (sad)**, se sentir (triste); **to feel like (doing), to feel inclined to (do)**, avoir envie de (faire); **to feel for (something)**, tâter (quelque chose), fouiller pour trouver (quelque chose)
fees, les honoraires (*m.*)
to **fell**, abattre, couper
fellow, le garçon; l'homme; **fellow traveller**, le compagnon de voyage
female companion, la compagne
fencing, l'escrime (*f.*)
to **fetch, to go and fetch**, aller chercher; **to come and fetch**, venir chercher
a **few**, quelques; **quite a few**, bon nombre de; **not a few of**, bon nombre de
field, le champ
fight, le combat; **to fight**, se battre; **to fight against**, combattre

figure (= *form*), la silhouette
to **fill**, remplir (*conj. like* finir); (*pipe*) bourrer; **filled with**, rempli de
to **filter**, tamiser
finally, enfin, à la fin
financially, au point de vue financier
to **find**, trouver; **to find out**, apprendre, découvrir
to **finish**, finir; achever, terminer; **to finish (doing)**, finir de (faire)
Finland, la Finlande
fire, le feu; **to catch fire**, prendre feu; **to fire** (*with a weapon*), tirer; **to fire at**, tirer sur; **to fire** (= *dismiss*), mettre à la porte; **fireman**, le pompier
firm, la maison, la firme
first (*adj*), premier; **first floor**, le premier (étage); **at first, first of all**, d'abord
fish, le poisson; **to fish**, pêcher; **to go fishing**, aller à la pêche; **fisherman**, le pêcheur
to **fit** (*tyres, etc.*), poser
to **fix**, fixer
flake, le flocon
flanked by, flanqué de
flash, un éclat; **flash of lightning**, un éclair
flat, un appartement
flat-heeled shoes, des souliers plats
to **flatter**, flatter; **flattering**, flatteur
to **flee**, s'enfuir (*conj. like* fuir)
flickering, vacillant
flooded with, baigné de
floor (= *storey*), un étage
florid, fleuri, rubicond
to **flow**, couler; **to flow** (= *drift*) **away**, flotter au loin, se dissiper au loin
flower, la fleur
to **fold** (*arms*), croiser; **fold**, le pli
folk, les gens
to **follow**, suivre; **following**, suivant; **the following day**, le lendemain

food, la nourriture; **to give food,** donner à manger
fool, un imbécile
foot, le pied; **to rise (get) to one's feet,** se mettre debout; **to set foot in,** mettre les pieds dans; **footpath,** le sentier; **footwear,** les chaussures (*f.*)
for (*prep.*), pour; (*conj.*) car; (= *during*) pendant; (= *since*) depuis
to forbid s.o. to (do), défendre à qn de (faire); **forbidden,** défendu
force, la force; **to force to (do),** forcer à faire
forehead, le front
foreigner, un étranger, une étrangère
to foresee, prévoir
foreshore, le rivage, la plage
forest, la forêt
to forget, oublier
to forgive, pardonner (à)
to fork (*of roads*), bifurquer
formerly, autrefois
fortnight, quinze jours
fortune, la fortune; **to make a fortune,** faire fortune
forward; to move forward, s'avancer
fragile, fragile
frank, franc, *f.* franche; **frankness,** la franchise
free, libre; (= *unpaid*) gratuit; **to free,** libérer
French (*adj.*), français; (*language*) le français; **in French,** en français; **Frenchman,** le Français; **the French (people),** les Français
fresh, frais, *f.* fraîche
friend, un(e) ami(e); **friendly** (*tone, etc.*), amical; **friendly** (*person*), aimable, sympathique
fright, la frayeur
to frighten, effrayer; **to be frightened,** avoir peur, être effrayé
frock, la robe
from house to house, de maison en maison

front (*of building*), la façade; **front door,** la porte d'entrée
frontier, la frontière
to frown, froncer les sourcils
frozen, glacé
fugitive, le fugitif
full, plein; (*hotel, compartment, etc.*) complet; **at full speed,** à toute vitesse
fun; to make fun of, se moquer de
fundamentally, foncièrement
funds, les fonds (*m.*), les ressources (*f.*)
funicular, le funiculaire
funny, amusant, drôle
furious (at), furieux (de)
furniture, les meubles (*m.*); **piece of furniture,** un meuble
fury; in a fury, furieux
future, l'avenir (*m.*); **in the future,** à l'avenir

g

gadget, le truc, le machin
gaff, la gaffe; **to gaff,** gaffer
gaily, gaiement, gaîment
to gallop, galoper
garage, le garage
garden, le jardin; **little garden,** le jardinet; **back garden,** le jardin de derrière
gas-cooker, la cuisinière à gaz
gate, la porte; (*iron*) la grille; (*farm, etc.*), la barrière; **gateway,** la porte cochère
to gather (= *assemble*), s'assembler, se réunir (*conj. like* finir); **gathering,** la réunion
gaudy, voyant, criard
gay, gai
to gaze at, dévisager, contempler
gear (= *things*), les affaires (*f.*)
general, le général (*pl.* –aux)
generous, généreux
gently, doucement
German, allemand
gesture, le geste
to get, chercher; (= *obtain*) obtenir, se procurer; **to get**

away, s'en aller; **to get back,** reprendre possession de; **to get into,** entrer dans, pénétrer dans; (*conveyance*) monter dans; **to get married,** se marier; **to get near,** arriver près de; **to get out,** sortir; (*vehicle*) descendre; **to get out a word,** proférer une parole; **to get ready,** préparer; **to get up,** se lever; **to get used to,** s'habituer à; **he is getting on for fifty,** il approche de la cinquantaine

gifts (*abilities*), les capacités (*f.*)

gimlet, la vrille

gipsy, le bohémien, le romanichel

girl, la jeune fille

to give, donner; **to give a cry,** pousser un cri; **to give away** (= *denounce*), dénoncer; **to give back,** rendre; **to give up** (= *yield*), céder; **to give up** (**doing**), renoncer à (faire); **to give way,** s'effondrer.

glad, content; **gladly,** volontiers

to glance, jeter un coup d'œil

to glare at, regarder fixement

glass, le verre

to glide, glisser

glimmer, la lueur

glimpse; to catch a glimpse of, entrevoir

glitter, l'éclat (*m.*); **to glitter,** étinceler, miroiter

gloomy, sombre, morne

glove, le gant

glow, la lueur; **to glow,** briller

glum, morose

to go, aller; (= *depart*) partir; (*cars*) marcher; **to go by** (= *pass*), passer; **to go by** (*time*), s'écouler; **to go down,** descendre; **to go for** (= *attack*), s'attaquer à, s'en prendre à; **to go in,** entrer; **to go off,** partir, s'en aller; **to go on** (= *happen*) se passer; **to go on** (*in speech*), continuer; reprendre; **to go on** (*of lights*), s'allumer; **to go out,** sortir;

to go up, monter; **to go up to** (= *approach*), s'approcher de

goat, la chèvre

gold, l'or (*m.*); **golden,** d'or

good, bon, bonne; (= *worthy, decent*) brave; (= *well-behaved*) sage; **to do good,** faire du bien; **good-looking,** beau, bien

goodbye; to say goodbye, faire ses adieux

goods, la marchandise

government, le gouvernement

to grab, saisir, empoigner

gracious me! mon Dieu!

gradually, peu à peu, graduellement

grammar, la grammaire

grandfather, le grand-père

to grasp, saisir (*conj. like* finir)

grass, l'herbe (*f.*); (= *turf*) le gazon

grateful, reconnaissant

grave, grave; sérieux, sévère

great-grandmother, l'arrière-grand'mère

greedy, avide

green, vert; (= *greenery*) la verdure

to greet, saluer

grey, gris

grimly, sévèrement, sardoniquement

to groan, gémir (*conj. like* finir), geindre (*conj. like* craindre)

grocer, un épicier; **grocer's shop,** une épicerie

to grope, tâtonner; **to grope one's way forward,** avancer à tâtons

ground, le sol; (*piece of ground*) le terrain

group, le groupe; **in groups,** par groupes

to grow darker, s'assombrir; **growing,** croissant

growl, le grognement; **to growl,** grogner; grommeler

growth, la croissance

guard, la garde; **to stand on guard,** monter la garde; **to be on one's guard,** être (se tenir) sur ses gardes

to guess, deviner
guest, un invité
guide, le guide
guilty, coupable

h

habit, une habitude
to hail, héler,
hair, les cheveux (*m.*); **her hair is nicely done,** elle est bien coiffée.
half, la moitié (de); **half a dozen,** une demi-douzaine; **half an hour,** une demi-heure; **half dead,** à demi mort; **half-closed,** mi-clos, à demi fermé; **half open,** entr'ouvert
hall; Town Hall, l'hôtel de ville
hallo! holà! (*on the phone*) **allô!**
to halt, s'arrêter
hamlet, le hameau
hand, la main; **in one's hand,** à la main; **to hold hands,** se tenir par la main; **on the other hand,** d'autre part; **handshake,** la poignée de main
handkerchief, le mouchoir
handsome, beau, *f.* belle
to hang, pendre (*conj. like* vendre); **to hang (hover) over,** planer sur; **to hang out washing,** étendre du linge
to happen, arriver, se passer
happy, heureux; **happiness,** le bonheur
harbour, le port
hard, dur; (= *difficult*) difficile; (= *with vigour*) fort; **hard work,** le travail assidu, la peine; **hard-working,** travailleur; **to work hard,** travailler dur (ferme)
hardly, à peine; ne ... guère
in haste, en hâte
to hasten to (do), se hâter de (faire), s'empresser de (faire); **to hasten up,** accourir
hastily, en hâte
hate, la haine; **of hate,** haineux; **to hate,** détester, haïr

hay fever, la fièvre des foins
head, la tête; **head** (*man*), le chef; **headmaster,** le directeur, le proviseur
health, la santé
to hear, entendre; **to hear of (about),** entendre parler de; **to hear that . . .,** entendre dire que . . .
heart, le cœur.
heat, la chaleur; **heatwave,** la vague de chaleur, la grande chaleur; **to heat,** chauffer
heavens; good heavens! mon Dieu!
heavy, lourd; onéreux; **heavily,** lourdement
hedge, la haie
heel, le talon; **high-heeled shoes,** des souliers à hauts talons; **flat-heeled shoes,** des souliers plats
help, le secours, l'aide (*f.*); **he comes to my help,** il me vient en aide, il vient à mon secours; **to help,** aider; **I can't help laughing,** je ne peux pas m'empêcher de rire; **helplessly,** n'y pouvant rien, impuissant
hen, la poule
here, ici; là; **here and there,** çà et là
to hesitate to (do), hésiter à (faire); **hesitation,** l'hésitation (*f.*)
to hide, (se) cacher
high, haut; **high road,** la grand'route; **High Street,** la rue principale, la grand'rue
hill, la colline; (*on a road*) la côte
to hire, louer; (*persons*) embaucher
history, l'histoire (*f.*); **historic,** historique
to hit, frapper, atteindre (*conj. like* craindre)
hoard, le magot
to hobble, boiter; **to hobble away,** s'en aller en boitant
to hold, tenir; **to hold out,** tendre;

to hold up, lever en l'air, lever à bout de bras

hole, le trou, *pl.* les trous

holiday(s), les vacances (*f.*); **on holiday,** en vacances; **to go on holiday,** partir en vacances

at home, à la maison; chez moi (nous, etc.); **to come (get) home,** rentrer à la maison; **home-coming,** le retour à la maison

honest, honnête

honey-coloured, couleur de miel

honour, l'honneur (*m.*); **in his honneur,** en son honneur

to hook, accrocher

hope, l'espoir (*m.*); **to hope,** espérer

horrible, horrible; **horribly,** horriblement

hospitable, hospitalier

hospital, un hôpital

hostelry, une hôtellerie, une hostellerie

hostess, une hôtesse

hot, (très) chaud

hotel, un hôtel

house, la maison; **to move house,** déménager

how, comment; **how much,** combien; **how are you?** comment allez-vous?

however, cependant, pourtant

howling, les hurlements (*m.*)

hubbub, le brouhaha

huddled, serré, entassé

huge, énorme

hullo! tiens!

hum, le brouhaha

humble, humble

a hundred, cent; **hundreds of,** des centaines de

to hunt, chasser; **to hunt for,** chercher

to hurl, lancer

hurriedly, en hâte

to hurry (up), se dépêcher, se hâter, se presser; **to be in a hurry,** être pressé

to hurt, faire mal à; **hurt,** blessé

husband, le mari

hush, le silence

hypnotic, hypnotique

i

idea, une idée

identity, l'identité

idiotic, idiot, *f.* idiote

ignorant, ignorant

ill, malade; **to speak ill of,** médire de

illusion, une illusion

imaginary, imaginaire

to imagine, s'imaginer, se figurer

to imitate, imiter

immaterial, immatériel

immediately, immédiatement, aussitôt, tout de suite

immensely, immensément, énormément

impatient, impatient; **to be impatient,** s'impatienter; **impatiently,** avec impatience

imperial, impérial

imperturbable, imperturbable

impolite, impoli

importance, l'importance (*f.*); **important,** important

impossible, impossible

impression, une impression

impressive, impressionnant

incessantly, sans cesse, incessamment

incident, un incident

inclined; to feel inclined to, avoir envie de

including, y compris

increasingly, de plus en plus

incredible, incroyable

to incriminate, incriminer, inculper

indeed, en effet

indefinite, indéfini

independence, l'indépendance (*f.*)

to indicate, indiquer

indignantly (*adj. normally used*), indigné, e.g. Non! dit-elle, indignée

indistinct, indistinct

individual, un individu

industrial, industriel
inexpensive, peu coûteux, bon
marché, pas cher
infantry, l'infanterie (*f.*);
infantry officer, un officier
d'infanterie
infinite, infini
to **inflict,** infliger
influence, l'influence (*f.*)
to **inform,** informer, renseigner;
information, les
renseignements; (*piece of
information*) le renseignement;
informative, instructif
to **injure,** blesser
inn, une auberge
inside, à l'intérieur; dans
to **insist on (doing),** insister pour
(faire); **to insist that,**
insister pour que
inspector, un inspecteur;
chief inspector, le
commissaire
**instance; in the present
instance,** en l'occurrence, en
cette occasion, dans cette
circonstance
instead of, au lieu de
instruction, l'instruction (*f.*)
instrument, un instrument
to **insult,** insulter
intelligent, intelligent
to **intend to,** avoir l'intention de;
intended to, destiné à; viser à
intense, intense; **intensely,**
intensément
intently, attentivement, avec
attention
**interest; to take interest (be
interested) in,** s'intéresser à;
interesting, intéressant
interruption, une interruption
to **interview,** interviewer
intrigued, intrigué
to **introduce,** présenter
intruder, un intrus
to **invent,** inventer
investigation, une enquête
invisible, invisible
to **invite to (do),** inviter à (faire)
inwardly, intérieurement; en
son for intérieur

iron, le fer; (= *of iron*) de fer
irresolute, irrésolu
irrevocable, irrévocable,
irréparable, irrémédiable
to **irritate,** irriter, agacer
isolated, isolé

j

to **jab,** piquer
jacket, le veston
jealous, jaloux
jerk, la secousse
job, un emploi, une place;
(= *occupation*) le métier;
(= *piece of work*) le travail
to **join,** rejoindre (*conj. like*
craindre); **to join in,** prendre
part à, se mêler à, se mettre
de la partie
joke, la plaisanterie; (*practical*)
la farce; **to joke,** plaisanter
jolly, gai
jolt, la secousse
journalist, le journaliste
journey, le voyage, le trajet
joy, la joie
juice, le jus
to **jump,** sauter; **to jump up,** se
lever d'un bond
jungle, la jungle
just, juste; exactement; **just as,**
(juste) au moment où; **just as
well,** tout aussi bien; **just then,**
juste à ce moment-là; **I have
just seen,** je viens de voir; **I
had just seen,** je venais de
voir
to **justify,** justifier; **that justifies
me in (doing),** cela me
met en droit de (faire)

k

to **keep,** garder; retenir; (*hotel,
shop, etc.*) tenir; **to keep quiet,**
se taire; **to keep up** (=
maintain), entretenir; **to keep
waiting,** faire attendre; **he
can't keep still,** il ne tient
pas en place

kettle, la bouilloire
key, la clef
to kill, tuer
kilometre, le kilomètre
kind, le genre, la sorte, une
  espèce
kindly, bienveillant
king, le roi
to kiss (*a person*), embrasser;
  (*hand, etc.*) baiser
kitchen, la cuisine
knee, le genou (*pl.* –oux); **on
  one's knees,** à genoux; **to
  fall on one's knees,** tomber
  à genoux
to kneel, s'agenouiller, se mettre à
  genoux; **kneeling,** agenouillé,
  à genoux
to knock, frapper; **to knock down,**
  renverser; (*with a blow*)
  assommer; **I hear a knock,**
  j'entends frapper
to know, savoir; (= *be acquainted
  with*) connaître; **to get to
  know,** connaître, faire la
  connaissance de; **well known,**
  (bien) connu
knowledge, la connaissance;
  to have (get) knowledge of,
  avoir connaissance de

L

label, une étiquette
to labour, travailler
ladder, une échelle
laden, chargé
lake, le lac
lamp, la lampe; (*street*) le
  réverbère
land, la terre; **to land** (*of planes*),
  atterrir (*conj. like* finir)
language, la langue
lantern, la lanterne; **dark
  lantern,** la lanterne sourde
to lash, attacher, lier
last, dernier; **at last,** enfin
to last, durer
late, tard; (= *after time*) en
  retard; **later,** plus tard; **it is
  getting late,** il se fait tard
latter, celui-ci, *f.* celle-ci

to laugh, rire; **to laugh at,** se
  moquer de, rire de;
  laughter, le rire
to launch, se lancer
law, la loi; **Law Courts,** le
  palais de justice
lawn, la pelouse
lawyer, un avocat, un homme
  de loi
to lay, poser; (*eggs*) pondre (*conj.
  like* vendre)
laziness, la paresse
to lead, conduire, mener; **to lead
  a life,** mener une vie
to lean, s'appuyer; **to lean back
  against,** s'adosser à; **leaning
  back,** adossé; **to lean
  backwards,** se pencher en
  arrière, se renverser; **to lean
  forward,** se pencher
to leap, sauter, bondir
to learn to (do), apprendre à
  (faire)
leash, la laisse; **on a leash,** en
  laisse
at least (*quantity*), au moins;
  (*reservation*) du moins
to leave (*a place*), quitter, partir
  de; (= *depart*) partir;
  (= *forsake*) délaisser,
  abandonner; **to leave alone,**
  laisser tranquille; **to leave
  out,** exclure (*p. part.* exclu),
  omettre
ledge, le rebord
left, gauche; **to the left,** à
  gauche
left; **there is nothing left,** il
  ne reste plus rien
leg, la jambe
leisure, les loisirs (*m.*)
to lend, prêter
length; **at full length,** de tout
  son long
less, moins
to let, laisser, permettre; **to let out
  (a cry),** pousser (un cri)
letter, la lettre
to levy (*taxes*), prélever, percevoir
  (*conj. like* recevoir)
liar, le menteur
at liberty, libre

library, la bibliothèque
lie, le mensonge; **to lie** (*tell an untruth*) mentir (*conj. like* dormir)
to lie down, se coucher, s'étendre, s'allonger;
to lie (= *to be lying*), être étendu (couché); **to lie** (= *to rest*), reposer
life, la vie; **in his lifetime,** de son vivant
to lift, soulever
light, la lumière; (= *daylight*) le jour; (= *radiance*) la clarté; **it is light,** il fait jour; **the light comes on,** la lumière s'allume
to light, allumer; **to light again,** rallumer; **to light up** (= *illumine*), éclairer; **to light up** (= *brighten*), s'animer
light (= *bright*), clair; (*colour*) clair; (*sound*) grêle, léger
lightning; flash of lightning, un éclair
to like, aimer; vouloir; **to like to do,** aimer faire; **to be liked by,** plaire à
like, comme; **to be like,** ressembler à; **to feel like (doing),** avoir envie de (faire)
likeable, sympathique
likely; very likely, sans doute
likeness, la ressemblance
lime tree, le tilleul
line, la ligne; **to line,** border
to linger, s'attarder
lion, le lion; **lioness,** la lionne
lip, la lèvre
to listen, écouter; (*prolonged*) prêter l'oreille
lit, lighted, éclairé
a little (*quantity*), un peu; **little,** peu
to live, vivre; **to live on,** vivre de; **to live** (= *dwell*), habiter, e.g. il habite Marseille
lively, vif, *f.* vive
living, vivant
local, du pays
lock, la serrure; **to lock (up),** fermer à clef

lodger, le pensionnaire, le locataire
log, la bûche
Loire, la Loire
London, Londres
lone, isolé
lonely, bien seul; **a lonely person,** un(e) solitaire
long, long, *f.* longue; **long since,** depuis longtemps; **a long time (while),** longtemps; **no longer,** ne . . . plus
look, le regard
to look, regarder; (= *appear*) paraître, avoir l'air; **to look like,** avoir l'air de; **to look for,** chercher; **to look up,** lever la tête (les yeux); **to look out of,** regarder par; **to look away,** détourner la tête; **to look after** (*thing*), s'occuper de; (*person*) soigner
loose earth, la terre meuble
Lord, lord
to lose, perdre (*conj. like* vendre); **to lose one's way,** perdre son chemin, s'égarer; **lost** (= *unable to find one's way*), perdu, égaré
loss, la perte
loud, loudly, fort
lounge (*of hotel*), le hall
love, l'amour (*m.*); **to love,** aimer; **lover,** un amant, un bon ami
lovely, beau, *f.* belle
low, bas, *f.* basse; (*sound*) sourd; **in low voices,** à voix basse, à mi-voix
to lower, baisser
luck, la chance; **to wish (s.o.) luck,** souhaiter bonne chance (à); **to be lucky,** avoir de la chance; **luckily,** heureusement, par bonheur
lukewarm, tiède
lull, un moment de calme
lunch, le déjeuner; **to (have) lunch,** déjeuner
lung, le poumon
luxuriant, luxuriant
lying (*untruth*), le mensonge
lying, couché, étendu

m

machine, la machine
made-up (*with cosmetics*), maquillé
magazine, le magazine
magic, magique
magistrate, le magistrat
main, principal
major (*army*), le commandant
to make, faire; **to make for** (**towards**), se diriger vers; **to make out** (= *distinguish*), distinguer; **to make believe**, faire semblant
make (= *brand*), la marque
male, le mâle
to manage, se débrouiller, se tirer d'affaire; **to manage to** (**do**), réussir à (faire), parvenir à (faire)
manor (**house**), le manoir
march, la marche
marked, marqué
market, le marché; **market-day**, le jour de marché; **market-place**, la place du marché
marriage, le mariage
to marry, épouser; **to get married**, se marier; **married**, marié
marshal, le maréchal
marvellously, merveilleusement
Mass, la messe
mass, la masse; (*of trees*) le massif; **mass** (*adj.*), en masse; **to mass**, se masser
master, le maître; (*school*) le professeur; **mastery**, la maîtrise; **masterful**, autoritaire
match, une allumette; **to strike a match**, frotter (craquer) une allumette; **match** (*game*), le match; **rugby match**, le match de rugby
mate, l'époux, *f.* l'épouse
matter; **what is the matter?** qu'y a-t-il? **what is the matter with you?** qu'avez-vous? **what does it matter?** qu'importe? quelle importance cela a-t-il? **as a matter of fact**, à vrai dire

mature, mûr
meal, le repas
mean (*adj.*), avare; chiche, pingre
to mean, vouloir dire; **that means nothing to me**, cela ne me dit rien; **what is the meaning of this?** qu'est-ce à dire?
meaningfully, d'un air entendu
means, le moyen; **by means of**, au moyen de
meanwhile, pendant ce temps; (= *for the time being*) entretemps, en attendant
measure, la mesure; **to measure**, mesurer
meat, la viande
mechanic, le mécanicien
medicine, le médicament, la médecine
to meet, rencontrer; **meeting**, la réunion, le meeting; **meeting-place**, le rendez-vous
member, le membre
memento, le souvenir
memory, le souvenir; (*faculty*) la mémoire
to mention, parler de
mercy; **to throw oneself on the mercy of**, s'abandonner à la merci de
merely, seulement, (tout) simplement
merry, joyeux
message, le message
metre, le mètre
middle, le milieu; **in the middle of**, au milieu de; **middle-aged**, d'un certain âge; **Middle Ages**, le moyen-âge
midnight, minuit
mile, le mille
milk, le lait
milliner, la modiste
million, le million
mind, l'esprit (*m.*); (= *memory*) la mémoire; **to make up one's mind**, se décider (à); prendre son parti
mine (*pron.*), le mien, la mienne, etc.

minister, le ministre

minute, la minute

mirror, la glace

misadventure, la mésaventure

miserable, malheureux

to miss, manquer; **I miss you,** tu
me manques

mission, la mission

mist, le brouillard, la brume;
misty, brumeux, embrumé

mistake, la faute, une erreur;
to be mistaken, se tromper;
to mistake the number,
se tromper de numéro

mistress, la maîtresse; la
patronne

misunderstanding, le
malentendu

to moan, gémir (*conj. like* finir),
geindre (*conj. like* craindre)

model, le (la) modèle

modern, moderne

modest, modeste; **modestly,**
modestement, pudiquement

moist, mouillé

moment, le moment, un instant

momentarily, momentanément

money, l'argent (*m.*)

monk, le moine

monkey-like, de singe

monotonous, monotone

monster, le monstre

moon, la lune; **in the
moonlight,** au clair de la lune

to moor, amarrer

more, plus (de); **what is more,**
qui plus est

morning, le matin; la matinée;
to say good morning, dire
bonjour, souhaiter le bonjour

most (= *majority*), la plupart;
most (= *greater portion*), la
plus grande partie

motorway, une autoroute

to mount, monter (sur)

mountain, la montagne

mourning, le deuil; **house of
mourning,** la maison
endeuillée

mouth, la bouche; **mouthful,**
la bouchée

to move, bouger; (*a thing*) déplacer;

to move away, s'éloigner;
to move aside, écarter; **to
move forward,** s'avancer; **to
move round** (= *circulate*),
circuler; **to move house,**
déménager; **to start to move,
to make a move,** se mettre
en mouvement (en chemin);
movement, le mouvement;
moved, ému; **moving,**
émouvant

to mow (*lawns*), tondre (*conj. like*
vendre)

much, beaucoup; grand'chose,
e.g. il n'a pas dit grand'chose

mud, la boue

in muffled voices, à voix basse

to mumble, grommeler

murder, le meurtre; (*political*)
un attentat;
murder! à l'assassin!

murmur, le murmure; **to
murmur,** murmurer

music, la musique; **musician,**
le musicien

mutton, le mouton

mystery, le mystère;
mysterious, mystérieux

n

name, le nom; **to name,**
nommer

narrow, étroit

nation, la nation

natural, naturel; **naturally,**
naturellement

nave, la nef

near, près de; **to get near,**
arriver près de; **nearby,**
voisin

nearly, presque; **nearly an
hour,** près d'une heure; **he
nearly fell,** il faillit tomber

necessary, nécessaire;
necessity, la nécessité

neck, le cou

need, le besoin; **to need,**
avoir besoin de; **you are
needed,** on vous demande

neighbour, le voisin;
neighbouring, voisin;

neighbourhood, les
environs (*m.*)
nephew, le neveu
nerve, le nerf; **nervous,**
nerveux, inquiet
neutral, neutre
nevertheless, néanmoins
new, nouveau (nouvel *before a
vowel*), *f.* nouvelle; **the New
Year,** le nouvel an; **new**
(= *unused*), neuf, *f.* neuve
newcomer, le nouveau venu
news, les nouvelles (*f.*);
piece of news, la nouvelle
newspaper, le journal;
newspaper reporter, le
reporter, le rédacteur
next (*adj.*), voisin, d'à côté;
next moment, le moment
d'après; **next day,** le
lendemain; **next morning,**
le lendemain matin; **next to,**
à côté de
nice (*person*), gentil, *f.* gentille,
aimable; (*thing*) joli; **nicely,**
joliment
night, la nuit; **by night,**
(pendant) la nuit, de nuit;
last night (*during the night*),
cette nuit; (= *yesterday
evening*) hier soir; **night
before,** la veille (de); **it is
night,** il fait nuit
nimbly, lestement
noble, noble
to **nod one's head,** hocher la tête
noise, le bruit; **noiseless,**
silencieux; **noiselessly,**
silencieusement, sans bruit;
noisy, bruyant
nonsense; to talk nonsense,
dire des bêtises, déraisonner
nook, le coin
Normandy, la Normandie;
Norman, normand, de
Normandie
north, le nord; **north-west,** le
nord-ouest; **north face,** la
face nord; **North Cape,** le
cap Nord
Norway, la Norvège
nose, le nez

to **notice,** remarquer;
(s') apercevoir; **to take no notice
of,** ne faire aucune attention à
novel, le roman
now and then, de temps en
temps, de temps à autre
nowadays, aujourd'hui, de nos
jours
numbed, transi, engourdi
number, le nombre; (*in a
series*) le numéro
numerous, nombreux
nurse, une infirmière

O

oak (tree), le chêne
occasion, une occasion;
occasionally, parfois, de
temps en temps
occupied, occupé
to **occur,** arriver, se passer, se
produire
object, un objet
to **object,** objecter
obliged to (do), obligé de (faire)
to **observe,** observer
obstacle, un obstacle
obstinately, obstinément
to **obtain,** obtenir, se procurer
obvious, évident; **obviously,**
évidemment
off; day off, le jour de congé
offence, le crime, le délit
to **offend,** offenser
to **offer,** offrir (*conj. like* ouvrir)
office, le bureau
officer, un officier
official, le fonctionnaire
oil, l'huile (*f.*); **holy oils,** les
saintes huiles
old, vieux (vieil), *f.* vieille; âgé,
e.g. âgé de 20 ans; (= *former*)
ancien; **old man,** le vieillard;
yes, old chap, oui, mon vieux;
old-fashioned, démodé; **in the
old days,** autrefois; **to grow
old,** vieillir (*conj. like* finir)
once, une fois; **at once,** tout
de suite, aussitôt
one by one, un(e) à un(e)
onlooker, le curieux

only, seulement, ne . . . que;
   the only one, le seul
open, ouvert; **wide open,** grand
   ouvert; **slightly open,**
   entr'ouvert; **in the open,**
   au large; **to open,** ouvrir; **the
   door opens,** la porte s'ouvre
operation, une opération
opinion, un avis; **in my
   opinion,** à mon avis
opponent, un adversaire
opportunity, une occasion
opposed; to be opposed to,
   s'opposer à
opposite, en face (de); opposé;
   the house opposite, la
   maison d'en face
oral, l'oral (*m.*), l'examen oral
orchestra, un orchestre
order, un ordre; **with orders to,**
   avec ordre de; **order**
   (= *requirement*), la commande
to order s.o. to (do), ordonner
   à qn de (faire); **to order a
   drink,** commander à boire
ordinary, ordinaire; **ordinary
   soldier,** le simple soldat
or else, ou bien
organ, les orgues; **organist,**
   l'organiste
original, un original
ornamented, orné
other, autre; **of others,** des
   autres, d'autrui
ought; I ought to do it, je
   devrais le faire; **I ought to
   have done it,** j'aurais dû le
   faire
out of (*motion*), hors de; **out of**
   (*position*), en dehors de;
   outside, dehors; **out of
   breath,** essoufflé; **out of**
   (= *through*), par, e.g. par
   habitude; **he is out,** il est
   sorti; **the light is out,** la
   lumière est éteinte; **to be out
   for a walk,** se promener;
   to get out (*of a place*), sortir;
   (*of a vehicle*) descendre; **to
   look out of,** regarder par; **to
   run out,** sortir en courant;
   to see out, reconduire

outdated, démodé
outlined, dessiné
outraged, outragé
outset, le début; **from the
   outset,** dès le début
outskirts; on the outskirts of,
   à la limite de
outstretched, tendu
over, sur; **over** (*a wall, etc.*),
   par-dessus; **over** (= *finished*),
   fini, terminé; **over there,**
   là-bas
to overcome, surmonter, vaincre
overgrown, agrandi
to overhaul, remettre en état
overhead, au-dessus
overjoyed, plein (transporté)
   de joie, ravi
to overlook, donner sur; (= *rise
   above*) dominer
to overthrow, vaincre, renverser,
   déposer
to owe, devoir
own, propre
owner, le (la) propriétaire

p

pace, le pas; **at a good pace,**
   d'un bon pas
packed, serrés; **packed together,**
   serrés les uns contre les autres
packet, le paquet
page, la page
to paint, peindre (*conj. like*
   craindre); **painted green,**
   peint en vert; **painter,** le
   peintre
pal, le copain
pale, pâle
in panic, pris de panique, affolé
paper, le papier; (= *sheet of
   paper*) la feuille
parallel, parallèle
parasol, le parasol
parcel, le paquet
pardon; I beg your pardon!
   je vous demande pardon!
Parisian, le Parisien, la
   Parisienne
park, le parc
parrot, le perroquet

part, la partie; (*played*) le rôle;
to be a part of, faire partie de;
to take part in, prendre part à
particular, particulier; **in particular,** en particulier, notamment
partition, la cloison
partner, le partenaire, le danseur
party (*of people*), le groupe
to pass, passer; (*from opposite directions*) croiser; **to pass through,** passer par, traverser
passage, le couloir
passenger (*train, bus*), le voyageur; (*ship, aircraft*) le passager, la passagère
passer-by, le passant
past; to go past, passer près de, passer à côté de; **to drive past,** dépasser
path (*narrow*), le sentier; (= *drive*) une allée
patience, la patience
patient, patient
patient (*doctor's*), le client, la cliente; le patient
patriotism, le patriotisme
to pause, s'arrêter (un instant), marquer un temps d'arrêt
pavement, le trottoir
paw, la patte
to pay, payer
peace, la paix; **in peace,** en paix
peasant, le paysan; **peasant woman,** la paysanne
pebbled, caillouteux
peculiarly, particulièrement
pedestrian, le piéton
to peer, risquer (jeter) un coup d'œil
to penetrate, pénétrer; **penetrative,** pénétrant; **penetration,** la pénétration
people, les gens; **young people,** les jeunes; **three people,** trois personnes
per, par; **per cent,** pour cent
perch (*fish*), la perche
to perch, se percher
percolator, le percolateur
perfectly, parfaitement

peril, le péril, le danger
period, une époque
to perish, périr (*conj. like* finir)
permission, la permission
to permit, permettre
to persist, persister
person, la personne
persuaded, persuadé
philosophy, la philosophie
phone, le téléphone; **on the phone,** au téléphone; **phone bell,** la sonnerie du téléphone; **to phone,** téléphoner, donner un coup de téléphone
photograph, la photographie; **photo,** la photo; **to photograph,** photographier
piano, le piano; **to play the piano,** jouer du piano
to pick up, ramasser
picture, le tableau
to picture, imaginer
piece, le morceau
to pierce, percer; (*right through*) transpercer; **piercing,** perçant
pile; to make one's pile, amasser une fortune
pillow, un oreiller
pine, le pin
pinned down, acculé
pint, la pinte
pipe, le tuyau; la pipe
pistol, le pistolet
pit of the stomach, le creux de l'estomac
piteous, pitiful, pitoyable
to pity, plaindre (*conj. like* craindre); **it is a pity that,** c'est dommage que + *subj.*
place, un endroit, le lieu; **in my place,** à ma place; **to take place,** avoir lieu; se dérouler
placid, placide
plain, simple
plan, le projet
plane (*aircraft*), un avion
plane tree, le platane
planet, la planète
to plant, planter
plate, une assiette
platform (*in a hall*), une estrade; (*station*) le quai

platter (*for washing*), le battoir

play (*stage*), la pièce de théâtre

to **play**, jouer; **to play the piano,** jouer du piano; **player,** le joueur

pleasant, agréable

to **please,** plaire (à); contenter; (**if you**) **please,** s'il vous plaît; **come in, please,** entrez, je vous en prie

pleased, content

pleasure, le plaisir; **it is a pleasure to,** cela fait plaisir de; **to be a pleasure to,** faire plaisir à

plight, la situation (difficile), l'embarras (*m.*)

to **plunge,** plonger

pocket, la poche; **breast pocket,** la poche de poitrine

poet, le poète

point, la pointe; **pointed,** pointu; **to point out,** indiquer, désigner

police, la police; **police officer, policeman,** le policier; (*uniformed*) un agent (de police); **police force,** la police, la force publique; **police car,** la voiture de police

to **polish** (*shoes*), cirer

polite, poli; **politely,** poliment; **politeness,** la politesse

political, politique; **political murder,** un attentat; **politician,** un homme politique

poor, pauvre

poplar, le peuplier

popping out (*eyes*), écarquillé

port (*sea-port, harbour*), le port; **to touch at a port,** faire escale à un port; **port** (*wine*), le porto

porter (*station*), un employé

portrait, le portrait

position, la situation

positively, positivement

to **possess,** posséder

possible, possible; **possibility,** la possibilité

to **post a letter,** mettre (porter) une lettre à la poste; **to post oneself** (= *take up a position*), se poster; **postman,** le facteur; **post office,** le bureau de poste

to **postpone,** renvoyer, remettre à plus tard

potato, la pomme de terre, *pl.* les pommes de terre

pound, la livre

to **pour out,** verser; **to pour out one's heart,** épancher son cœur

poverty, la pauvreté, la misère

power, le pouvoir

practically, pratiquement

to **practise,** s'exercer

to **pray,** prier

prayer, la prière

precaution, la précaution

to **precede,** précéder

to **prefer,** préférer, aimer mieux

premises, les locaux (*m.*)

preparation, le préparatif

to **prepare,** préparer

presbytery, le presbytère

prescription, une ordonnance

presence, la présence

present, actuel

present (*gift*), le cadeau

presently, tout à l'heure

Press, la presse

to **press,** presser

to **pretend to** (**do**), faire semblant de (faire)

pretender, le prétendant

pretentious, prétentieux

pretty, joli; **pretty well,** assez bien

to **prevent,** empêcher

price, le prix

pride, l'orgueil (*m.*)

priest, le prêtre

principal, principal; **principal** (*head*), le directeur, la directrice

print, la gravure

privacy, l'intimité (*f.*)

private, particulier

probable, probable; **probably,** probablement

problem, le problème

to proceed to (do), se mettre à (faire)
process, une opération
procession, le cortège
professional, professionnel
to profit by, profiter de
profoundly, profondément
programme, le programme
progress, le progrès, les progrès
to promise to (do), promettre de (faire)
promptly, promptement
to pronounce, prononcer
property, les biens (*m.*)
proposal, la proposition
to propose to (do), se proposer de (faire)
proprietor, le (la) propriétaire
to protest, protester; **protest,** la protestation
to protrude, sortir, dépasser
proud, fier, fière
provided that, pourvu que + *subj.*
province, la province
to prowl, rôder
public, le public; **public,** public, *f.* publique
to publish, publier
puddle, la flaque d'eau
puff, la bouffée
to pull, tirer; **to pull hard,** tirer fort; **to pull away,** arracher, enlever
punt, le bateau plat
purple, violet, *f.* violette
on purpose, à dessein; exprès
purser, le commissaire
pursuit, la poursuite; **to start in pursuit,** se mettre à la poursuite
to push, pousser; **to push off,** repousser
to put, mettre; **to put on** (*garment*), mettre; (*light*) allumer; **to put back,** remettre; **to put down,** poser, déposer; **to put out** (*light*), éteindre; **to put up** (= *erect*), dresser: **to put up with,** supporter
puzzled, intrigué, perplexe; embarrassé

q

quarrel, la querelle, la dispute, la brouille; **to quarrel,** se quereller, se disputer
quarter, le quart; **three quarters,** les trois quarts; **quarter of an hour,** le quart d'heure; **at close quarters,** de près
quay, le quai
queer, étrange
question, la question; **it is a question of,** il s'agit de; **to question,** questionner, interroger
quick, rapide; brusque; **quick** (*adv.*), vite
quiet (*noun*), le silence; **quiet** (*adj.*), silencieux; (*person*) calme; **to keep quiet,** se taire; **quietly** (= *silently*), silencieusement; (= *gently*) doucement; (= *calmly*) tranquillement; (= *in a low voice*) à voix basse
quite, tout à fait; **quite a few,** bon nombre de

r

rails, railings, la grille
rain, la pluie; **raincoat,** un imperméable; **to rain,** pleuvoir; **it is raining in torrents,** il pleut à verse
to raise, lever
rank, le rang, le grade; **high-ranking,** supérieur, de haut grade
to rap, frapper
rapid, rapide; **rapidly,** rapidement
rash, imprudent, téméraire
rate; third-rate, de troisième ordre
rather (= *to a fair degree*), assez; (= *if anything, sooner*) plutôt
ravenously, voracement
ray, le rayon
to reach, arriver à, atteindre (*conj. like* craindre); **to reach out,**

tendre; **within my reach,** à
ma portée

to read, lire

    ready (to), prêt (à); **to get
ready,** préparer; **readily,**
volontiers

    real, réel, *f.* réelle; (= *undoubted*),
vrai, véritable; **really,**
réellement, vraiment

to realize, se rendre compte,
comprendre

    reason, la raison; **reasonable,**
raisonnable

to reassure, rassurer

to rebuild, rebâtir (*conj. like* finir)

to recall, rappeler

to receive, recevoir

    receiver, le récepteur; **to lift
(take up) the receiver,**
décrocher le récepteur

to recognize, réconnaître

    recording, un enregistrement

to recover, retrouver, recouvrer;
    to recover from, se remettre de

    red, rouge; **red-rimmed,** bordé
de rouge, à bordure rouge

    reed, le roseau

    reference; terms of reference,
les attributions (*f.*)

to refrain from, se retenir de, se
garder de

to refuse to (do), refuser de (faire)

as regards, quant à; à propos de;
en ce qui concerne

to regret to (do), regretter de
(faire); **regret,** le regret

    rejoinder, la réplique

to relate, raconter

    relation, relative, le parent

    relative, relatif

    relief, le soulagement

to relieve, soulager

to relight, rallumer

to rely on, compter sur

to remain, rester; **to remain silent,**
rester silencieux, se taire

to remark (= *pass a remark*),
faire remarquer; **remarks,** les
propos (*m.*); **remarkable,**
remarquable

to remember, se souvenir (de),
se rappeler

to remind, rappeler

    reminiscence, le souvenir

to renew, renouveler

to rent, louer

to repeat, répéter

    repeatedly, à plusieurs reprises

to replace, replacer

    report, le rapport

    reporter, le reporter

to represent, représenter

to repulse, repousser

    rescue, la rescousse, le secours

to reserve, réserver

to resign (= *give up office*),
démissionner; **to resign
oneself,** se résigner; **resigned,**
résigné

to resist, résister (à); **resistance,**
la résistance

to resolve, résoudre; **resolved to
(do),** résolu à (faire)

    resort (*seaside*), la plage

to resound, retentir (*conj. like* finir)

    respect, le respect; **in this
respect,** à cet égard; **to respect,**
respecter; **respectable,**
convenable

    responsible, responsable;
responsibility, la
responsabilité

    rest, le reste

to rest, se reposer

    result, le résultat

to resume, reprendre

to retire, se retirer; **retired** (*from
work*), retraité, en retraite

to retort, répliquer

    retreat, la retraite; **to retreat,**
se retirer

    return, le retour; **on my return,**
à mon retour; **to return**
(= *to come back*), revenir;
(= *go back*) retourner;
(= *give back*) rendre

    Reverend, monsieur l'abbé

to revive, ranimer

    reward, la récompense

    rib, la côte

    rich, riche

    rid; to get rid of, se
débarrasser de

    right (*noun*), le droit; **right**

(*adj.*), droit; **on (to) the right,** à droite; **right and left,** à droite et à gauche; **right at the bottom,** tout au fond; **all right,** très bien; entendu; **all right with,** bien avec; **to be right,** avoir raison

rimmed, bordé

to **ring (the bell),** sonner; **to ring for,** sonner; **the phone bell rings,** la sonnerie du téléphone retentit; **ring me,** appelez-moi, donnez-moi un coup de téléphone

to **rip through,** transpercer, déchirer

to **rise,** se lever; (= *go up*), monter; (*of things high*) se dresser; **the wind rises,** le vent s'élève

to **risk,** risquer; **to take (run) the risk,** courir le risque

river, la rivière; **river-bed,** le lit (le fond) de la rivière

road, la route; le chemin

to **roar,** rugir (*conj. like* finir)

rod, la canne

roof, le toit

room (*any room*), la pièce; la salle; (= *bedroom*) la chambre; **room** (= *space*), la place

roseate, rose

rose-bush, le rosier

rosy, rose

to **rot,** pourrir (*conj. like* finir)

round, autour de; **all round,** tout autour de; **to walk round,** faire le tour de

routine, la routine; **routine question,** la question routinière

row (= *line*), le rang; (*of houses*) la rangée; **row** (= *quarrel*), la querelle, la dispute

to **rub,** frotter

rude, impoli

to **ruin,** abîmer

rule, le règlement

ruler, la règle

to **run (about),** courir; **to run out,** sortir en courant

to **rush,** se précipiter, s'élancer, se ruer.

Russia, la Russie

to **rustle,** bruire (*imperf.* bruissait), passer en bruissant

S

sack, le sac; **to sack, to give the sack,** mettre à la porte

sacrifice, le sacrifice

sad, triste; **sadly,** tristement

safe, en sûreté, en sécurité; **safe and sound,** sain et sauf; **safety,** la sûreté, la sécurité

sagacity, la sagacité

to **sail** (*of clouds, etc.*), planer, voguer

sake; for the sake of, pour le plaisir (la satisfaction) de

salary, le traitement

salmon, le saumon; **salmon fishing,** la pêche au saumon

same, même; **all the same,** tout de même; **he does the same,** il en fait autant

sand, le sable; **sandbank,** le banc de sable

satisfaction, la satisfaction; **satisfied,** satisfait

to **save,** sauver

saxophone, le saxophone

scale; large-scale, sur une grande échelle

Scandinavia, la Scandinavie

scar, la cicatrice

scarcely, à peine

to **scare,** effrayer

scene, la scène; (*of crimes, etc.*) les lieux

scent, le parfum

scholarship, la bourse

school, une école; (*grammar, public*) le collège; **schoolboy,** le collégien; **schoolmaster,** le professeur

scientific, scientifique

to **scoff,** dire avec mépris; railler

scoop, le coup

a **score of,** une vingtaine de

scoundrel, le coquin, le scélérat, le gredin

scout, l'éclaireur, le boy-scout

scraping, le grincement

screen, le rideau
script, la copie
sea, la mer
in search of, à la recherche de;
    searchlight, le projecteur
season, la saison
seat (*in vehicle, etc.*), la place;
    (= *bench*) le banc, le siège;
    to take one's seat, prendre
    place
second (*adj.*), second; **second**
    (*time*), la seconde; **second** (*in*
    duel), le témoin; **second-hand,**
    d'occasion
secret, le secret; (*adj.*) secret,
    –ète; clandestin; **secretly,**
    secrètement, en secret; **to keep**
    secret, tenir secret, garder le
    secret sur
secretary, le (la) secrétaire
to see, voir; **to see s.o. out,**
    reconduire qn; **seeing that,**
    vu que
to seek, chercher; **to seek to (do),**
    chercher à (faire)
to seem, sembler; **it seems,** il
    semble, il paraît; **seemingly,**
    apparemment
Seine, la Seine
to seize, saisir (*conj. like* finir)
seldom, rarement
to sell, vendre
semi-darkness, la
    demi-obscurité
senator, le sénateur
to send, envoyer; **to send for,**
    envoyer chercher; **to send**
    to bed, envoyer se coucher
sensation, la sensation
sentence, la phrase
sentinel, la sentinelle, le
    factionnaire
serious, sérieux; grave; **seriously,**
    sérieusement, (*ill*) gravement;
    to take seriously, prendre au
    sérieux
servant, le (la) domestique
to serve, servir (*conj. like* dormir)
to set out (off), partir; **to set off**
    again, repartir; **to set out**
    (*things*), disposer, placer; **to set**
    foot in, mettre les pieds dans;

to set oneself up as, s'ériger
    en
setting, le décor, la mise en scène;
    setting of the sun, le coucher
    du soleil
to settle (*accounts*), régler; **to settle**
    down, se ranger
several, plusieurs
sewn, cousu
to shade, ombrager
shadow, une ombre
shady, louche
to shake (off), secouer; (*nerves*)
    ébranler; **to shake one's**
    head, hocher (secouer) la
    tête; **I shake hands with**
    him, je lui serre la main
to sham, faire semblant (de),
    feindre (de)
shameless, cynique;
    shamelessly, cyniquement
to share (out), partager
shark, le requin
sharp (*tone*), sec; **sharply,**
    sèchement
sheep, le mouton
shelter, un abri; **to shelter,**
    s'abriter
to shift, bouger
shimmering, étincelant,
    miroitant, luisant
to shine, briller
ship, le navire; **to ship,** embarquer
shirt, la chemise
shoal, la bande
shock, le choc, le coup
shoe, le soulier
to shoot down, abattre (à coups
    de revolver)
shop (*small*), la boutique;
    (*large*) le magasin; **to go**
    shopping, aller faire son
    marché
shore, le rivage
short, court; **to cut s.o. short,**
    couper la parole à qn;
    shortly afterwards, peu
    après
shot, le coup (de feu)
shoulder, une épaule; **to shrug**
    one's shoulders, hausser les
    épaules

to shout, crier; shouting, les cris
shovel, la pelle
to show, montrer; a light shows,
    une lumière se montre; to
    show in, faire entrer,
    introduire; to show round,
    faire les honneurs
to shriek, pousser des cris, crier
shrill, aigu
to shrug one's shoulders,
    hausser les épaules
to shut up (= be quiet), se taire
shutter, le volet
shy, timide; shyness, la
    timidité
sick, malade; to sicken,
    écœurer
side, le côté; (of boat, etc.) le
    flanc; (in a quarrel) le parti;
    on all sides, de tous côtés,
    de toutes parts; sideways,
    de côté
sidelight, la lanterne
sigh, le soupir; to sigh,
    soupirer
sight, la vue; (= something seen)
    le spectacle; to lose sight of,
    perdre de vue
sign, le signe; (= indication) un
    indice; (of an inn) une enseigne;
    to make a sign, faire signe;
    to sign, signer
signature, la signature
silence, le silence; silent,
    silencieux; silently,
    silencieusement
silly, stupide
silver-gilt, le vermeil
silvery, argenté; d'argent
simple, simple; (= innocent)
    naïf; simply, (tout)
    simplement
since, depuis; (= for the reason
    that) puisque; long since,
    depuis longtemps
sincere, sincère
to sing, chanter
a single, un(e) seul(e)
to sit (down), s'asseoir; to sit down
    again, se rasseoir; to sit up,
    se redresser; to sit (= to be
    seated) être assis; sitting, assis

situated, situé
situation, la situation
skeleton, le squelette
sketch, le croquis
skilfully, adroitement
to skim, effleurer
sky, le ciel
sleep, le sommeil; to sleep,
    dormir; to go (get) to sleep,
    s'endormir; to go to sleep
    again, se rendormir; sleepily,
    l'air endormi, l'air somnolent
to slide, glisser
slight, léger; slightest, le (la)
    moindre
slim, mince, svelte
to slip, glisser; (= escape) échapper
slipper, la pantoufle
sloping, en pente
sloppy, niais
slow, lent; slowly, lentement;
    to slow down, ralentir (conj.
    like finir)
sluggishly, paresseusement,
    léthargiquement, lourdement
smack; I smack his face,
    je le gifle
smallest (= slightest), le (la)
    moindre
smart, élégant
smell, une odeur; to smell,
    flairer; sentir l'odeur de
to smile, sourire; smile, le sourire
to smoke, fumer
to smuggle, passer en fraude,
    passer en contrebande
to snap, dire sèchement
to snatch, arracher
to sniff at, flairer
snow, la neige; to snow, neiger
so (= thus), ainsi; (= therefore)
    donc; (= to such an extent)
    tellement; so many, tant;
    and so on, et ainsi de suite;
    so to speak, pour ainsi dire;
    so that (= in such a way that),
    de sorte que
soap, le savon
society, la société; high
    society, le grand monde
sodden, détrempé
soft, doux, f. douce; (of sound)

feutré; (= *yielding*) moelleux;
(= *muddy*) mou, boueux,
marécageux; **softly,**
doucement; (*voice*) tout bas;
(*music*) en sourdine

soil, le sol, la terre

soldier, le soldat; **ordinary
soldier,** le simple soldat

solemn, solennel, *f.* –elle

solid, solide

solitary, solitaire

solitude, la solitude

somebody, someone, quelqu'un;
something, quelque chose;
some time, quelque temps;
somewhere, quelque part;
somewhat, un peu, quelque
peu

song, la chanson

soon, bientôt; **sooner,** plus
tôt; **sooner or later,** tôt ou
tard; **as soon as,** dès que,
aussitôt que; **he will soon
come back,** il ne tardera pas
à revenir

sooty, noirci (encrassé) de suie

sorrow, le chagrin

sorry; to be sorry, regretter

sort, la sorte; le genre

sound, le bruit; (*bells, music,
etc.*) le son

space, un espace

spade, la bêche

spare, de réserve; de rechange

to **spatter,** éclabousser

to **speak ill of,** médire de

spectator, le spectateur

speech, le discours

speed, la vitesse; **at full speed,**
à toute vitesse; **to gather
speed,** prendre de la vitesse

to **spend one's time (doing),**
passer son temps (à faire)

to **spin** (*fishing*), pêcher au lancer

spinet, une épinette

spit, la broche

to **spit,** cracher

to **spite,** contrarier; **in spite of,**
malgré

to **spoil,** gâter; (*things*) abîmer

spot (*place*), un endroit

to **spot,** repérer, apercevoir

spruce, pimpant

to **squall,** brailler

square (= *open space*), la place

staff, le personnel

stag, le cerf

stage, la scène; **on the stage,**
en scène

stained glass window, le
vitrail, *pl.* les vitraux

staircase, stairs, l'escalier

stall, un étalage en plein vent

to **stammer,** balbutier

to **stand,** se tenir, être debout;
(*in a certain place*) se placer;
to stand (= *to bear*), supporter;
to stand up, se lever, se mettre
debout; **to stand on tiptoe,**
se dresser sur la pointe des
pieds; **the sweat stands out,**
la sueur perle; **standing,**
debout

star, une étoile; **star** (*performer*),
la vedette

to **stare at,** regarder fixement,
fixer

to **start** (= *begin*), commencer;
to start again, recommencer;
to start off for, se mettre en
route pour; **to start towards,**
se diriger vers

start; to give a start,
tressaillir, sursauter; **with a
start,** en sursaut

startled, surpris, alarmé

to **starve,** mourir de faim

state, un état; **the State,** l'État

stately, imposant

station, la gare

statue, la statue

to **stay,** rester; (*in a place*)
séjourner, loger

steady, fixe, soutenu; **to walk
steadily,** marcher d'un pas
ferme (posé)

steak, le bifteck

to **steal,** voler; **to steal away,** se
dérober, s'esquiver

step (= *pace*), le pas; (*of stairs*)
la marche; **to take a step,**
faire un pas; **step** (= *action*),
la démarche; **to step over,**
enjamber

stern, sévère
sterterous, stertoreux, ronflant
stick, la canne
to stick, coller
stiff, raide
still, encore, toujours
still (adj.), immobile, sans
    mouvement; tranquille; **he can't
    keep still,** il ne tient pas en
    place; **stillness,** le calme
to stir, remuer
stoical, stoïque
stomach, l'estomac (m.);
    (= abdomen) le ventre
stone, la pierre
stool; **camp stool,** le pliant
to stop, (s') ârreter; (= cease)
    cesser; (= prevent) empêcher;
    to stop (doing), s'ârreter de
    (faire), cesser de (faire)
straight off, tout de suite
strained, tendu
strange, étrange; **stranger,** un
    étranger, une étrangère
straw, la paille
stream, la rivière; (= brook)
    le ruisseau
strength, les forces (f.)
to stretch (the limbs), s'étirer; **to
    stretch out** (e.g. the hand),
    tendre
to stride on, marcher à grands pas
to strike, frapper, atteindre (conj.
    like craindre); **to strike a
    match,** frotter (craquer) une
    allumette; **striking,** le
    frottement, le craquement
stripe, la raie; **with red stripes,**
    rayé de rouge
to strive to, chercher à
stroke, le coup; **to stroke,**
    caresser, flatter, passer la
    main sur
to stroll, se promener
strong, fort, puissant
stronghold, la place forte, la
    forteresse
struggle, la lutte; **to struggle**
    (= fight), lutter; (= make wild
    efforts) se débattre
student, un étudiant
studies, les études (f.)

studio (painter's), un atelier
to study, étudier; lire avec attention;
    study (room), le cabinet de
    travail
stupid, stupide
subject, le sujet
to subsist, subsister
subtlety, la subtilité
suburb, le faubourg; **suburban,**
    de banlieue
to succeed, réussir (conj. like finir);
    (in exam) être reçu
success, le succès
such, tel, f. telle
to suck up to, lécher les bottes à
sudden, soudain, subit;
    suddenly, tout à coup,
    soudain, subitement
to suffer, souffrir (conj. like ouvrir);
    suffering, la souffrance
to suffice, suffire
to suggest, suggérer, proposer
suit (man's), le complet;
    (woman's) le tailleur
to suit, convenir; **suitable,**
    convenable
suitcase, la valise
to sulk, bouder
summer, l'été (m.); (= of
    summer) d'été
sun, sunshine, le soleil; **sunset
    sky,** le couchant; **sunset glow,**
    les feux du couchant
sunk (in a chair), affalé;
    sunken, creux, f. creuse
supernatural, surnaturel
to suppose, supposer
sure, sûr; certain; **surely,**
    sûrement, à coup sûr; **to
    make sure,** pour être bien
    certain
surface, la surface
to surmount, surmonter
surplice, le surplis
to surprise, surprendre, étonner;
    to be surprised, s'étonner;
    surprise, la surprise,
    l'étonnement (m.)
to surround, entourer; cerner;
    surrounded by, entouré de
to suspect, soupçonner; se douter
    de; **suspect (person),** le suspect

suspended, suspendu
suspiciously, avec méfiance,
d'un air méfiant, d'un air
soupçonneux
to swallow, avaler; **to swallow
down one's anger,** ravaler
sa colère
to swear, jurer
sweat, la sueur; **the sweat stands
out,** la sueur perle; **to sweat,**
suer
Sweden, la Suède
sweep (*of hand, etc.*), le
mouvement
sweet (= *pleasant*), doux,
charmant, agréable;
sweetheart, un amoureux
swiftly, rapidement
to swim, nager; **to have a swim,**
se baigner.
Switzerland, la Suisse; **Swiss,**
suisse
sword, une épée; **swordfish,**
un espadon

t

tailor, le tailleur
to take, prendre; (= *carry*)
porter; (= *lead*) conduire;
(*to a place*) emmener; **to take
away,** emporter; **to take off,**
ôter, enlever; **to take in,**
faire entrer; **to take up** (*a
person*), faire monter; (*e.g. a
song*) reprendre; **to take out**
(*a thing*), sortir; **to take out of,**
tirer de; **take that!** attrapez!
to tap, taper
taper, la cierge
taste, le goût; **tasty,** savoureux,
plein de saveur
tax, un impôt; **to tax,** imposer;
faire payer des impôts (à)
taxi, le taxi
tea, le thé
to teach, apprendre; (*in school*)
enseigner; **teacher** (*primary*),
un instituteur
tear, la larme
to tear (up), déchirer

to tease, taquiner
technological, technologique
telephone, le téléphone; **to
telephone,** téléphoner
television, la télévision; **the
"telly",** la télé
to tell, dire; (= *relate*) raconter
temper, la colère; **to lose one's
temper,** se mettre en colère,
s'emporter
to tempt, tenter; **temptation,** la
tentation
tender, tendre
tent, la tente
terms of reference, les
attributions (*f.*)
terrace, la terrasse; **on the
terrace,** à la terrasse
terrible, terrible, effroyable
terrified, effrayé, terrifié
terrorist, le terroriste
to thank, remercier; **thank God!**
Dieu merci!
theatre, le théâtre; le spectacle
then (= *next*), puis; (= *at that
time*) alors; **since then,**
depuis ce temps-là
up there, là-haut
thermometer, le thermomètre
thermos, lé thermos; **thermos
flask,** la bouteille thermos
thick, épais, *f.* épaisse; (*rain,
snow*) dru
thicket, le fourré
thief, le voleur
thigh, la cuisse
thin (*person*), maigre;
(= *not thick*) mince
thing, la chose; **things**
(= *possessions*), les affaires (*f.*)
to think, penser, croire;
(= *reflect*) réfléchir (*conj. like*
finir)
thirsty; to be thirsty, avoir soif
thorn, une épine
though (*conj.*), bien que, quoique;
(= *however*) cependant; **as
though,** comme si
thought, la pensée; **on second
thoughts,** à la réflexion;
thoughtful, pensif;
thoughtfully, pensivement

thousand, mille

to **threaten to,** menacer de

threshold, le seuil

throat, la gorge; **to clear one's throat,** s'éclaircir la gorge

through, par; à travers

to **throw (out),** jeter

to **thrust in,** enfoncer

thunder, le tonnerre; **clap of thunder,** le coup de tonnerre; **thunderstorm,** un orage

thus, ainsi

ticket, le billet; **ticket inspector (collector),** le contrôleur

tie, la cravate

to **tie,** attacher

tiger, le tigre; **tigress,** la tigresse

time, le temps; (*by the clock*) l'heure; (= *occasion*) la fois; **at times,** parfois; **at the same time,** en même temps; **from time to time,** de temps en temps; **before time,** avant l'heure; **for the time being,** pour le moment; **it is time that,** il est temps que + *subj*.

timidly, timidement

tinkle, le tintement

tint, la teinte

tip (= *advice*), le tuyau

to **tip up,** basculer

to **tiptoe out,** sortir à pas de loup, sortir sur la pointe des pieds; **to stand tiptoe,** se dresser sur la pointe des pieds

tired, fatigué; **to get tired,** se fatiguer

tobacco, le tabac

together, ensemble

tolerant, tolérant

tone, le ton; **toneless,** blanc, atone

tongue, la langue

tool, un outil

top, le haut; (*hills, mountains*) le sommet; **on the top of,** en haut de; **to get to the top,** arriver en haut; **top** (*adj.*), supérieur

torch, la torche; (*of fire*) le flambeau; **electric torch,** la torche électrique, la torche de poche

torrential, torrentiel; **it rains in torrents,** il pleut à verse

to **torture,** torturer

to **toss,** jeter, lancer

to **touch,** toucher (à); **to touch at a port,** faire escale à un port

a **tough,** un dur; **tough** (*adj.*), coriace

to **tour,** être en promenade; **tourist,** le touriste

towards, vers; (= *in the direction of*) du côté de; **to make towards,** se diriger vers

Town Hall, l'hôtel de ville; **in (to) town,** en ville

trader, le marchand; (*market*) le camelot; **tradespeople,** les marchands, les fournisseurs

tradition, la tradition

train, le train; **by train,** par le train.

to **train** (*animal*), dresser; (*weapon, light*) braquer; **trained** (*for test*), entraîné, exercé

tramlines, la voie du tramway

to **translate,** traduire

trap, le piège

to **travel,** voyager; **to travel on,** continuer son voyage (son chemin); **traveller,** le voyageur

tray, le plateau

treatment, le traitement (médical)

to **tremble,** trembler

trick, la ruse

trimmed with, orné de, paré de

trip, le voyage; **to take a trip,** faire un tour (une promenade)

troop, la troupe

troubles, les ennuis, les soucis; **to trouble to (do),** se donner la peine de (faire)

trousers, le pantalon

trout, la truite

true, vrai; **truth,** la vérité

trust, la confiance; **to trust,** se fier à, avoir confiance en

to **try to (do),** essayer de (faire)

trying, fatigant, accablant

tune, un air; **in tune,** d'accord,
en accord; **in tune** (*rhythm*),
en cadence; **to tune,** accorder
tunnel, le tunnel
turn, le tour; **to turn,** tourner;
to turn about, faire demi-tour;
to turn away, se détourner;
to turn round, se retourner;
to turn on (*e.g. pursuers*),
se retourner sur; **to turn to,**
se tourner vers; **to turn out
the light,** éteindre la lumière
to type, taper à la machine
tyre, le pneu, *pl.* les pneus

u

umbrella, le parapluie
unavowed, inavoué
unbearable, insupportable
to unbutton, déboutonner
to understand, comprendre;
entendre, e.g. nous nous
entendons, *we understand each
other*
to undertake, entreprendre
undoubtedly, sans aucun doute,
indubitablement
to undress, se déshabiller
unexpected, inattendu
unfailing, inaltérable
unfaithful, infidèle
to unfasten, détacher
unfortunate, malheureux
ungrateful, ingrat
unhappy, malheureux
universe, l'univers (*m.*)
university, une université
unjust, injuste
unless, à moins que + ne *before
verb in subjunctive*
unmistakable, facilement
reconnaissable
unoccupied, inoccupé
unreasonable, peu raisonnable
unstuck; **to come unstuck,** se
décoller, se détacher
until (*prep.*), jusqu'à; (*conj.*)
jusqu'à ce que + *subj.*
unusual, insolite, extraordinaire
unwise, imprudent

up and down, de long en large;
up there, là-haut; **to walk up,**
remonter; **to go up to**
(= *approach*), s'approcher de
to upset, déranger
urgent, urgent; **urgently,**
d'urgence
to use, employer; se servir de;
to get used to, s'habituer à,
s'accoutumer à; **it's no use,**
cela ne sert à rien; **it's no use
my waiting,** il m'est inutile
d'attendre, cela ne me sert à
rien d'attendre
useful, utile
usual, habituel, *f.* –elle; **as
usual,** comme d'habitude,
comme toujours; **usually,**
d'habitude, généralement, en
général
to utter, prononcer
utterly, complètement,
absolument

v

vacant, vacant, libre
vacation, les vacances (*f.*)
vague, vague; **vaguely,**
vaguement
in vain, en vain
vale, le vallon, la vallée
valet, le valet
van (*large*), le camion; (*small*)
la camionnette; (*police*) le car
vehemently, avec véhémence
vehicle, la voiture, le véhicule
vertical, vertical
very; **at this very moment,**
à ce moment même
victory, la victoire
in view of, en vue de; **lost to
view,** perdu de vue; **to view,**
envisager
vigil, la veille
villa, la villa
village, le village; **villager,**
le villageois
vineyard, le vignoble, la vigne
violence, la violence; **violent,**
violent; **violently,** avec
violence, violemment

visit, la visite; **to visit,** visiter;
visitor, le visiteur
vitality, la vitalité, la vigueur
voice, la voix

W

wage(s), le salaire
to wait, attendre; **to keep
waiting,** faire attendre;
waiting-room (*doctor's*), une
antichambre, le salon
d'attente; **a wait,** une attente
waitress, la serveuse
to wake, (se) réveiller, (s')éveiller
to walk, marcher; (*for pleasure*) se
promener; **to walk in,** entrer;
to walk up, remonter; **to
walk down,** descendre; **to
walk away,** s'éloigner; **to
walk towards,** se diriger vers;
to walk across (through),
traverser; **to walk along,**
longer, suivre; **to walk round,**
faire le tour de; **walk,** la
promenade; **to take (go for,
be out for) a walk,** se promener,
faire un tour; **to take for a
walk** (*e.g. a dog*), promener
wall, le mur, la muraille
to wallow, se vautrer
to wander, errer; **to wander
about,** errer dans
war, la guerre
warm, chaud; (*lukewarm*) tiède;
to warm, (faire) chauffer; **to
keep warm,** se chauffer, se
réchauffer; **warmth,** la
chaleur
to warn, avertir (*conj. like* finir),
prévenir
to wash, laver; **to wash up,**
faire la vaisselle; **to do the
washing,** laver du linge,
faire la lessive; **to hang out
washing,** étendre du linge
to waste, perdre
watch, la montre
to watch, regarder; (= *keep watch
over*) surveiller
watchman, le veilleur

water, l'eau (*f.*); **waterfall,**
la cascade
wave, la vague
to wave, agiter
way, le chemin; la route; **on the
way to,** en route pour; **to lose
one's way,** perdre son chemin,
s'égarer; **to make one's way
to,** se diriger vers; **way**
(= *manner*), la manière, la
façon; **by the way,** à propos;
in the way (= *unwanted*), de
trop
weakness, la faiblesse
wealthy, riche
to wear, porter; **wearing** (*on the
head*), coiffé de
weary, las, *f.* lasse
wedding, le mariage, la noce;
wedding present, le cadeau
de noces
week, la semaine; **week-end,**
le week-end; **at the week-end,**
en fin de semaine
to weep, pleurer
to weigh, peser; **to weigh down,**
peser lourd dans
weighted with, chargé de
welcome; to make welcome,
faire bon accueil à
well, le puits
well, bien; **as well as,** aussi
bien que; **to look well,**
avoir bonne mine
west, l'ouest (*m.*)
whenever, chaque fois que,
toutes les fois que
whereas, tandis que
whether, si
while (*conj.*), pendant que;
(*with idea of contrast*)
tandis que; **a while,** un
moment, un temps; **a long
while,** longtemps
whilst, tandis que
whip; to have the whip hand,
tenir les rênes, avoir la haute
main
whiskers (*cat's*), les moustaches;
whiskers (*man's*), les favoris
to whisper, murmurer; chuchoter;
to speak in a whisper,

murmurer, parler bas;
whispering (= *rustling*),
bruissant
whistle, le coup de sifflet
white, blanc, *f.* blanche;
whitened, blanchi; **whitish,**
blanchâtre
whoever, quiconque, celui qui
whole, entier; **wholly,**
entièrement, tout à fait; **the
whole day,** toute la journée;
on the whole, en somme,
à tout prendre, d'une façon
générale
why, pourquoi; **why not,**
pourquoi pas; **why, of course!**
mais bien sûr!
wide, large; (*sea*) vaste,
immense; **wide open,** grand
ouvert, tout grand; **to open
one's eyes wide,** ouvrir de
grands yeux
widow, la veuve
wild (= *untamed*), sauvage;
(= *crazy*) fou, *f.* folle; **the
wilds,** le désert, les solitudes,
la brousse
will you (do)? voulez-vous
(faire)?
to **win,** gagner
wind, le vent; **wind-screen,**
le pare-brise
to **wind** (*road*), serpenter; **to wind
in,** ramener
window, la fenêtre; **stained
glass window,** le vitrail, *pl.*
les vitraux
wine, le vin; **wine-waiter,** le
sommelier
winged bonnet, la cornette
to **wipe,** essuyer
wisely, prudemment
to **wish,** vouloir, désirer; (= *to
express a wish*) souhaiter, e.g.
souhaiter le bonjour
wisp, la traînée
with, avec; **what have you done
with the hammer?** qu'as-tu
fait du marteau?
withered, flétri
to **withhold,** retenir
to **witness,** être témoin de;

witness-box, la barre des
témoins
witty, spirituel
wolf, le loup
to **wonder,** se demander
wonderful, merveilleux
wood, le bois; **woods,
woodlands,** les bois; **wooden,**
de bois; **wooded,** boisé
word, le mot; **without a word,**
sans mot dire; **to get in a word,**
placer un mot; **I have a word
with him,** je lui dis un mot
(deux mots), je lui touche
deux mots; **in a word,** bref,
enfin
work, le travail; **to get to work,**
se mettre au travail (à
l'œuvre); **to work hard,**
travailler dur (ferme);
working hours, les heures de
travail; **workman,** un ouvrier
world, le monde; **World Cup,**
la Coupe du Monde
to **worry,** s'inquiéter, se tourmenter;
to worry about, se soucier
de; **don't worry!** soyez
tranquille! **worried,**
tourmenté, tracassé, inquiet,
soucieux
to **worsen,** empirer
worst, le (la) pire
worth, la valeur; **to be worth,**
valoir; **that isn't worth
doing,** cela ne vaut pas (la
peine) d'être fait
wound, la blessure; **to wound,**
blesser
wretchedness, la misère
wrinkled, ridé
to **write,** écrire; **writing,** l'écriture
(*f.*)
wrong; to be wrong, avoir tort;
to do wrong, faire du mal

Y

yard, le cour
yard (*measure*), le mètre
(*approx.*)
year, un an, une année; **New
Year,** le nouvel an

to **yell,** hurler
yellow, jaune
yesterday, hier; **yesterday
evening,** hier soir
yet, pourtant; **and yet,** et
pourtant
to **yield,** céder

young, jeune; **their young,**
leurs petits
youth, la jeunesse

Z

zebra, le zèbre